Aaron Henry

Margaret Walker Alexander Series in African American Studies

Aaron Henry
The Fire Ever Burning

Aaron Henry with Constance Curry
Introduction by John Dittmer

University Press of Mississippi / Jackson

www.upress.state.ms.us
Copyright © 2000 by University Press of Mississippi
All rights reserved

08 07 06 05 04 03 02 01 00   4 3 2 1

Library of Congress Cataloging-in-Publication Data

Henry, Aaron, 1922–
Aaron, Henry : the fire ever burning / Aaron Henry with Constance
Curry ; introduction by John Dittmer.
p.   cm. — (Margaret Walker Alexander series in African American studies)
Includes index.
ISBN 1-57806-212-8 (cloth : alk. paper)
1. Henry, Aaron, 1922– . 2. Afro-American civil rights workers—
Mississippi Biography. 4. Civil rights movements—Mississippi—History—20th
century. 5. Afro-Americans—Civil rights—Mississippi—
History—20th century. 6. Afro-Americans—Civil rights—
Mississippi—Clarksdale—History—20th century. 7. Mississippi—
Race relations. 8. Clarksdale (Miss.)—Race relations. I. Curry,
Constance. II. Title. III. Series.
F350.N4H46   2000
323'.092—dc21
[B]   99-36984
CIP

In the Old Testament, God told Moses to speak His word through Aaron.
He then told Moses and Aaron to build a fire
to light the way to freedom and to keep
THE FIRE EVER BURNING.
Leviticus 6:13

Contents

Introduction

In its broad outline, Aaron Henry's life is the personification of the American Dream: the sharecropper's son and hotel porter who pulled himself up by his bootstraps to become a successful businessman and political leader. Of course there is much more to the story than that, for Henry grew up black in the Mississippi Delta during the age of segregation, where racial proscription and violence were the order of every day, and simply surviving this oppressive environment was all that most Negroes could hope for. World War II, however, served as a catalyst for social change in America, and Henry was one of many black veterans who "returned home fighting," vowing to destroy Jim Crow and everything it symbolized in the Magnolia State. He remained active in that struggle until his death more than five decades later.

It is ironic—and regrettable—that although Aaron Henry contributed in so many ways to the successes of the civil rights movement, he is not well known today, even in his home state. Other black Mississippi activists like Fannie Lou Hamer and Medgar Evers have commanded the attention of historians and Hollywood. Equally as dedicated but less charismatic (and more fortunate—he was never seriously hurt in the attacks made on his life), Henry spent the 1950s and much of the 1960s working in relative obscurity. Although he was involved in civil rights work long before most of his contemporaries, and played a major role in the establishment of the Council of Federated Organizations (COFO), the umbrella organization that coordinated movement activities in Mississippi during the early 1960s, Henry preferred to stay out of the limelight. Occupying the middle ground between the conservative national leadership of the National Association for the Advancement of Colored People (NAACP) and the militant activism of the Student Nonviolent Coordinating Committee (SNCC), Henry knew that his effectiveness depended on tact and quiet diplomacy, hardly the qualities that attract national attention.

Scholars, too, have focused on the more dramatic Mississippi stories: the assassination of Medgar Evers; the "Freedom Summer" of 1964, with the lynching of Chaney, Schwerner, and Goodman; and the Meredith March of 1966, where Stokely Carmichael proclaimed "Black Power" to the world. Henry's involvement in these and other important movement events have not received the attention they deserve. He emerged onto the national scene briefly during the 1964 Democratic National Convention in Atlantic City, but there his role was secondary to that of Mrs. Hamer, whose powerful testimony before the credentials committee remains the most poignant memory of that convention. For the next three decades Henry labored—not in obscurity, but largely out of the spotlight.

Aaron Henry's position in the Mississippi movement was both unique and essential. An NAACP activist who became state president in 1959, Henry exhibited a commendable independence. He took on the job of COFO president against the wishes of national NAACP leaders like Roy Wilkins and Gloster Current. (Unlike state field secretary Medgar Evers, Henry was an unpaid official elected by Mississippi NAACP members. He would often observe that "Ain't nobody hired me, ain't nobody can fire me.")

More than any other Mississippi leader, the Clarksdale pharmacist united blacks across lines of age, ideology, and social class to present a consolidated front against the forces of white supremacy. A man of tremendous personal courage, Henry faced down death threats, spent time in jail, and survived Klan bombings. All these qualities came together in his leadership of the Clarksdale boycott and direct action campaign in the early 1960s.

Overshadowed by similar campaigns going on in Jackson and Birmingham, the Clarksdale movement nonetheless quietly sustained itself for more than two years against intractable white opposition. The boycotters demanded integration of all public facilities, school desegregation, voting rights, and formation of an interracial committee. Determined not to budge on any of these issues, white officials responded by arresting Henry and four other local NAACP activists, charging them with conducting an illegal boycott. Shortly thereafter Henry's wife, Noelle, was fired from her teaching job in the Clarksdale school system.

The most ecumenical of all civil rights leaders, Henry called upon the national civil rights organizations for support. Martin Luther King was the first to respond, urging local people to "stand in, sit in, and walk by the thousands." The Congress of Racial Equality (CORE) sent in staff members, and SNCC organizers were in and out of town to help when needed. (National NAACP officers, who accepted as an article of faith the idea that Mississippi was "NAACP territory," became apoplectic when they learned of Henry's heresy!) The Clarksdale pharmacist also enlisted virtually every black advancement group in the county, from the Mississippi Progressive Voters' League to the Coahoma County Ministerial Council. A respectable and successful businessman with a down-home manner, Henry had won the endorsement of the black middle class to pursue a militant program, no small achievement.

During the spring of 1963 black Clarksdale was subjected to an unprecedented reign of terror. In early March someone broke out the front windows in Henry's pharmacy, and on Good Friday two white men firebombed the Henrys' home. As he tells us in his memoir, Henry enlisted the assistance of his house guest, Detroit congressman Charles Diggs, in extinguishing the flames. Later that month an explosion ripped a hole through the roof of Henry's drugstore. There followed a series of demonstrations and sit-ins that jolted the city throughout the summer. After defying a court injunction prohibiting picketing, Henry was arrested, jailed, and assigned to a garbage truck work detail, an attempt at humiliation that only increased his prestige in the black community.

Despite black Clarksdale's sustaining a boycott far longer than had any other movement operation in the state, white officials remained intransigent. Backed by the police and courts, and believing that the Kennedy administration would not intervene, segregationists were confident that they could break the boycott without making concessions. Faced with this reality, Henry and other COFO leaders agreed that if the movement in Clarksdale—and in the rest of Mississippi—were to survive, they must reach out to the largely indifferent national public and shock it into demanding federal intervention. To do so meant attracting the media to Mississippi and providing television cameras with action footage. The Mississippi movement was about to enter a new stage.

The first step was the "Freedom Vote" in November of 1963, a mock election designed to prove to the nation that blacks would vote if given the opportunity. Henry was the COFO candidate for governor, the only person who had widespread support among the black middle class as well as connections to the younger militants in the movement. More than 80,000 blacks cast their ballots, in the face of white harrassment and violence.

Unfortunately, the Freedom Vote marked the high point of inter-organizational cooperation in the Mississippi movement. The "Freedom Summer" of 1964 did bring national and international attention to the Magnolia State, but fissures in the movement were beginning to show. Under increasing pressure from Wilkins and Current, Henry began to distance himself from his COFO allies. At the Democratic National Convention at Atlantic City Henry headed the Mississippi Freedom Democratic Party delegation that was challenging the seating of the white Mississippi segregationists. Under pressure, a reluctant Lyndon Johnson proposed a "two-seat compromise" whereby Henry and white activist Ed King would be seated as at-large delegates while the rest of the MFDP group would be "honored guests" of the convention. The MFDP rank and file, led by Mrs. Hamer, angrily denounced the proposal as both inadequate and insulting. Henry, on the other hand, influenced by national leaders ranging from Hubert Humphrey to Martin Luther King, supported the compromise and was so distraught when his delegation rejected it that he left for home before the convention ended. How one stood on the Atlantic City compromise became a litmus test of movement militancy, and Henry had clearly failed.

The following year Henry supported the state NAACP's decision to withdraw from COFO and found new allies in a group of white moderates, including Hodding Carter III, who had been on the sidelines when the freedom movement was fighting its toughest battles. This faction lobbied the national Democratic party to become its official voice in Mississippi, a position that put it squarely at odds with the grass-roots Freedom Democratic Party. Henry and Carter also joined forces to replace the besieged Child Development Group of Mississippi (CDGM), the movement-based statewide Head Start agency under attack from powerful Mississippi segregationists like Senator John Stennis. Here again movement activists like Mrs. Hamer denounced Henry as a sell-out when he and Carter agreed to head up the rival Mississippi Action for Progress (MAP), which won both state and federal support and became the major Head Start provider in Mississippi.

The last half of the 1960s was a painful time, both for Henry and for the young militants, who believed their movement had been betrayed by erstwhile allies at home and in Washington. Most of the SNCC and CORE organizers left the state to pursue activist agendas in other areas.

Aaron Henry stayed put. In the late sixties he was part of a coalition that successfully challenged the re-licensing of Jackson's major television station, WLBT, which had a long history of anti-black programming and policy. He was the key figure in building an interracial state Democratic party in the late 1970s, and served as party co-chair. In 1979 he won election to the state legislature, a position he held until 1995. Henry used his electoral office as a platform to call attention to the continuing pattern of racial injustice in the Magnolia State, introducing legislation to remove the Confederate battle flag from the Mississippi state flag and calling for the reopening of the 1960s murder cases of Medgar Evers and Vernon Dahmer. In the twilight of his career, as age and infirmity began to take their toll, Aaron Henry remained the dedicated activist, taking to the streets one final time to lead a demonstration against a state-sponsored plan to close two of the state's historically black colleges.

It is time that scholars take a closer look at the career and legacy of Aaron Henry. Viewed from the perspective of history, his position at Atlantic City and his decision to found MAP as a rival to CDGM seem more understandable, less like acts of betrayal. People of good will differed on whether to accept the two seats at Atlantic City and declare victory, or to reject the compromise on principle. That the issue became so divisive has much more to say about the perfidy of liberal northern Democrats than it does about the choices made by Henry and his followers. Unfortunately, Henry was tarred with the same brush, and his influence in the Mississippi movement declined.

As for the Head Start controversy, here again the choices were not simple. Had Henry and Carter not set up MAP, the alternative facing War on Poverty officials in Washington was either to end Head Start in Mississippi or to put it firmly under the control of white segregationists in state government. The total and unprincipled attack on CDGM by John Stennis had doomed that agency, despite the heroic efforts by local people and their national allies to save it.

So what are we to make of Aaron Henry's role in the history of the civil rights movement? The historian August Meier once referred to Martin Luther King as a "conservative militant," a person who put his life on the line daily in the struggle for civil rights, but who was also willing to compromise on issues of strategy, even though it meant alienating him from more outspoken activists. I believe that label fits Aaron Henry, too, and—unlike in the 1960s—it is no longer an epithet. The successes of the civil rights movement resulted from the cooperation of people with different backgrounds and agendas. As a link between black middle-class Mississippians and the younger full-time activists in SNCC and CORE, Henry played a crucial role during the years 1961-1965. That he stayed in Mississippi, and for the next three decades fought for human rights in a different political environment, is a tribute both to his commitment and to his under-appreciated role as Mississippi's most important black politician since Reconstruction.

We all owe Constance Curry a debt of gratitude for taking on the difficult task of editing and organizing Aaron Henry's autobiography, gathering interviews from his associates, and writing new material dealing with Henry's career after 1964. In her preface Curry talks about how she came across the 300-page manuscript of interviews with Henry conducted in 1965 by Bill Silver and Henry Hurt. This was and is an amazing document. Aaron Henry's voice comes through in every sentence. His descriptions of growing up black in the Mississippi Delta are some of the most moving and poetic passages I have read on the subject. For example, in discussing the great Delta flood of 1927, he observes that ". . . that old Mississippi river has never had one ounce of racial prejudice. It will drown or wash away a white man just as quick as a Negro and never think twice about it. When it comes to bursting over those levees, it doesn't stop and ask where the colored section is, it just takes it all. There's a particular equality about the river." The subsequent recollections of his coming of age in Mississippi, his army service in World War II, and his civil rights activism over the next two decades are of as much importance to the historian as they are of interest to the general reader.

Most oral interviews give us pieces of a person's life, interesting snapshots that provide source material for scholars. Of the "movement" oral histories I have come across, this is the only one that stands on its own as autobiography. Silver and Hurt did a masterful job of conducting the original interviews and doing the initial editorial work. Connie Curry has taken the process one step further, further editing the document while keeping Henry's voice in command throughout. What emerges is a mesmerizing first-person account of an African-American life in Mississippi from the era of the Great Depression to the mid-1960s.

Henry did not sit down for another series of sessions to reflect on his life after the Atlantic City convention. He did give other formal interviews, none of them remarkable, all paling in comparison with his memoir. In the spring of 1981 John Jones (then the oral historian for the Mississippi Department of Archives and History) and I made the journey to Clarksdale to interview Henry. Like other historians and journalists before us, we spoke with him as he waited on customers in his drug store. Kind, friendly, and considerate, Henry was everything but forthcoming, particularly when questions focused on the post-1964 years. He refused to respond to those activists who had publicly criticized some of his decisions since Atlantic City, and his answers to questions about the earlier movement years contained few new insights. Maybe he was saving this material for a full-scale autobiography; as an active politician he was no doubt wary of divulging information and opinions that opponents might use against him; or perhaps he had just had his fill of giving interviews to outsiders asking the same questions, wasting his time.

At any rate, the post-1965 oral histories with Henry are disappointing, and it is to Curry's credit that she did not cobble them together and pass the finished product off as "the autobiography of Aaron Henry." Still, it is unfortunate that Henry did not tell us more about his later career. Had he lived, no doubt he would have spoken candidly and at length with Connie Curry, herself a 1960s civil rights activist who had first-hand experience in Mississippi. The result of this collaboration would have been rewarding, to say the least.

Denied that opportunity, Curry has done the next best thing, soliciting remembrances of Aaron Henry from his friends, family, and colleagues in the civil rights movement. These interviews give us anecdotal insight into Aaron Henry's character and conduct. Several of them also provide new information on the black freedom struggle in Mississippi and are valuable primary source documents in themselves.

Aaron Henry was among the last of that generation of black leaders who came out of World War II dedicated to cracking open Mississippi's "closed society." After Henry's death in 1997 Benjamin Hooks, former NAACP executive secretary, called him a "giant" who devoted his life to the movement. Robert Clark, the first African American to serve in the Mississippi legislature in this century, summed up his feelings toward Henry quite simply: "I had more admiration for him than for any other living human being on the face of this earth." We come away from reading *The Fire Ever Burning* with respect and admiration for this unassuming, kind and courageous local leader, who left behind a legacy future generations should both know and honor.

John Dittmer
DePauw University

Prologue

I first met Aaron Henry at his drugstore in Clarksdale, Mississippi, one day in the summer of 1964. My friend Winifred Green and I had driven up to the Delta from Jackson. We were working then for the American Friends Service Committee and wanted to visit the few white contacts who might be interested in getting involved with Mississippians for Public Education, an organization formed to foster peaceful school desegregation in the state. The people we had approached on the Bobo plantation just outside Clarksdale were not interested—they asked us to leave before we finished our presentation. The ubiquitous pickup truck with gun rack had followed us on the deserted dusty road through the cotton fields until we hit the main road. We hightailed it to Clarksdale.

The drugstore on Fourth Street was dark, cool, and welcoming. As we two white women entered, a young handsome black man emerged from the back of the store. He introduced himself, and we told him what we were about. He gave us a cold Coke and told us to rest awhile.

Thirty-three years later, a group of Aaron Henry's friends in Jackson called me at my home in Atlanta and asked if I would be interested in telling his story. Aaron, as well as his friends, had read my book *Silver Rights*, about the Carters, a black family in a neighboring Delta county, who had also worked for civil rights. Aaron Henry liked the book because, as he told me, "It's about ordinary people—the people who made the freedom movement real—not just about the big-name leaders."

At first, the task of telling his story seemed daunting. There isn't one aspect of the fight for freedom and equality in the state of Mississippi over the past fifty years that does not reflect the influence of Aaron Henry. This became apparent as I interviewed the friends who were so intent on getting his story told. It had not been easy for them to convince Aaron to cooperate. "You can't write history when you are still making it," he told them. At the time, in 1996, along with his many other activities, he was serving in the Mississippi state legislature and chairing the board of WLBT, the TV station he had sued on charges of racism in 1964.

Aaron was born in 1922 on the Flowers plantation in Coahoma County, outside Clarksdale. His parents were sharecroppers, and he spent his early years picking cotton. He told me of being in the cotton field when a bright shiny school bus carrying white children whizzed by. When he asked his mother why he wasn't going to school for seven months as the white children did (black kids went for five months), his mother told him, "Aaron, you're my boy and you're smart and you just don't need to go as long." Then he looked at me and added, "I've been cocky ever since."

He also told me of his father's anger over the death of blues singer Bessie Smith. One of the few pleasures in the hard lives of Delta sharecroppers was attending minstrel shows. Bessie Smith, even after she became famous and known as "the Empress of the Blues," continued to star in shows in forgotten places in the rural South. In 1927, on her way to Darling, Mississippi, ten miles from Clarksdale, she was severely injured in an automobile accident. One story widely believed but since proven untrue is that she died because she was refused treatment at the white hospital in Clarksdale. The perception of the black community at the time was that the death of a beloved friend had occurred at the hands of a cruel system. Ed Henry and a group of his friends immediately started plans for a small clinic to provide emergency medical services for black people.

In December 1996, after Aaron and I agreed that we would do the book together, arrangements were made for us to spend ten days together in a secluded spot where I could interview him at length and without interruption. On Christmas Day, he had a stroke, which impaired his speaking ability. He died five months later. In the meantime, I had come across a treasure in the archives of Tougaloo College—over three hundred pages of autobiographical material, written in his voice, taken from interviews with Aaron done in 1965 by Bill Silver and Henry Hurt. Bill Silver is the son of Dr. James W. Silver, who taught at the University of Mississippi until 1966.

Dr. Silver left the university in the midst of a raging controversy over his book *Mississippi: The Closed Society*, which includes his meeting Aaron for the first time and learning from him about the "other side of life" in Mississippi. Bill Silver had just graduated from Harvard, was home for the summer, and went with his father to visit Aaron in Clarksdale. He became interested in Aaron's life, and, along with his friend Henry Hurt, at the University of Mississippi, interviewed him, and then transcribed and wrote a draft manuscript of Aaron's autobiographical material, which went through 1964. In going over the material, I found that there were clumps of pages missing. After some interesting detective work, I found Bill Silver in California. He directed me to Henry Hurt in Virginia. Henry Hurt, through a near miracle, found his copy of the work, including the missing pages, in his basement. Both Hurt and Silver have given their blessing to my use of their work, and I am grateful. I have revised, edited, and reorganized that oral history to serve as the first section of the book. It tells, in Aaron's voice, the story of his boyhood days on the Delta plantation and in Clarksdale, of his time in the Army and in college, and then of his emergence as an extraordinary leader in the Mississippi NAACP and the civil rights movement of the 1960s.

The last chapter of the book includes interviews that illuminate his life after 1968, when "everyone wanted a piece of Doc," as one of his friends said. The interviews show the variety and number of people and organizations he served; among many other activities, he chaired the boards of the Jackson TV station and of the National Caucus and Center on Black Aged, and served terms in the state legislature. It is clear that his work has changed not only Mississippi but also systems and policies of national import.

I have also included material from interviews that show the personal side of this man—his relations with his wife, Noelle, his daughter, Rebecca, and his grandsons, Aaron and DeMon. He evoked deep loyalty from the black people whose lives were so much better because of his work. He inspired fear, respect, and reverence in a white community that he helped change forever. The white power structure in Clarksdale, Jackson, and Washington, D.C., paid attention to Aaron, because, as a friend said, "He always followed through—no empty threats from Aaron Henry." But the two themes that echoed over and over in my interviews were "the most forgiving man I've ever known" and "the most courageous person I ever met."

He was a complex man who brooked no pretense but shone with warmth and humor. "I've been in jail thirty four times," he told me, "but you always get out." He had a unique way of greeting men he knew (and many he didn't know) with a head butting or a banging of foreheads in addition to a routine handshake.

He knew and loved music, poetry, and books and, near the end, asked to see a copy of his favorite poem, "Invictus" ("I am the master of my fate.")

Aaron never recovered from the stroke on Christmas Day, and he died on May 19, 1997. I had visited him in the hospital in Jackson and in his house in Clarksdale. During the Clarksdale visit in April, I played a tape for him of the prologue of a National Public Radio series called *Will the Circle Be Unbroken*. The twenty-six segments tell the stories of the "foot soldiers" in the civil rights movement from the 1940s on. The stories are taken from interviews done over the years, and Aaron speaks in the prologue as well as several times in segments on Mississippi. The speaking parts are interspersed with music of the times, and, in the prologue, right before Aaron talks, we heard those haunting lines from Sam Cooke—"I was born by the river/change is gonna come, oh yeah." Then there were echoes of "People, get ready, the train's a-comin' " and "Will the circle be unbroken." As Aaron listened, he tapped his fingers on the bedcovers in time to the music, and, as it faded away, I saw tears in his eyes.

At the memorial services for Aaron Henry, I was looking at the program and saw that his favorite farewell—one that he had been using in speeches for years and years—was an Irish blessing that my parents had passed on to me and that has been hanging on my office wall for thirty years:

> *May the road rise to meet you,*
> *May the wind always be at your back,*
> *May the sun shine warm upon your face,*
> *May the rain fall soft upon your fields,*
> *And until we meet again,*
> *May God hold you in the palm of his hand.*

There couldn't have been a clearer message from Aaron to me regarding the writing of this book. I felt as if he were looking over my shoulder, giving his blessing but saying in his insistent way, "Well, we've just got to get on with it."

This book does not pretend to be a definitive biography of Aaron Henry. I have not interviewed many of the people who knew him well, and I have not included all of the interviews that I did conduct. In remaining true to his request that the book be accessible to everyone and "not be one of those big academic ones," these pages are a mere taste of his life. I hope others will be inspired to fill in the rest.

Constance Curry
Atlanta, Georgia 1999

Aaron Henry

Chapter 1

The Bible, The Almanac, and the Sears Catalogue

White people used to say we didn't mind that hot Mississippi sun, beating the strength out of our backs and drawing the sap from our souls. They said our black skins kept us from knowing that suffering—that we didn't mind working fifteen hours a day in thick heat and stinging dust. They said we were able to withstand the drudgery because we were made that way and were capable of little else besides that work.

When I was growing up in Mississippi, on the Flowers brothers' plantation about twenty miles east of Clarksdale in Coahoma County, the sharecropping system was firmly established. Its tap root ran straight down through history to the first time man discovered what tactics could be employed to press his fellow man into servitude. The branches of the system were entangled in every field Negro's brain, back, and soul, and we never questioned it, because it was all we knew. We had to work all day in those green-and-white blistering cotton fields if we wanted to live. It was work or starve or get run off the place, and the work was simpler than the uncertainty of the outside. Nobody ever asked how we felt. They would hear us singing about the heat and the work and the life, and they would turn and tell each other how happy we all were. Of course, singing and religion were about all we could do for entertainment, and I think most people will admit that we got pretty good at those two things.

The Mississippi Delta was developed by the constant overflow of the Mississippi and Yazoo rivers over hundreds and hundreds of years. The continuous overflow created a swampy, wooded area, sparsely inhabited until late in the nineteenth century. After the Civil War, Negroes could not buy land in many areas in Mississippi, and the first land that became available to the freed slaves was in the Delta. Few whites were willing to suffer the hardships of almost uncivilized country, the undeterminable factor of an unmanageable river, and serious health problems. The flooding rivers would often destroy an entire year's labor, and the heavy infestation of mosquitoes made malaria and yellow fever recurring and deadly problems. As methods were developed to control the almighty river, more whites began moving in. That uninhabitable swamp had been cleared and was soon cultivated into the most fertile cotton land in the state—the Mississippi Delta.

As far back as I can trace, my family has been in Mississippi. I remember my maternal grandmother telling stories of slavery days, of murders and lynchings and white authority that went completely unchallenged. When I was born in 1922, my father had about forty acres to farm on the Flowers plantation.

Thirty or so members of our family also lived there, including ten or twelve adults and the rest children. My mother died when I was three, and my father two years later, and I was raised by Mother's brother, Ed Henry, and his wife Mattie. I considered them my parents and Merryll, a niece they were also raising, as my sister. All of my relatives on the plantation—aunts and uncles and cousins—pitched in and helped each other in the endless plowing, chopping, and gathering of the cotton—it was our life. Between times dictated by Master Cotton, the family operated as a unit, banding together to go into the woods and cut trees for fuel for winter. The men and boys made sure they left a load of wood at each of our houses.

When working in the fields, we were up before the sun, and Mother fixed us eggs if we had them and filled our empty spaces with grits. That was to hold us until dinner. On special occasions we had butter for our grits, but usually it was just salt. Sometimes after hog-killing time, we would have a big treat of bacon.

If it was time to plow, before going to the fields each day, we would go get our mule from an enclosure called "the lot." All of the plantation mules were kept there, and I can still see what looked to a child like an acre of mules. We would get ours hooked up and go to the field and plow and bring the mule back to the lot at noon and again in the evening.

Usually the walk to the fields in the early morning would be at least comfortable, if not cool. But by the time we got there, the sun would be rising and the sweat would be coming. When I dressed in the morning, my clothes were usually damp and cool from the previous day's sweat, but they were warm and sticky again by the time we reached the fields.

As far back as I can remember, I have detested everything about growing cotton. When we would pick, I was one of the slowest workers. My hands were never as large as the other boys', and one time a white man told me that I might make a musician some day. He said that my hands were smaller and my fingers longer than those of most white men. I told him that maybe that was the reason I detested cotton working so much. I never learned to play an instrument, and maybe dreaming about it slowed me down even more. I just know that I would start down my row picking that cotton and stuffing it into my sack and never looking up. The older field hands always told us that once we bent over, to stay down as long as we could, because the bending and unbending made your back the sorest. So, I went along the row picking as best I could, head down, and, after a while, I would just know I was halfway to the end of the row. Then I would look up and see that I was only about twenty yards from where I had started, that I was twenty yards behind everybody else, and that my sack was only about half as full as the others.

There were two or three white families on the plantation who worked as sharecroppers and lived under the same conditions that we did. We had a common bond in our impoverishment, and color made no difference between us—no segregation and no white supremacy. We all stood in the same line to get our goods at the commissary. The men sat around and chewed tobacco together and drank whiskey that they sometimes made together. The white and Negro women frequently had quilting bees. The families shared when bad weather was expected or any sort of emergency existed. A Negro midwife on the plantation named Granny delivered white and Negro babies. No courtesy titles entered the picture, because white and Negro sharecroppers called each other by first names.

As a child, all of this seemed perfectly natural, but later, when I operated my drugstore, I fully understood the absence of racial prejudice among the sharecroppers. Race simply made no difference as long as you were dirt poor—white and Negro tenants simply suffered their destinies together. I found in my own store that the really poor whites were just as humble as Negroes at that economic level. I have known whites so poor that they didn't object to going to a Negro's home, sitting at his table, and even sleeping in the same bed with him.

One of the white sharecropper families on the Flowers place was named Smithers, and they had a son, Randolph, who was my age, and a daughter about the age of my sister. My mother later told me that when Randolph and I were babies, I sometimes was left at the Smithers house, and Mrs. Smithers nursed us both. When Randolph was left at our house, my mother did the same. I cannot remember the time that Randolph and I were not the closest of friends.

The manager of the plantation, Mr. Baker, was a short, fat white man with a red face and a thick neck. He sweated a great deal, and when he held his chin up, I could see black lines of grit across his neck where his double chins had folded in the sweat and dirt. We all accepted Baker as the head of the plantation, but he never interfered with family units. My father was the head of our family. My parents were hardworking and loyal people. I was never directly abused in any way by the Bakers, and I don't believe my father was. However, if he was mistreated, Father would not have told us, because he always tried to spare us from unpleasantness. Baker had a son, about my age, and he was usually a part of our nuthunting and berrypicking. We always felt that the son was a little above the rest of us, white and Negro, because he had so many more things and did not have to work.

Life support on the plantation was meted out from the heart of the system—the commissary. We got our food supplies and clothing here and at the same time wrapped ourselves in debts from which it was nearly impossible to escape. We were charged for the supplies, and, at the end of the crop year after the cotton had been harvested and ginned, Mr. Baker would inform us what sum our part of the crop had brought. If we earned more than we owed, we got the difference. If we owed more than we had earned, the difference was charged to us. There was only one set of records, which were kept by the plantation owner, and we had to pay or get whatever he said. There was no contract, and, over the years, many tenants found themselves so deeply in debt that they could never leave the system.

We bought rice and flour, salt and pepper, and salt meat from the commissary. We ground corn into meal ourselves, but it was never enough to last the year, so we had to buy meal, too. We bought cloth, and Mother made shirts and dresses and underclothes. Trousers, coats, and caps were purchased.

We had room on our forty acres to raise chickens and hogs. The hogs were slaughtered and salted down, but chicken was a delicacy because we used them mostly for eggs. Pork was the only fresh meat until September, when the first bales of cotton were ginned. Then, if we got a share of the money, we went to the butcher shop in town and bought beef or liver. Steak and gravy were the treats at this time of year.

There are other pleasant recollections of fall when everybody, young and old, went blackberry picking or hunting for muscadines, persimmons, hickory nuts, and walnuts. We also dug up peanuts that we had grown, but, once they left the ground, they were kept by the adults so the children wouldn't get stomachaches from eating green peanuts. The raw nuts were spread out on the flat roof of the house to dry.

One time after my father had spread the nuts to dry, he took the ladder up to Mr. Baker's storehouse so we couldn't use it to climb onto the roof. I was determined to get up there and get a pocketful of peanuts, but I knew I couldn't get the ladder. My father had planted a tree beside the house about the time I was born and had taken every precaution to protect it so that someday we would have shade. I guess the tree was six by then, and it reached well above the top of the house. It wasn't very big around, but I figured it was surely large enough to hold me. I waited until my parents had gone away, and I started to shinny up the tree. I got almost to the point where I could have moved over onto the roof when the tree started bending and swaying. I knew that I was bound to go down with the tree, but I didn't know if it would be a gentle fall or if the tree would simply break and drop me straight to the ground. So I lunged toward the roof and grabbed it by the edge, and the tree swung away from me. There I was, hanging by my fingertips on the edge of the roof, unable to draw myself up and unsure if I could drop without hurting myself. I was trying to decide how to get down and thinking what my father would do if he caught me.

Just then someone came along laughing to beat hell. Because of the way I was hanging, I couldn't look down, but I asked the boy to help me down to the ground. The rogue just kept laughing and accusing me of trying to steal peanuts and finally told me that there were rocks and broken glass under me and that if I dropped, I would cut my feet badly. I was tired of hanging and terrified and started bawling as hard and as loud as I could. I started yelling for my mother while the boy below kept laughing—almost as loud as I was crying. Before long I heard my father calling my name, as he ran towards the house. He reached up and grabbed me by my feet, and I let go of the roof. I was thankful to be down, but when my father realized what I had been doing, I got one of the sharpest whippings of my life. The other boy was still standing there laughing, and I told Daddy how he had lied about the glass and rocks beneath me. As was the custom, my father didn't lay a hand on the other boy and went straight to his father to tell what had happened. I could hear the other boy getting his whipping, but Daddy said he would whip me again if I went over there and watched and laughed.

During those years, the Bible, the Ladies' Birthday Almanac, and the Sears and Roebuck catalogue served as standard references. They composed the family library. The Bible was the basic guideline, and it could work either way—to tell us what we couldn't do and then to show that our parents had done the right thing. It usually didn't work too much in my favor, but I held the Bible in complete respect. The almanac told us what to do and what not to do according to phases of the moon. We planted vegetable crops only on certain days that were indicated in the almanac. We were careful not to get our teeth pulled at times when the blood was in the head.

The Sears catalogue was the real treasure as far as the children were concerned. We would sit for hours and look at the pictures of trains and trucks and hats, and we would talk about wanting this or that more than anything else on the page. Then we would turn the page and find something else that we wanted even more. Our parents would laugh at us and tease us when we told them we were going to order from the catalogue. But when we weren't looking they would spend more time than the children, looking at the pictures and wishing. Sometimes, it sounded like a ladies' church social when several of the women would get together and all be trying to look at the catalogue at the same time. They would talk at the same time, and then their voices would get louder and they would be scrambling around, each one trying to point out what she wanted most on the page. I guess one of the most joyous times of the year was when the new catalogue arrived, but I cannot recall a single time when my family ordered anything through the mail.

Many of the sharecroppers on the plantation were improvident in handling their money. After a long year and dull days of hard work, many tenants would take their settlement money and toss it away frivolously rather than save it to buy their own land. That's one reason why there were so many automobiles in rural areas, even when there was no money to buy gas. A car was a symbol—"we have arrived; we have amounted to something." Later the symbols would be indoor plumbing and a radio. Or some sharecroppers would buy whiskey and drink it immediately. Perhaps because the plantation owner controlled their lives so completely and sometimes capriciously, many sought to get what little pleasure they could the moment it was available. Others were more disciplined, and my father, in fact, was something of a penny-pincher.

Most plantation owners did not deal honestly with their tenants, and this formed the basic inequity of the sharecropping system. The owners were dealing with people whom they felt were subhuman, and they felt no moral obligation for fairness in the treatment of their tenants. The Bakers considered us only as instruments or machines that were needed to help them make a living. They were quite willing to take care of every need that was essential to our full productivity. In another respect, they treated the Negroes like mules—kind to them when the animal worked hard, but, if the mule balked, he was in trouble.

The system was not a condition of actual servitude, but escape meant a willingness to throw basic security to the wind—the basic plantation security that assured food, clothing, and medical attention. Forget about the little things that often aren't actually needed but would be so very nice to have anyway. I remember that I always wanted a white wide-brimmed felt hat like Mr. Baker had, but I was told that a yellow wide-brimmed straw hat was good enough for me, and it was a long time before I even had that.

I was not aware that plantation life was a peculiar way to live. It was all that I had ever known and appeared to be the way the whole world operated. If my father had been satisfied with only basic securities, I might have spent all of my life on a plantation, never knowing if I would have had the initiative to break with the system.

One major weakness of the sharecropping system, however, was the white man's failure to recognize the factor that could destroy this bondage—education. The roots of the system, so tangled up in the generations of black ignorance and white supremacy, sometimes produced an almost childlike innocence, where a white planter found it acceptable, if not useful, for a Negro tenant to learn a trade. When my father realized this and the near impossibility of prospering within the system, he learned the cobbling trade, and we moved into the nearby town of Webb. Our family was relatively small, and I am not sure how valuable we were to Baker. Perhaps Baker could have prevented my father from learning the trade, but I rather believe that Baker did not realize the full significance of even a smattering of education. Whites used to laugh and say that we bred like flies, but they were not aware of the multiple progression that comes when tiny bits of education are connected and put to use.

I don't know why my father decided to try shoe cobbling. I suppose that it was either from reading about it in a magazine or hearing people talk about it. It was the era when Tuskegee Institute in Alabama taught cobbling and other trades of the hands following Booker T. Washington's philosophy that Negroes should be content to work with their hands. Perhaps someone was talking about Tuskegee and convinced my father that cobbling was a trade that he could learn. He toyed around during his spare time putting together pieces of leather and saw that he had a talent for it. He got in touch with the Southern Leather Company in Memphis who sent a white representative to talk with Father. The company was interested in setting up a cobbler in Webb, and we moved from the plantation in the spring of 1927.

Father drove a borrowed truck up to our house one hot September morning. Behind the truck was the rest of our family who lived on the plantation and a host of neighbors. We had packed our belongings in boxes, done the breakfast dishes, and dismantled the beds. Everybody helped us load up, and, when the truck was full, Mother made us wear our shoes and hats and coats to save space. We were hot and uncomfortable, and at first Father wanted me to stay in the back of the truck to make sure nothing fell off. I wanted to ride on the front seat—the second time in my life—but, before I could complain, Mother told him that I was too little to ride in back, and Merryll rode there instead. As we drove off, I heard someone holler, "Aaron, they ain't got no flat roofs with peanuts on them in town." It was the little rogue who had left me hanging off the roof the time I was trying to steal peanuts. Word about that incident had spread, and I had been teased without mercy. Everybody was laughing at the remark, except for me and Father—I still didn't think it was funny. Father seemed to understand, and I felt as close to him as I ever had.

We drove off amidst the hollering of good-byes and best wishes. I was between my parents in front and turned to look out the back window of the truck. Our belongings were piled too high to see, so I just hollered my good-byes at the top of my lungs until Mother told me to hush. I am sure my father had dreamed for years about the day when he would put down the hoe and cotton sack, stop walking behind a mule, and have no need to pray about enough wood for the winter. We had all of the money from the last crop, all the meat we had was cured, and all the provisions we had were stored. We were more free and economically secure than we had ever been. After we moved from the plantation, the family left behind also began to move. My grandparents moved to Clarksdale, and the rest scattered to St. Louis and Chicago. They had been talking for years, and, after we did it, they took heart and followed.

We moved into a small, four-room house in Webb. It was in the Negro section of town but very close to the white area. Merryll slept in the front room, and my parents and I slept in the bedrooms in the back of the house. There was a combination kitchen and dining room and a narrow front porch that went the length of the house. The porch had a swing, which was a great novelty for me and the source of many bad spills. When it was put off-limits for me, I would try to swing anyway, and, if I fell, I was careful to cry so softly that Mother couldn't hear me. A wood stove heated the house, and, for the first time, we could buy wood rather than chopping it. The one great addition to our regular utensils and furnishings were the Christmas gifts from the Southern Leather Company—a beautiful lamp and a leather wall hanging.

We had a garden in back with apple and plum trees that were as taboo for me as the peanuts on the plantation.

Webb was a small Delta cotton town to the left of Highway 49 going towards Greenwood, not far from the plantation but in Tallahatchie County. It had about a thousand people, majority Negro, but the whites controlled the town and owned most of the businesses. Negroes owned cafes, a beauty shop and the barbershop, and Father set up shop on the dusty main road that dead-ended at the cotton fields. He rented his space from a Chinese grocer.

The Southern Leather Company provided Father with all of his machines and was willing to bide its time on the payments. The agreement was that Father would continue to buy all his leather from them, and the company gave him a rebate on the price of leather, which went towards paying for the machines. When Father was first getting started, the representative from the leather company frequently came by to teach him how to operate the machines and how to work with the leather. The soles for the shoes came two ways—either they were ready-cut, or, if there were no appropriate size, the correct size was cut from rolls of crude leather. Father had to be prepared to provide both. His main work was repair, and, when he occasionally tried to make a pair of shoes from scratch, I thought they never did look worth a damn.

Father's hours at the shoe shop were longer than they had been on the plantation. He would go to work before dawn and work until eight or nine o'clock before coming home at night. The difference to the family, of course, was that we weren't obligated to help—no more servitude to the cotton fields. I only had the not-very-difficult job of cleaning the shop. By Christmas after our move, Father had become proficient in cobbling and was doing better than he had ever done on the plantation.

The year we lived in Webb, the white people accepted my father as a competent businessman. In most instances, the white leaders of the town were civil and even cordial to him, although they were always "Mister" and he was always "Ed." No matter what equality there might be in a business dealing, the differentiation of the courtesy titles for whites persisted for no other reason than race, and it bothered me from an early age. Both Negro and white were willing to pay Father for his work, but there were times when neither could pay him with money, and then he accepted payment in goods—a dozen eggs or a sack of potatoes. More often than not our diet consisted of the goods which Father had accepted in lieu of money. There was a time that I fell out with eating pumpkin. It seemed that most of the non-paying customers were able to give a pumpkin for Father's cobbling work, and Mother never did learn to cook it so that it was palatable.

Every now and then there would be a white fellow who would get his shoe work done on credit and then decide not to pay. Father was always very insistent that he be paid for his services. When that didn't work out, he never created any real trouble over it, and I am not sure that he could have. But for those people, Father refused to do additional work unless they paid for work done previously.

Shortly after we moved to Webb, Mother took a course in beauty culture. She began to dress hair at home, and she and her customers were often at it until late at night. As I lay in bed, I sometimes thought that they did more talking than anything else, and it reminded me of the times the women on the plantation used to pore over the Sears catalogue.

The Smithers family had moved from the Baker plantation at the same time we did and remained our closest friends in Webb. Mr. Smithers worked for a company delivering wood and coal, and Mrs. Smithers became a waitress in a restaurant right across the street from the shoe shop. She served both whites and Negroes, but there was a work area in the center with seats on one side for whites and on the other for Negroes. We would sit on our side and see her over on the other side.

For a long time, Randolph and I didn't know anyone but each other. I found other Negro friends and white friends, but I never felt as close to them as I did to Randolph. The Smithers family lived in the white part of town, and our house was in the colored section, but in actuality the houses weren't very far apart. Their house was between our house and the shop, so I passed it twice every day going to the shop and coming home. Our families had visited back and forth on the plantation, and this continued in town. There were never any objections. My parents and Randolph's parents were on a warm, first-name basis, and this never altered.

During the spring and summer that I was in Webb, Randolph and I spent a lot of time together. Sometimes we would play with other kids and swirl a rope, and at other times somebody would have a pocket knife and we would play mumblety-peg. If we didn't have a pocket knife, one of us would get a paring knife from our kitchen, but to be caught doing this was equivalent to stealing peanuts or swinging too hard on the porch swing. We shot marbles, and still picked berries and went hickory nut hunting. We swam in the creek and did a thousand other things. We had a great time talking about when we would start school in September and we looked forward to enjoying it together. But when the time came, we were told that we would have to go to separate schools. That was one of the greatest heartbreaks of my life.

There was a school for whites in Webb, but Negroes had to go to school on a nearby plantation. Our school was held in a Baptist church, and two teachers were in charge of all grades. The teachers would go from one group to another while we sat on our benches and waited. Each grade had a time during the day to recite and have its lessons heard by the teacher. My grade was called "primer," and our lessons were in McGuffey's reader. During that time, my mother said that school did Merryll and me no more good than to keep us quiet.

In contrast, the school that Randolph attended was made of brick, and it looked like a school. It was directly across the road from where we lived, and I would look at the white children laughing and playing outdoors and not understand. Randolph and I never discussed it, but it was then I began to realize that my family and I were considered something less than our white counterparts. I was considered inferior to Randolph simply because his skin was white and mine was black. In every other respect we were the same— our cultural background, our economic status, and even our social status were all about the same. In fact, I think probably Father's business gave us a financial independence that the Smithers family did not enjoy.

In short, I experienced my first racial segregation in Webb and became aware that schools, housing, restaurants, washrooms—everything was completely segregated. Yet there was always that strange business of friendship between the races. We had so many hardships and problems in common that the kinship was bound to exist. It flourished in private but was denied to the end in public or when the chips were down. I am sure that I was confused by all of this and my emotions were strong, but I began to learn to forget the things that are most unpleasant.

My year in Webb also taught me about life under another kind of tension. It was 1927, the year that the Mississippi River flooded. All up and down the Delta, that old river came swirling and snorting out of its bed and washed away almost everything people had, except their sins. There was talk about thousands of people getting killed and drowned, and they said that the river left the white folks as poor as the colored. We lived across the railroad tracks from the real high water and had to use a boat to get downtown to the shop. I watched people working on the levees, piling up sandbags to keep water from coming into the town. The flood itself was not too hard on the people of Webb. The worst part was the stories that we heard. We heard rumors that people in towns up and down the river might come and dynamite our levees in order to relieve the pressure on theirs. There were armed guards on the levee, and there was even talk of murdering anybody from a neighboring town who might be in Webb for that reason.

I realize, thinking back, that that old Mississippi River has never had one ounce of racial prejudice. It will drown or wash away a white man just as quick as a Negro and never think twice about it. When it comes bursting over those levees, it doesn't stop and ask where the colored section is, it just takes it all. There's a particular equality about the river, an equality that comes in something so great and powerful and so potentially good that no man can change it. The Mississippi gave both whites and blacks their water and food, and it accepted our waste—the giving and the taking were all on an equal basis. It was like the sun and rain and death and God, the things that even the biggest cotton planter in the Delta could not control. But the example did not wear off on him. If there was ever real authority in Mississippi, it was the river, and the white people seem to have been born with a resentment of its authority. A mystical person might say that the inherent rebelliousness of the white Delta people comes from a heritage of having to deal with the river on the river's terms—no questions asked.

Chapter 2

A Boy Scout General

Father and Mother worked hard in Webb, and within a year or so we were able to buy our own lot and house and move to Clarksdale, Coahoma County seat, about twenty-five miles west of Webb. We made the move during late summer, so Merryll and I would have time to settle in and get ready to start school in the fall. My parents' interest in education is not easy to explain, but they were determined that my sister and I take advantage of a better education in the Clarksdale system. Mother finished only six grades at Vance, Mississippi, where she was raised, and went to Tuskegee Institute for a year, but her parents never had money to send her back. Father's schooling was limited, but he and Mother had seen that Father's knowledge of cobbling had enabled him to break from the system. They knew what people could do with some education and figured their own children must have it in order to prosper.

We had our house built for about five thousand dollars, obtained through the Home Owner's Loan Corporation, a federal agency. It was fairly easy to borrow money from them—you had to earn about ten dollars a week and want to build your home. We were so thankful for that loan, and I went happily each week for five or six years to the post office for the postal money order forms we used for payments.

Clarksdale was a busy world after our life in the rural area, but I liked our neat little house at 742 Garfield, only seven houses away from Highway 61, the main thoroughfare to Memphis. The house was in the midst of the colored section and right across from Myrtle Hall School, the public school for blacks. Life was also different because we missed my father during the week. He kept the shop at Webb and only came to Clarksdale on the weekend.

If I didn't have a summer job, I would go to Webb with him to help in the shop, and it reinforced my lack of desire to be a cobbler. The hard part came when Father tried to teach me the skills. I learned how to sew up a rip in a shoe, and, after a great deal of effort, I was able to half-sole shoes. I was best at putting plates on shoes—an easy job because the plates came with three prongs attached, and all I had to do was hold them straight and drive them in. But I couldn't operate the machines, and whenever Father would leave the shop in my charge it seemed like the machines would break down, and there I would be, stuck like a fool, unable to fix anybody's shoes. The equipment that we had wasn't the best, but my father had learned to tinker with it and make it work. It was like the case of an old car that will not run except for one certain man.

Soon after our move to Clarksdale, I saw even more vividly the real position of the Negro in a white-controlled but predominantly black community. The schools were separate and unequal; movies for colored were upstairs and dingy. Negro boys could not be in the Boy Scouts, even in a separate troop. If we paid social calls on whites, it was through the back door, because it was through the front door that courtship possibly could occur.

Church was a big thing in Clarksdale, and the Haven Methodist Church, where my parents were staunch members, took up a lot of time. A regular Sunday was a pretty good workout in itself, but I had to start doing my part at home on Saturday by cutting the grass and trimming up the yard. I had to scrub the kitchen floor and do heavy work around the house. Sunday mornings were a big rush, and my sister and I always got into a fuss over something. I guess it was because we were always ready to go too early and had to sit around with Sunday clothes on and nothing to do. Sunday clothes meant doing Sunday things or going to a funeral.

After Sunday school came church. The preachings were hellfire and damnation, and when you left you were sure you had no chance of getting to heaven. The emphasis was strictly otherworldly—little concern for a good life here but a lot for getting to heaven in the next life. The theory was that the worse off you were on earth, the better chance you had at the pearly gates. A lot of people said they believed that, but I never saw anyone turn down good money to improve their chances for the here and now. Possibly the Negroes' situation on earth seemed so hopeless that the church felt it could do nothing of significance to change their lives.

On Sunday afternoons, I would have to go to the Epworth League, our youth group, and, later that night, the whole family would go to night service. During the year, there was the Easter pageant, the Mother's Day plays, and the Children's Day plays. One year I was a wise man in the Christmas play, and the next year I moved up to Joseph. All year long, I had to learn verses of biblical characters for various presentations, and after a while I would get mixed up about which role I was playing. I had to be in all of the plays, and each part required long hours of memorization and practice. I had so much church that it was coming out my ears.

In addition to official church functions, Mother had all sorts of related activities at home. She worked with the Women's Missionary Society, a world-service program sponsored by the Methodists. This group, with separate chapters in the white and colored church, collected money to support missionaries. When I was growing up, their goal was to Christianize the Japanese. So, the segregated Negro and white Methodist churches of Clarksdale were supporting the same missionaries for the same cause. Never in my recollection has anybody objected to integrated money. White and colored may not be able to put it in the same plate at the same time, but once it is there it matters not where it came from.

The Women's Missionary Society held study sessions on this burning issue of offering the advantages of Christianity to the Japanese. The national church headquarters would send the women literature to read and discuss. The women spent a great deal of time looking at pictures and slides of Japanese people, and I even had to be in a church play on Japanese culture. They were concerned over the Japanese not knowing the teachings of Jesus Christ, while some of their own people were almost starving under the burden of secondary citizenship in a country racked by the greatest economic depression in its history. And even though the Japanese were also needing food, the women in Clarksdale, white and Negro alike, were more interested in indoctrinating heathens in the saving grace of Christ than they were in feeding them.

Often these talking sessions between Mother and her friends lasted until late at night, and this had a bearing on one of my main chores. During the cool months, my job was to make sure there was enough coal and kindling in the house at night to keep the house warm until we went to bed and then to start the fire the next morning. When Mother and her friends sat up late and burned up all the coal and kindling, I would have to get up early in the morning in the cold and go outside to get more material to start the fire. I used to voice my objection, but it never did any good. Mother would just laugh and say that the only bad thing would be my getting a little cold and she didn't see that it would do me any harm. We always bought our wood in "blocks," and I would have to chop it up, so I finally learned that the more you chopped, the more wood got burned. It was then possible for me to send the women home whenever I wanted by calculating when they would run out of heat from the fire. I would lie there in my bed and hear them talking, or they'd be quilting or playing cards. The worst time was when they would raise their voices and yell over how much money to send the Japanese. I'd listen to them still talking about taking care of the Japanese and wonder where I was going to get the money to buy a new pair of trousers to wear to school in September, and I was glad that they would soon be running out of wood.

The missionary zeal of these Methodist women reminds me of the interest of southern white Christians a century earlier when they decided that they and their forebears had brought heathen Africans here in order to Christianize them. In my childhood, the white ladies were willing to come over and make charitable offerings, as long as they were able to pat our kinky heads and go back home and say they had done some good. I wonder about the nobility in helping the underprivileged. That nobility comes easy when your community is overflowing with destitute people and you are in sympathy with a system that keeps them that way.

When we first became involved at Haven Methodist Church, I wondered why we bypassed the three Baptist churches within five blocks of our house. It always seemed to me that one of them would be just as good. But my parents insisted that we walk all the way to the Methodist church, and after a few years I became convinced that the Methodists must be the most likely to take care of a few of our problems on earth and get us all to heaven as well.

But as I grew older I realized all the churches failed to play the role that they should have—trying to close the gulf between Negroes and whites within the same denomination. Had the churches tried to better race relations during the early thirties, possibly they could have held a light through the racial turbulence of the sixties. They could have provided competent leadership, respected by members on both sides of the issues.

All the church doings, and not-doings, and fear of my not being a good Christian left me with little desire for the fun most kids should have. I had learned from my father to hide a nickel for a long time and not to spend it the first time I thought I needed to. I waited and spent it only the second or third time that it seemed necessary. Saving money, going to school, and working in my father's shop were foremost in my mind. By the time I was twelve my aunts and uncles would see me coming with my serious face, and say, "Why, here comes that little old man, Aaron."

We were able to prosper in Clarksdale, even within the system—still a better one than the plantation system from which we had escaped. And even as the Great Depression crept in, there was more talk about it—as with the great flood—than there was actual hardship. Perhaps it was because things were already so bad in Mississippi that they couldn't get much worse. Father did begin to get more bartering payments than money. There were more eggs and milk and the despised pumpkin, and meat became a rarity. A favorite trick of some youngsters was to grease their mouths when they came out to play after a meal to give the impression that they had eaten meat for dinner. Most of us were eating turnip bottoms.

I started to school at Myrtle Hall, across the street from our house in Clarksdale. It offered only eight grades—there was no high school for Negroes in Clarksdale until 1950. The first five grades at Myrtle Hall were only for the children from below the railroad tracks, and the last three had Negro students from all over the city. The other Negro elementary school, Booker T. Washington, went through the fifth grade, and when children completed that, they came to Myrtle Hall. My first-grade teacher was a lady named Mrs. Stone, whom I remember for a big blue mole on her lip. She taught us reading, writing, and numbers. There were about a thousand students at Myrtle Hall, and many of them lived in the rural. Their parents sent them to town to school at a tuition of two dollars a month. There were schools in the rural areas, but the schools in Clarksdale were considered the best in the county and had a good reputation across the state. We had a separate teacher for each grade, which was quite an improvement over the school system at Webb.

The principal of the school was the only one on staff who had some college work. Most of the teachers had not finished high school. The best system that could be arranged was to make sure that each teacher finished at least a grade higher than he or she was teaching. Schoolteachers were paid only thirty-five or forty dollars a month. The colleges for Negroes in Mississippi, until the establishment of the Mississippi Vocational College at Itta Bena, were all located outside of the Delta. The students who graduated from these colleges and went into teaching usually went to other parts of the state because of higher pay.

One of the main attractions of school in Clarksdale for me was play period and organized activities during the school year and sometimes on into the summer. I had never had any desire for organized recreation on the plantation or in Webb, but I guess it was because I had never been exposed to it. On the plantation my friends and I had always been content to amuse ourselves wherever we were and with whatever equipment was handy. We had always had plenty of room for play since there were always vacant fields, but it was so much better to play on school playgrounds, and competitive sports were good because there was someone there to make sure the rules were obeyed. When the sun was shining, there was beanbag tossing and horseshoes, and when the weather was bad we could go in and read or color.

At home, my sister and I were busy through the week with chores. It was my job to keep the grass cut and to scrub the kitchen, and she and I took turns at washing the dishes. My sister had to keep the rest of the house clean and help Mother prepare meals. But it wasn't long before I started getting jobs after school and in the summertime. I still had to do my chores at home, but I did the housework at night and yard work on Saturdays.

The Crystal Ice and Fuel Company delivered coal to our house. It was my job to walk down to the company and order five hundred pounds or a half ton of coal. Then I would ride back with the Negro man who delivered it to make sure he didn't stop by his own house and throw off a few shovelfuls for his own use. This was a precaution almost all of the families took. The coal and wood were for the fireplaces in the house. We used a kerosene stove for cooking, and it was also my job to go get the kerosene. A little store about a block from the house sold kerosene for fifteen cents a gallon, but there was a place about ten blocks from home that sold it for ten cents a gallon. I wasn't allowed to stop at the fifteen-cent store and walked the eighteen extra blocks to save that nickel.

After we had been in Clarksdale for two or three years, Mother went to work for the white-owned Roy Crisler Real Estate Company. They had a home-owners' program, and Mother's job was to encourage Negroes to buy their own home. Her angle was that if her family could own their home, then there was little reason why other Negro families couldn't also. The job required Mother to be away from home quite a bit visiting communities all over the state. Grandmother would come take care of us, and Mother would leave us money to buy groceries, or we would use our charge account at one of the local stores where either my sister or I would shop.

At first, my father wasn't too happy about Mother working outside of the house, but she convinced him that it would help liquidate our debts. She was paid on a commission for every house or lot that she sold, and a good portion of our income came from her work. Because of that added income, Father finally agreed, and she was hired on the assumption that she would know prospective Negro customers and that they would be more willing to trust the real estate company if she was the go-between. Knowing my mother, I believe that the company dealt fairly with her.

To my dismay, even after our move to town, my days of working in cotton were not over. At ten years old I was able to hire out as a day laborer, and, for a while each summer, I went back to the fields. Trucks would come through the city every morning to pick up the laborers, and those who wanted to work that day just got on and went. Ordinarily the driver was paid for the number of laborers that he could deliver each morning, but some of the plantations sent their own trucks. There was no contract—you just went on the days that you wanted to and were paid at the end of the day. Cotton picking began the last week of August, so we were able to get in three or four weeks of picking before school began. After that, we would work on Saturdays.

Some of the most unpleasant times of my life were spent standing on the corner waiting for the truck to come take us to the fields. A big crowd would be standing there waiting—a lot of laughing and general foolishness—but all I could think of was those sweltering and boring fields waiting for us. We would usually leave around five in the morning and get to the fields about seven. We would work steadily through the morning until noon and then take off an hour for lunch. Sometimes I would carry my lunch from home, but if there was a store nearby I would take some money and buy bologna sausage, cheese crackers, sardines, and some kind of drink. On the plantation I had learned to accept the long, backbreaking day, and I actually thought that maybe I was out of step in disliking the work so intensely. And there I was back in the fields again, hating it more than anybody and doing the worst job. I doubt if I ever picked a hundred pounds in one day. The other laborers were always kind to me, and even at some sacrifice to their total day's work, they would help me out when I got too far behind. I was better at chopping cotton because everybody got the same pay, while for picking you got paid according to how much you picked. We were paid fifty cents a day for chopping and fifty cents per hundred pounds for picking. Whatever money I earned in the fields went to support the family.

My sister finished at Myrtle Hall when I was in the sixth grade, and she went off to Rust College at Holly Springs. This was a shock for me, because we had become quite close while living in Clarksdale. Mother's real estate work kept her away from home the last two years of Merryll's school, and Father was in Webb most of the time. With the money left for us for food and coal, we shared the responsibility of shifting for ourselves, and when it came time for her to leave for college, I was going to be left at home all by myself—without her and with all the chores. I was very unhappy and I cried for days, which was probably very foolish for a twelve-year-old. My parents were thirty years older, so I grew up with adults who were not only much older but also pretty serious-minded. That also might have added to my close attachment to my sister.

A white school was about four blocks from Myrtle Hall, and generally there was harmony. We seldom crossed paths with whites that we didn't know, and we had no desire to associate with white children simply because they were white. But when there was a white boy or girl that we knew and wanted to be with, we put ourselves out to go and find them. So there was little possibility of racial conflict when social intercourse was kept on a one-to-one level. Difficulties were apt to rise, however, when there was a gathering of white and Negro boys. Any such confrontation, like at an athletic event, would raise the possibility of a racial flare-up. There were times that these difficulties reached such magnitude that the parents had to intercede. Sometimes white men would come to talk to my father about things they thought I had done wrong, and, on occasion, Father would go talk to the white men about things their children had done which he thought were wrong. Usually, a matter handled in this manner was the end of it. A discussion between parents would decide whether we should get a whipping or not. Justice was usually nonexistent, but at least it was equal. The parents would usually decide: "If we give them both a whipping, maybe they won't do it anymore." Father would come home, and I'd get a whipping and the white boy would get the same medicine. These parental negotiations stayed within the master-servant relationship, but at least the discussions were on the basis of "your child and my child" where we were equal. I never heard of an instance where a white father claimed his son in the right simply because he was white and his adversary black. But then I believe that if that had ever occurred, my father would have tried to keep me from knowing about it.

Whatever happened between our parents, there was no noticeable degree of master-servant relationship between the children, particularly when we were young. We called each other by our first names and used the same cusswords. But the white children did imitate their parents by calling Negro adults by their first names. They called my father "Ed," but I had to use a courtesy title and his first or last name when I addressed their father. The white children seemed to carry this on with an air of superiority. Now the equality between the children was maintained only by the fact that the Negro children, just through human nature, weren't going to be pushed around by another child of their own age. A certain innocence allowed the Negro child to push and pull and scrap and bite, regardless of his opponent's color. It was only as we grew older and came to realize that we had to consider much greater pressures than the blow of a small white fist that we gradually fit into our role of secondary citizens. I am sure that the white children could have suppressed the Negro child into an immediately inferior position had the Negro child permitted them to do so.

After moving to Clarksdale, I saw Randolph Smithers less and less, because our paths rarely crossed and our spare time was increasingly filled with school work and outside jobs. He didn't go to the fields—Negro work—but he would come visit us, I would visit him, and our families still visited back and forth. The relationship held from the plantation time and Webb. My mother and Mrs. Smithers would visit and gossip about everyone else's business, but Mr. Smithers was usually out of town on his job, and we saw very little of him.

All the new friends that we made in Clarksdale were Negro. The racial lines were pretty strictly drawn to prohibit easy development of new social connections between the races. No one seemed to object to old friendships being maintained, but open cultivation of new interracial ones on an equal social basis would cause great objection.

In the white school, Randolph was exposed to a greater variety of subjects and to better instruction than I'd dreamed of. He took lessons in playing the bass violin, and I don't think I had ever seen such an instrument until one night I went to see him and he had brought the thing home from school. Randolph and I started drifting apart when we were thirteen or fourteen years old—the same time we started seeing girls. He and I accepted segregation as something that we just had to do—the way things were supposed to be. Whites went their way and Negroes another. We just did it without much to say about it. The most difficult thing for me to understand was *who* decided these things. It was all so nebulous that it seemed that God was responsible, but I knew that he wouldn't sponsor anything that spawned so much unpleasantness and misery. It was impossible to pinpoint who drew the lines of racial separation, and it was equally impossible to understand the reasoning behind it. The lines just seemed to be there, and they seemed to be accepted, if not endorsed, by both races. As with so many things that are complex and totally beyond comprehension, it was simpler to just accept them as the way things are supposed to be. And that is what we did.

The city of Clarksdale considered itself quite progressive in the thirties because it sponsored a recreation program for white youth. In the summer of 1937, organized recreation for Negroes became a project of the Association of Church Women. Mrs. Mary D. Martin was a member of the Women's Society of Christian Service of the white Methodist church. My mother was still a member of that group in the Negro Methodist church. There was some association between the two groups, but always with a representative of the white group coming to the Negro church, and never vice versa. The need for organized and supervised recreation for Negro children, beyond that which was provided by the school, was a matter of concern to both groups, and they got together to discuss it. My grandmother owned a small building not in use at the time, but that had been used as a candy and cookies store. The woman who had operated it had closed down the shop and gone to Chicago. The white and Negro women got together and hired Mrs. Lottie Hamer to be the supervisor. She got a small salary and operated the center for three or four years. We had dances, shuffleboard, horseshoes, croquet, and beanbag tossing. And all of us, both girls and boys, would go on hikes with Mrs. Hamer for swimming and general recreation. The building was called the Myrtle Hall Recreation Center and operated during the summer. White ladies brought modeling clay, coloring books, and other toys. To us, everything they brought, which was usually secondhand, seemed like new. The work of these women was greatly appreciated in the Negro community. I believe that their behavior was motivated by an awareness of the need. Conscience required that something be done, and they did it.

But the attitude of the white women towards the Negro children remained paternalistic. They would come and pat us on the head and say, "Look what we brought you." They were adults, and since I'd always been taught to respect older people, white or black, this didn't disturb me or seem unnatural. Undoubtedly, they went back to their churches and talked about all the cute little "pickaninnies" they had seen and what nice things they had done for them. Whites have always had a great fondness for Negro children, but they seem to want them to continue to behave like children after they are adults. What they don't want is for us to grow up.

One of my bitterest feelings came when I found out that I could not be a Boy Scout. Like most boys, I had always had a great admiration for uniforms. When there were parades in Clarksdale, there was always a unit of World War I veterans with uniforms on and some with medals and stripes. Then there were some white boys who went off to military school, and they would come home on vacation and walk around the town in their pants with the black stripe down the side and a few stripes on their sleeves. But the most impressive of all was the Boy Scout parade. They were boys my own age, regular boys who hadn't been off to military school, but they had uniforms and medals hanging from their shoulder or their stomach as well as stripes going all the way down their sleeves. They would march along high-stepping to fast march music, and it made bubbles run up and down my spine. I used to dream of saving money and buying some sort of uniform— not sure of what kind it would be.

When I was twelve, I heard that a delegation from the national Boy Scouts office was coming to Clarksdale to organize a Negro Scout troop. That was more exciting to me than Christmas coming. Weeks before, I was thinking about my uniform and how I would look in it, about all of the medals that I would work for and win, and soon in my imagination I was a full-fledged general in the Scouts, if there were such a thing.

The day the officials arrived, the Myrtle Hall principal let all the boys out of school to meet with them. They told us how much we could learn by being a Scout, including how to get along with people. But the major point would be teaching us to be good Americans and to appreciate our country. They conducted sessions for about a week, and, by the end of it, we knew what it meant to be a U.S. citizen. They also taught us how to march, and the climax of the program was a march all over town when I believe that we outstepped every marcher ever seen in Clarksdale. We were determined to show the white community that we could be as good Scouts as anyone.

The organizers left the day after our march, did not come back, and were never heard from again. It turned out that the white community had asked them to leave. (Whites seem to have an aversion to Negro marchers—is it leftover fear of slave rebellions?) Yes, Boy Scouting meant cultural development, a step toward equality, and Clarksdale whites felt we weren't ready for it. The decision was made without consulting the Negro community—*they* were the authorities on our welfare. When it came to food and medicine, they might help, but they retreated from any connection that might improve our position in the community or country.

There was so much exclusion under the practice of segregation. In the courthouse, Negroes had to sit on one side, and very few seats were allotted to us. The judges called Negro defendants by their first names, and proceedings often degenerated into a paternalistic admonishment of the Negro before sentencing: "Now, James, you know you shouldn't have stolen Joe's check—you know better than to go around here stealing, and if you come in here again, I'm going to put you in jail. This time I am only fining you ten dollars and putting you on probation. You understand that?" James would nod and say "yassuh" as many times as he could and go back to stealing chickens or whatever else he might need. He knew that the treatment he got next time would be about the same—as long as the victim was not white. And in many cases, a short stay at the penitentiary, even Parchman, was welcome relief from the drudgery of looking for the next meal.

Travelling circuses and carnivals were segregated by opening one night for whites and the next for colored. At outdoor spectator sports events, better seats were always for whites, and we often couldn't even see the field from our seats. At the theater, white people went through the great big brightly lit front door, while we went up the fire escape to a dinky balcony.

Social segregation was enforced strictly by custom. No rules were ever written, and there was no need to explain them. We were never told we couldn't come in a front door, and we didn't know what would happen if we tried to violate the customs. This fear of the unknown kept the Negro community in its place. We did know, however, that Negroes were lynched for more flagrant violations of the code, such as speaking an alleged obscenity to a white lady or even looking at her the wrong way.

Chapter 3

"As Good As Anybody"

As I grew older and spent more time away from the family, I was exposed to bloodcurdling accounts of white mob violence against individual Negroes. There were stories of shootings and hangings and drownings and cuttings that ended in immediate or prolonged death. There were the frequent beatings and, most common, verbal abuses, and the stories drifted up and down in the Delta river mists or hot sun, usually told in lowered voices, becoming entirely different tales at the end of the forty-mile trip. But it was an effective communication of fear, and it enforced the codes and the system.

Most frightening to me were the stories of Negro men being castrated and their groins swabbed with kerosene. The account was usually associated with a white woman or girl. The mob would seize the suspected Negro, take him to an isolated place, beating him and abusing him all the way. They would rip his clothes off, hold his legs wide apart, and then there would be more beating and kicking. While the helpless man was stretched out, one of the white men would take a razor or sometimes a fairly sharp knife and slash and gouge until the scrotum was completely severed. The butcher would step back amidst cheers, and another would step forward with a can of kerosene, pour it on a corncob or rag swab and poke the bleeding groin until it was saturated. There would be more kicking, beating and verbal abuse and then they would leave him writhing and squirming until someone happened along and found him, or until he died. Nothing would ever be said about any of this. Emasculation would occur if he looked at a white woman with "lust." If it were more serious than this, the Negro would be killed.

About this time, I heard of a Negro boy who was castrated when some whites found him in bed with a white girl. It seemed, however, that the relationship was mutual, so they didn't kill him. They both had been working at the Travelers' Hotel. He was a bellhop, and she was a maid. They had known each other for a long time and the intimacy had been in progress for some time. Then one night some whites who were staying in the motel charged into the room where the boy and girl were in bed, threw the girl aside, and castrated the Negro right there in the bed with a razor blade. By their standards she was innocent, and he was guilty. But what a double standard this was. I just couldn't understand why white men in Clarksdale had always felt free to drive through the colored section looking for Negro girls. They would stop and say, "Hey, girl, come here." Then she would walk over to the car, "yassuh" her way into the back seat, and off they would go to some secluded spot.

This has always bothered me—why can a white man have a black woman and a black man is usually killed if he has a white woman? I don't think there are any deeply intellectual reasons behind the white man's obsession to keep his women from Negro men. I think their reasons are immediate and petty—not connected to the eventual amalgamation of the races. That concept is a later rationalization for a reaction to an immediate displeasure—a simple matter of jealousy. Most rednecks think that Negroes, with so little social activity in their lives, spent most of their time singing in cotton patches or in bed and that we have developed a sexual ability superior to whites'. Thus many white men seem to think that Negro girls are good sex partners, and maybe in their simplistic logic they would conclude that the Negro male must be superior for the white female. White men don't like this, and they are willing to kill to protect their sexual superiority—real or unreal. We never discussed racial violence at my home, and I was dangerously naive.

While my sister was away at Rust College and before Father was able to send me to the Coahoma County Agricultural High School, I worked at the Silver Moon Cafe. An incident there brought me within a gnat's hair of being castrated or lynched.

The Silver Moon provided beer, girls, and poker for the white gentlemen of Clarksdale. I worked there the summer after I had finished the eighth grade at Myrtle Hall, and it was my job to serve the men foods that supposedly appealed to the masculine taste. I never knew if these pickled sausages and pigs' feet and chili peppers were supposed to be delicacies, but I served them along with beer and cigarettes, usually when the men were at the poker tables in the back room. I also had to keep the place cleaned up and deliver some takeout orders. It was probably one of the easiest jobs I've had, and I learned a lot of new things at the Silver Moon—things that I had never seen and things that I had never heard of. As a fifteen-year-old boy, I had a lot of questions. During the afternoon, when some of the white men would come in for beer, I would hang around in the back and listen to them talk about sex. They did a lot of talking and boasting and usually spoke in the most graphic terms. Since I was Negro, they would talk in front of me like I wasn't there, and, of course, they needed me at their beck and call.

Some white girls also worked as waitresses, and they were expected to do a little whoring on the side. I became friends with one of the girls, but the relationship never developed along sexual lines. We enjoyed talking to each other, and that was it. She was much older—about twenty—but we had the same amount of schooling, and we read the daily newspaper, which gave us something to talk about. Whenever we weren't busy and just sitting around peeling tomatoes and potatoes or shelling peas, we had conversations.

Neither of us even thought about anything more. Foremost in my mind was when I would be able to start school again. Almost every week, Father would say, "I'm going to let you go to school soon, but you're going to have to work at the Silver Moon for another week." This went on until Christmas, and I guess I was talking more and more to the girl. Then one day I came home, and Father said, "Well, Aaron, you are going to school Monday." I was elated and started preparing for my first day and never even questioned the quick decision. I assumed that someone had paid a long-overdue bill.

I learned much later the real reason for the rush. While I was working at the Silver Moon, some of the white customers got upset over the amount of time I spent talking to the white girl. An old Negro man named Nelse who worked at the place got worried when several white men expressed their displeasure at the relationship and said I was acting out of my place. Nelse got excited and went to my father and told him to get me out of there before something happened to me. I had never sensed the problem at all. Nobody at the cafe seemed to show any hostility towards me, and I never knew anyone noticed the girl and me talking together. Anyhow, the incident got me back to school.

I started part-time at the agricultural high school in December 1938, but Father couldn't afford to let me board there. I had to commute the four or five miles, and it cost about fifteen cents a day—a lot cheaper than living at the school. To help save money towards going to school full-time, I got a job at the Henderson Drug Store as a delivery boy—my first brush with pharmacy as a profession. I worked in the afternoon and on weekends and was paid five dollars a week, which was considered good money. H. W. Henderson owned the store and hired several other Negro delivery boys and one white boy as stock clerk. Mr. Henderson had an older white assistant named Sparks, who was always kind to me, but not so with Mr. Henderson himself. He was a rough character and had a rapid turnover in his help. I had heard talk about this mean old white man who frequently kicked and abused Negroes—knew it when I took the job and soon learned the truth.

One Sunday, while I was working, Mr. Henderson kicked one of the Negro delivery boys. There seemed no reason for it—he was just angry in general and took out his rage on the boy. But it frightened me, and I got the notion that I was next and ran home and told my father what had happened and that I couldn't stay if there was a chance I would be kicked. Father explained how badly we needed the money and persuaded me to walk back with him to talk to Mr. Henderson. Father told Henderson that I had gone home because I was afraid that he was going to kick me. Mr. Henderson said, "Yeah, I kicked that little nigger, but I wasn't going to kick Aaron. He's a pretty good little nigger, so I wouldn't bother him."

Father told Mr. Henderson that I needed the work to continue in school but that he would prefer that Mr. Henderson not kick me and, if it came to that point, to just send me on home to him. Mr. Henderson promised, and during the two years that I worked there, he never abused me physically, although he cussed me out a number of times.

It upset me inside that Henderson had referred to me as a "nigger" to my father. It didn't shock me, but that particular incident made me acutely aware of the constant unpleasantness we faced at the hands of whites. Perhaps Father was so accustomed to this that it seemed ordinary speech. Or, maybe he was burning inside and showing no outward discomfort to protect my job. The system dictated that my father beg Mr. Henderson to let me stay on rather than storm in and say, man to man, "I'll not have you mistreating my son."

One amusing sidelight to my delivery work developed soon after I began work at Henderson's. The white stock boy, Joe Wilson, went to work at the same time I did. His work was strictly in the stockroom, unpacking goods and marking and shelving them. There were enough delivery boys so that we frequently had spare time, and, whenever I wasn't busy, I went back to help Joe Wilson. At first Joe didn't say much one way or the other, but I could tell that he never felt very friendly towards me. Mr. Sparks, Henderson's kind assistant, noticed that I was helping Joe and encouraged me. Mr. Henderson never said anything, but it seemed to me that he preferred that we keep busy. After several weeks, Joe started pouting. Finally his resentment was open, and he told me he didn't want me back there doing his job. I told him that I didn't mind helping, but he pouted more and more and told me that he could handle the job alone. Finally, Joe decided that I should address him as "Mr. Joe" or "Mr. Wilson." Since we were about the same age, I just hooted at the suggestion and told him that I wasn't about to call him "Mr." anything. So I continued to call him Joe, and he continued to pout, and his resentment continued as long as I knew him. He was really upset when I opened my own drugstore.

The most unpleasant incident during my work at Henderson's occurred one Halloween night. I was riding along on my bicycle making deliveries and stopped along the sidewalk to talk to a friend. As we talked and laughed, a car pulled beside us and stopped. A white man leaned out of the window and hollered, "Nigger, what did you say to me?" I answered, "I wasn't talking to you." The white man got out of the car, busted me in the mouth, cussed me some more, and then drove away. He didn't break my teeth, but the blow caused my teeth to cut my lips badly. I was used to getting cussed out and verbally abused. All we had to do was walk down the street and not get off the narrow sidewalk to let a white pass. Particularly if you happened to bump up against one, he would turn around and start bellowing, "You black nigger son of a bitch, get off the street. You nappy-headed bastard, you know what I'll do to you." I always hurried on in case he might try to do some of the things that he was threatening.

Somehow I never felt powerless in the face of these people. It didn't occur to me that they had all of the authority and that they could indeed just kill me. Had I realized this, I am sure I would have been more cautious. Certainly my parents understood the severity of the code, but maybe they were so ashamed of such injustice that they never discussed it at home. They left it up to the good Maker to get me through whatever difficulties might arise. And for all the problems with working for Mr. Henderson, I believe that first job in the drugstore aroused my interest in going to pharmacy school. I carried prescriptions to people who were sick, and I saw them and talked to them. I watched the people who came in the store not feeling well ask for advice and medicine, and they usually got it. I was intrigued to see Mr. Henderson and Mr. Sparks go into the back and make preparations that could ease a customer's pain.

Besides my work at the drugstore, I began delivering papers, the *Memphis Press-Scimitar*, the first year that I went to Coahoma County Agricultural High School. There were two editions of the paper—one that arrived about midafternoon and the other that came on the train about seven o'clock in the evening. There were three Negro and eight white evening carriers. We all got along fine and did a lot of talking while waiting for the train to bring the papers.

Harvey Yaffe, a Jewish fellow about my age, was the manager of the evening route. The Yaffe family lived in the back of a store on Sunflower Avenue, and I visited them many times. Harvey had a number of brothers and sisters, and they all had a keen interest in music and literature. His sisters played the violin, and we would sit and listen to them read poetry. Sometimes, when I was especially tired, I would rest on Harvey's bed until time to get the papers. Mr. and Mrs. Yaffe were always as nice to me as could be; they had a genuine affection for me and not because Aaron is a good Jewish name. I wasn't aware that the Yaffes were Jewish. In some respects, the Jews in Clarksdale were a middle group between the whites and Negroes. They went to the white schools and were not barred from public facilities. Yet Jews were not fully accepted by the whites and were often criticized because they were friends with Negro families in the community. I guess that the Jews had had their share of suffering and didn't want any part of the persecution of Negroes.

About seven p.m., we would go to the station and meet the other carriers. We would sit on the baggage carts and talk about what we had done that day or what we were studying in school. We did a lot of horsing around, and someone was always running out and putting an ear to the track to see if he could hear the train coming. Once in a while when the train was late, and it was hard to tell when it would arrive, one of the boys would have a penny that he was willing to sacrifice and would place it on the track. The train would flatten it, and the smashed coin would be deposited in an already-well-filled pocket of junk. I never felt I could sacrifice a penny.

We would hear the train whistle first blowing on the north end of town, and then a few minutes later the porter would start calling, "Train's coming, train's coming on track one." We stood and watched the huge locomotive come lumbering into the station. When the engine passed us, the engineer would always wave and usually tap his whistle, not loudly, but just enough to answer our waves.

While we got our papers, the porter would start spilling out all of the towns where the train was bound: "Merigold, Mound Bayou, Cleveland, Hushpuckena, Greenville." We went our separate ways, with our routes, but sometimes when my load was too heavy, Harvey would go with me and carry some of my papers on his bicycle.

One of our white carriers, Winston Barnard, later became a physician in Clarksdale. I never understood how Winston turned out to be such a racist, but he was very outspoken. He grew up with us and shared in our work and talk, but he was a different man when he returned from medical school. I thought we would continue our friendship, but he was hostile and didn't seem to want to remember the old times.

By the time school started the following fall, I was entering the tenth grade and had saved enough money and was able to start boarding there. The Coahoma County agricultural high school at that time was, for the most part, a gigantic farming operation. The dirt roads on the campus were dusty, and when it was dry and windy, that dust would work its way into every building and every room on campus. The screens could keep out the insects but not the dust, and if you closed the doors and windows, the heat would suffocate you. There were four or five buildings on the campus, including a dining hall, one girls' dormitory, two boys' dormitories, and an administration building. The grades ranged from the eighth through the twelfth, and boys studied mostly agricultural subjects, while the girls took home economics. There was a smattering of history, English, biology, and chemistry, and classes met from eight in the morning until about midafternoon. The boarding facilities were good, and for some students the living was better than it ever was at home. The school produced a good bit of its own food, such as milk, butter, molasses, vegetables, chickens, hogs, and cows. A standard breakfast consisted of grits and gravy, hot biscuits and syrup, and milk, and the food varied for other meals in accordance with what crops were being raised.

My freshman class had five acres of cotton as its project, and I was returned to those damn fields again and hated them as much as ever. But I could at least tell myself that at last there was a useful reason for my labors. We chopped and picked after school, and, by the end of the season, our group had developed a real esprit de corps from our work together.

After-school jobs were available under a "work support" program, and it resembled today's scholarships. Whatever you made went to pay a part of your fees. My first job was in the gardens, which was much better than the cotton fields. Then I changed to the dining hall, washing dishes and serving, and I stuck with this, working during all three meals. I never minded this work and actually enjoyed it. I got to know as many people in the school as any one person because I saw them all three times every day. The work wasn't hard and only occasionally boring. I was paid around four dollars per month, which amounted to half of my eight-dollar-per-month fees for lodging and tuition.

Soon after I graduated from washing dishes to serving—a promotion although the same pay—I got the idea that I was pretty good at serving plates. I had watched some of the older servers and had learned just how to flick my wrist and make the vegetables land at the right spot on the plate. One day, Mr. J. B. Wright, our principal, whom I respected greatly, was coming down the line. I wanted to make a good impression on him. Nobody was in front of him, so I was able to plan my move. I stood there casually until he got right in front of me and then went into action. I slammed my scoop into the mashed potatoes with one hand, grabbed a plate with the other, brought the scoopful of potatoes about a foot from the plate, and flicked my wrist. The ball of potatoes sailed down toward the plate, and, about the time I looked up and spoke to Mr. Wright, I felt the potatoes hit my hand. They splashed all over the side of his plate and my hand. He laughed, so I did, too, and then just stood there grinning with my potato-covered hand in the air. He said, "You're dishing out those potatoes pretty fast, aren't you?" I just laughed a little more, since I couldn't think of a thing to say. Then I wiped off my hand and got another plate and served everything more carefully. From then on, I took it easy on the fast-serving, but sometimes I would speed up and show off when a pretty girl would come along.

When I enrolled at the agricultural high school, Mr. Dan Crumpton was superintendent of the county school system. His occasional visits caused quite a stir. "Mr. Crumpton is coming, get your desk in neat order and your belongings together." Down the hall he would come, "Morning, Bessie, hello, Delia," always addressing the teachers by their first names. He seemed to be a bustling, good-natured white fellow, and I always imagined him whistling constantly or chewing gum and shaking a lot of hands.

Mr. Crumpton held meetings in our auditorium—the only facility large enough—for all of the teachers in the county Negro elementary schools. Although they were supposed to be private, I stood many times by the auditorium door and listened. Mr. Crumpton usually started the meeting by wringing his hands and saying merrily, "I was thinking driving out here—I feel like hearing me a spiritual this morning. Ernestine, you're pretty good. Come on up here and start it off." Ernestine Powell, who was probably the best teacher in the Negro school system, would come up front and begin singing "Swing Low, Sweet Chariot," and the others would chime in. There they were, our teachers bellowing their lungs out with spirituals and field songs, and Mr. Crumpton standing there, tipped slightly forward from the waist up, chin poked out, beaming and smiling and rubbing his hands. After several songs, Mr. Crumpton would thank the song leaders by their first names, and they would proceed with business.

One of the teachers might raise her hand, stand and say, "Mr. Crumpton, I'm Ruth Davis and I teach at the Jonestown school. You got us some new blackboards for the fourth grade, and I know we ain't had them long, but it looks like the black part is peeling off. We can't hardly write on them any more. It gets so hot, the black boils up and flakes off, and then when it rains and the air gets right thick, the black part get soft and flabby and comes off more when you write on it."

"Now, Ruth, we just put them boards in there last year, and I don't see why they'd be doing that. You sure your children aren't messing with them?"

"Nawsuh, the children don't touch that blackboard. I keep the chalk in my drawer, and I catch any child fooling with the blackboard I get after him. When the board first started peeling, some of the children took to pulling off the flakes, but I whipped one of them and they ain't touched it since."

"Well, Ruth, a fellow came through here from Jackson selling those boards, and he gave us a good deal, and I know there's nothing wrong with them. You just keep watching out for them children."

Then Ruth would sit down, and she would keep her inferior blackboards and say nothing more until the next meeting, when she would say the same thing with the same replay from Mr. Crumpton, and nothing would change, until, perhaps, that blackboard salesman from Jackson came along with another good deal.

Those meetings were conducted to suit Mr. Crumpton's taste and personal fancies. If he felt the business had gone on long enough, he would call for another spiritual, and, as the teachers heaved themselves up and burst forth, he would grin his way out of the auditorium and go back to Clarksdale where he probably had to report to someone just like himself. As for the teachers, they could go back to their schools and say, "We had a meeting and Lord, it was hot"—back to their state-approved textbooks that mentioned Negroes only as criminals, just enough to justify the Ku Klux Klan's activity. Ruth Davis's blackboard would still be coming to pieces, and the teacher in the next room would be sitting on the front edge of her chair because one

of the back legs was broken. Or they might go back to find that some northern group had sent them a hundred boxes of superior quality carbon paper.

But underneath the surface of spirituals and subservience, something was
going on. Principal Wright had come to the school only a short time before
me, and he was soon in dutch with the county board of education. Negro
history and literature were being bootlegged into the high school, and we
were learning in biology that the Negro race was not inferior at all. He insisted on giving the students some liberal arts education to supplement the
technical and agricultural work. He would not stick to the Booker T. Washington program of teaching Negroes only to work with their hands. My first
year, every boy had an individual agricultural project, and mine was a corn-
testing experiment, where I took several grains of corn and determined
which was the most fruitful. I took the kernel from several different ears of
corn and germinated them to see which was the best to use for planting.
This was not just busywork, as all of the corn had to be tested before being
used for a crop. Later I had a chicken-raising project, and others had projects
dealing with cattle or hogs.

But by the time that I was a senior, these projects had gone by the board.
Mr. Wright had de-emphasized agriculture to the point that it was almost
secondary to the instruction that was officially prohibited by the board of
education. He was insisting on the arts, music, and the classics. He himself
taught a course in ancient and medieval history and translated enough Cae-
sar and Chaucer for us so that at least we knew who they were.

The home economics department was geared to teach girls how to wash
clothes, iron, and cook, and it was assumed that this training would help
them find a job working for a white family. Wright insisted that the girls be
taught to learn all of this house care, because they would have a family of
their own someday. These ideas were firmly implanted in every class and in
every student's mind—we were not inferior at any level. This was not what
the board had in mind for colored education, and Mr. Wright was finally
fired for his liberal ideas.

But his great contribution to the school was his leaving behind a faculty
that shared his beliefs. Some of the older teachers had some disagreements

with newer members, but they were never very vocal. All of them knew how the school was lacking. The science courses were rudimentary, because there was so little equipment available for laboratory work. The teacher was the only person in chemistry class who had a Bunsen burner. He would show us how to generate hydrogen and oxygen, and that was mastery of high school chemistry lab work. The equipment in biology was equally inadequate, and we spent a good deal of time on genetics. The teacher refuted white supremacist theories, and it was so important for me to learn from a book that we were inferior to no one.

We had an excellent football coach who won the state Negro championship several times as well as the Blues Bowl in Memphis. I enjoyed playing, but was never good enough to be one of the big starters. No matter how good or bad our team was, the coach could never get the white team in Clarksdale to play us. He asked them time and time again, but the white coaches always declined—they had a full schedule, or more frequently they would just admit that they weren't supposed to play Negro teams.

About this time I started having girlfriends, and it seemed like I was always having a crush on girls named Juanita. Juanita Washington was the first girl I ever cared about. She lived just down the street from me. Then, a little later, there was Juanita Johnson. She and I had been to Myrtle Hall School together. Around the tenth grade Juanita Chapman came along, and she was really something. We cared deeply for each other and probably would have married if I had not joined the service. When I was courting my last Juanita, a boy named Earl Barker was trying to move in and take her from me, but Juanita never paid him any attention. Then about a year after I had been in the service, I got a "Dear John" letter from her, saying that she was marrying Earl, who had not been called to serve his country.

The greatest single influence on me during high school was a young teacher named Thelma K. Shelby. Her influence catapulted me into being a serious contender in the civil rights arena. Mr. Wright had arranged to hire Miss Shelby as soon as she graduated from Dillard University in New Orleans. She had joined the NAACP while at Dillard, but our board of education did not know this, and they allowed Mr. Wright to hire her. It really wasn't until after the 1954 Supreme Court decision that Mississippi school boards began seriously checking employees for NAACP membership.

Miss Shelby had been a liberal arts major in college and taught English and economics at our high school. She also spoke French and would speak it to us during our free hours. I don't think any of us ever learned much French, since there were no textbooks and no regular classes, but oh, did we feel like we were going somewhere, when we knew that French was available as sort of an extracurricular activity. She talked with us inside and outside the classroom about the struggle for human dignity. She believed that Negroes should be allowed to vote, but, at the time, she did not advocate that Negroes should go to school with whites. Her feelings stemmed from her association with the NAACP, and they were pushing then for "separate but equal" facilities—the law of the land—not for school desegregation. The organization's main concern during that era was to instill racial pride in Negroes and try to raise the race's standards to the same level as any good middle-class American. There was little objection from whites when Roy Wilkins came down and solicited memberships in the NAACP. Some even thought it was a good organization. A few joined, and a few rare whites even made generous contributions, agreeing that things should be separate but indeed equal. But most whites knew that as long as things were separate they could always keep them unequal, because they controlled the power and the purse strings.

Miss Shelby spent all her time with us, and some of the older teachers frowned on some of her activities. Those were the days of jitterbug, and, when we had dances, Miss Shelby was always there and jumping around with the best of us. She was willing to take time to work with any of us on anything. Several times she joined us when we were eavesdropping on Mr. Crumpton's teachers' meetings. It disturbed her to hear the teachers in there singing, and she would say, " Now look at that. Just listen. Those teachers are the best people we've got, and that white man has them in there acting the fool." Her repugnance rubbed off on us.

Many things disturbed T. K. Shelby. There was no public transportation for Negro students. The bus for whites passed right by the school, but we were not allowed to ride on it. And she was always talking about the lack of foreign languages, the inferior quality of equipment and facilities, and the fact that what we were learning would not prepare us to compete if we went to college or even in our everyday lives.

One of my first assignments under Miss Shelby in English class was to give an oral report on Richard Wright's *Native Son*, and it made an unforgettable impression on me. It was a little hard for me to identify with Bigger Thomas, Wright's main character who was born in Mississippi and moved to Chicago at the age of eight, because of the immense environmental differences between Chicago and Coahoma County. The frightening aspect of the book, however, as I pointed out in my report, was that the plight of the Negro seemed almost universal, and we didn't stand a chance in the white man's society. As heinous and barbaric as Bigger's crimes were, they all related directly to his resentment and fear of whites. Bigger was hardly a civilized person as he walked and stalked the alleys of Chicago's Black Belt, but he was that way because the system had fostered it. Because of his ignorance and poverty, the only meaningful personal expression that he could achieve was through violence. Then when he is trapped in a corner and kills the white daughter of a prominent family, he is accused of raping her as well, and eight thousand whites join in a massive manhunt to capture him. They catch him, and the white system of justice begins simply because he is a black boy who has murdered a white girl. But he is falsely accused of raping her. No consideration is given for the clear fact that Bigger has acted in accordance with the way the system forced his development. In the trial, the whites point out that Bigger had murdered the daughter of a man who had been generous in giving money to help Negroes, but it never comes out that this same man had charged exorbitant rents for Negroes living in his shoddy tenement houses.

After several days of running from the eight thousand hunters, Bigger finds himself at the end of his line, trapped on the roof of a tenement house. He is crouching in a shadow, as two men approach, unaware of his proximity. The men talk about a Negro girl that they have just seen undressing through a window in the house and how they would like to drop out of the manhunt and stay with her a while. To me, this made universal the familiar theme—white men may behave as they please towards Negro women, Negro men are killed for any association with white women.

One sentence in the book was the most powerful I had ever read. Bigger had been captured, and the white state's attorney was trying to make Bigger show them just how he had committed the rape. Bigger says nothing at first and then asserts that he did not rape the girl. The attorney threatens to *make* Bigger show how he raped the girl. Bigger says to him, "You can't make me do nothing but die!"

The entire book fascinated us all, but one of the most revealing parts was about Mississippi. In the novel, there was a great deal of publicity before Bigger's trial, and a Jackson, Mississippi, newspaper had discovered that Bigger had lived in their state until he was eight years old. A story then came out in the *Chicago Tribune* that included a wire that they had received from the editor of the *Jackson Daily Star*:

"Thomas comes of a poor darky family of a shiftless and immoral variety. He was raised here and is known to local residents as an irreformable sneak thief and liar. . . .

"Our experience here in Dixie with such depraved types of Negroes has shown that only the death penalty, inflicted in a public and dramatic manner, has any influence on their peculiar mentality. Had that nigger Thomas lived in Mississippi and committed such a crime, no power under Heaven could have saved him from death at the hands of indignant citizens. . . .

"We of the South believe that the North encourages Negroes to get more education than they are organically capable of absorbing, with the result that northern Negroes are generally more unhappy and restless than those of the South."

Native Son had been published only a year before I made my report. The newspaper account set our class to thinking. We got the message that the white South and white North had had some serious and bloody differences, but it seemed they had one thing in common—they did not consider a Negro equal to a white. The book made us realize that our situation in the South in the forties was just a greatly magnified version of conditions all over the country.

A problem soon developed over our empathy with Bigger Thomas and our abhorrence of the white society that led him to his fate. The only people in the book who showed understanding towards Bigger were communists, and lawyers for the Communist Party in Chicago did all they could to save him. Wright clearly depicts white capitalists as villains and communists as champions of the downtrodden Negro. About the time I gave my book report, Miss Shelby had been lecturing on the NAACP and its difficulty with attempted communist party takeovers. She explained that the NAACP did not want to be a communist organization and how they fought against it. Then *Native Son* comes along and presents to a bunch of high school students a glowing picture of the communists as defenders of a helpless Mississippi Negro against cruel white supremacists.

We were pretty mixed up. Miss Shelby told us there were two kinds of people who were concerned with human rights: those who wanted to see progress made and those who wanted to see hell raised about it. She said that the NAACP wanted to work within the democratic system to alleviate the burdens of the Negro. We wanted that, too, and the entire class joined the youth division of the NAACP. It cost fifty cents each. I have retained my membership ever since.

Through Miss Shelby and other teachers, we became familiar with other prominent Negroes in history and literature. We learned about Langston Hughes, Benjamin Banneker, Crispus Attucks, Harriet Tubman, Frederick Douglass, George Washington Carver, Charles Drew, and Mark Epps. The lesson was "You are as good as anybody. You must believe in your personal worth and that you are equal to any other man. Racial superiority is a myth."

Segregationists were right. The fatal flaw in their system was education. If they wanted to preserve it forever, they should never have allowed us to be educated, even under Booker T. Washington's principles of staying in our place. They should have kept us in the fields and prevented us from ever becoming literate.

In the meantime, the sham of "separate but equal" continued as educational policy, but whites got new gymnasiums and finer facilities while we struggled with our inferior system. They were happy with the thought that we were all out there at the agricultural high school learning to be good farmers and homemakers or field hands and maids. They never realized or cared what was going on inside our school. As we learned about Bigger Thomas and the oppression of Negroes everywhere, we knew we were getting a bad deal right there in the school and in Clarksdale. It was up to us to change things, and those quiet rumblings from within the high school gave hope to many of us.

Chapter 4

The Cotton Boll Court

When I finished high school in 1941, I had to get a job to earn enough money for college. I went to work at a motel as a night clerk and changed from a boy into a man. I saw white people do things that I had been told were done only by Negroes. I heard prominent white men who publicly supported the system tell me to stand up and be a man, although I'm sure their advice did not mean for me to consider myself their equal. And while I was subjected to the sharpest verbal abuse that I had yet encountered, I began to learn how to handle problems that could flare up when a white is having to deal with a Negro who is giving the rules—like how to rent a room. It verified for me that, aside from the color of our skins, we are all just about the same.

My job as night clerk at the Cotton Boll Court required much more than simply renting rooms. I did everything from washing dishes to supplying guests with names and telephone numbers of local prostitutes. I reported for work at eight o'clock each evening, but the manager usually stayed until around ten. So I would go over to the restaurant and serve food, wash dishes, mop floors or do whatever needed to be done.

Mrs. Smithers, Randolph's mother, was a waitress at the restaurant, and sometimes Randolph would be there in the evenings. When I wasn't busy we would do a lot of talking and visiting—the first time since the sixth grade that we had been able to be together for long periods, and we had a lot to talk about. Although we never discussed it, we had known since high school that our relationship was unusual. It was a sensitive point for both of us, and we just didn't talk about it. Neither of us was on a crusade about

45

race, and we were satisfied to continue the friendship in a way that brought no hardship to us or our families.

The job at the motel was by far the best one I had ever had. I saw and heard so many new things. The motel manager would close the restaurant at ten o'clock, check the money at the lobby desk, and take it with him. From then until morning, I was in charge, and during these hours I made my friends and enemies. In most relationships in Clarksdale, I had been neither friend nor enemy—just a Negro. But now I was in charge of the motel for the night hours, and some whites didn't like it. Others were interested in someone to talk to, and friendships developed. This was during the war and it was exciting to talk to overnight guests who had been to London and Paris and California and New York—places that I had only read about. Frequently guests would come down to the lobby and talk to me late into the night, and I heard ideas and opinions that I never dreamed existed. Some of the most interesting people were instructors from the pilot training program at Fletcher Field. They talked constantly about the war and told me that I would make a good soldier. I got pretty enthusiastic and decided that I would like the merchant marines. I wrote to them, but I never got an answer. Much later I learned that my mother had intercepted my reply in hopes that I would forget about joining up.

But my position at the motel made me visible to the white community for the first time in my life, and, while some people resented me, the job enabled me to know Mr. S. H. Kyle. He was the owner of the motor court and one of the wealthiest planters in Coahoma County. He encouraged me more than any other white to get a college education and work to improve myself. Mr. and Mrs. Kyle lived most of the year on the plantation, but during the colder winter months they lived in an apartment over the office at the Cotton Boll. Occasionally, Mr. Kyle came down to talk while I was there at night, and usually we discussed me and my future. He was impressed that I brought along books to read during the night and liked the fact that during the early hours I stayed busy at the restaurant even when I wasn't paid for work done there. He made it clear that I should tell him if I was ever mistreated at the motel and advised, "Don't bow and scrape to anybody. Do your work, but be a man."

Specifically, he helped me most in studying simultaneous equations. We never had them in high school algebra, although they were covered in the book. Randolph had learned them, and I was interested but just couldn't figure them out by myself. I had gone over the book time and again, and I finally asked Mr. Kyle to help me. He was a little rusty himself, but he studied a while and then showed me how to do them.

Some of the guests who stopped at the court had never seen a cotton gin or a plantation, and Mr. Kyle liked to show people the county and the state. He had about two thousand acres in cotton, and one of my jobs was to take guests on a tour of the plantation. Often the guests would be a man and his wife. She would sit in the middle of the front seat between me and her husband, and we would talk the entire time. It was a breach of the code to have the woman in front with me, and many of the plantation whites complained when they saw us drive up. But they never dared to bother me, because I was following Mr. Kyle's request.

The whites would really get disturbed when I drove the guests to the plantation store. The storekeeper would have received orders from Mr. Kyle to serve the guests refreshments, but had been instructed to serve me also. There I would sit, at one of the tables for whites, talking to a white man and woman, answering questions, drinking the same thing they were and enjoying each other's conversation. No one ever said anything to me while I was with the guests but I felt their cold stares.

Another main stop on the tour was the cotton gin. Here, the gin master did most of the talking, but I would ask a lot of questions. Before long I had heard the explanation of the gin operation enough so that I knew it by heart. After that, I would do most of the explaining and let the gin master answer questions at the end. He was white and didn't like my taking away his job, but I used the same techniques learned from Joe Wilson at Henderson's drugstore—I tried to make him feel that I was just helping him out.

Word drifted back to me from the plantation whites. "That damned smart nigger," they would say. "He's gonna end up hanging off a tree or else in the ground. Y'all better talk to him." I think they resented the fact that I was Mr. Kyle's pet. They would have resented it if Mr. Kyle had shown special interest in a white boy, but it really burned them up that I was a Negro. When I heard the secondhand threats, I would laugh and dismiss them. I never made any concessions or altered my ways.

I am sure Mr. Kyle never intended to give aid to a person who would go on to do all that he could to destroy the system, but he was an aristocrat. Our relationship was the sort that white Mississippians always proudly point to as being the ideal of the South—with him taking a keen interest in my welfare as an individual, but not treating other Negroes as he did me. I believe he chose to help me because he saw constant evidence of my interest in getting an education and saw a way to keep me from fulfilling his stereotype of Negro men. He'd say, "You can be as great as anybody. All you've got to do is want to be somebody. You don't have to be riffraff. You don't have to go downtown on Saturday night and start cutting and fighting. Get an education." He insisted that I telephone him if I needed something. I doubt if it ever occurred to him that education would lead to my open discontent with the system. Regardless of his motives, I will always be grateful for his interest in me.

Most of the friends that I made at the Cotton Boll I saw only when they would stop by in the evening. One of the most pleasant men was John Duddy, a salesman for Ellis Bagwell Drug Company. When he learned my name was Aaron, he immediately said that his middle name was Aaron. I was always glad to see him and tried to make sure he got the room he wanted and everything else that he needed for a comfortable stay. He always treated me as an equal and never griped when something was wrong with his room—and, no small bearing on my feelings, he was a good tipper.

Most of the times when I really got cussed out, it was over some white man's resentment at having to pay for his room to a Negro at the front desk. If I didn't know the customer, I was instructed to always take the money in advance, and this just infuriated some of them. Some would even leave, and a few complained to Mr. Kyle or the manager. The standard comment was "I ain't never paid a nigger money in my life." On one occasion during a torrential rainstorm, a man became particularly furious over paying me room rent. He absolutely refused and said that he would sleep in his car before he would give the money. It really didn't matter to me, but it was clear that it was raining too hard for him to leave. He cussed for a few minutes and threatened to call the owner and the manager, neither of whom he knew. He even talked about calling the police. He finally came up with an idea and rushed over to the desk. He was so impressed with the idea, and he became almost friendly as he explained it. He instructed me to get an envelope and pencil, and then he scrawled on the envelope: "For the manager (white)." He put his two dollars inside, sealed it, and handed it to me with instructions to give it to the manager. I gave him a key and thanked him cordially for doing business with us, which seemed to irritate him all over again.

One morning I was standing in front of the office, and one of our regular customers drove in with his wife. He leaned out of the window and asked me something, and whatever the question was, I answered "yes." Gracious! I don't know if he had just awakened from a nightmare about Negroes chasing him or what, but he lunged out of the car, cussing my head off because I had failed to say "Yes, sir." His wife grabbed him and talked him into leaving, but he was still cussing and yelling out of the window as he drove away. I suspected some unpleasant experience that morning had caused him to vent his rage at the next available Negro.

Because of my dual role as night manager and bellboy, I was always busy on weekends and during the tourist season. I tried to greet guests courteously, with only a few failures. On one memorable occasion, I failed to take off my cap when I entered a guest's room. They had called asking for something to drink. I had both hands full when I got to the door, so I tapped it with my foot. Some fellow hollered for me to come in, and I called back that both hands were full and I couldn't open the door. I guess that was the wrong response, because the man jumped up, ran over, jerked open the door and said, "Get the hell in here, nigger. Where you been?" Before I could answer, he got right up in my face and was bellowing, "You black bastard, if you don't want to eat that hat, you better take it off before I knock it off." I decided the man was crazy and got out of there before anything could happen to me.

Before long, most of the regular guests were as glad to deal with me as with white employees. Some of them almost preferred having me serve for their parties, since the feeling still prevailed that it made little difference to us what we saw a white man doing. Some of the goings-on at those parties could have harmed a man's reputation if certain people heard about them. One night a group of men with several young women had come up from Cleveland, Mississippi, and were set to have a big time. One of the men had been to the motel before and I remembered him, because he acted like such a big shot. Several cars arrived from Cleveland and this one fellow got out and hollered at me, "Boy," which I was used to. I walked over to the car and addressed him by his name, using "Mr.," of course. I could see him just puff up all over when I knew his name and he started talking about all the parties he had thrown at the Cotton Boll. Then he started talking about the party he was having that night, and he wanted me to serve for it. Of course, he mentioned a big tip for me, and I knew I would get it because he had offered it in front of the others. I agreed to do the serving.

That night at the party the loudmouth got angry at me and started yelling that I had not brought what he had ordered. I looked at what I had written down on his order and explained that I was certain that I had brought exactly what he had ordered. The fellow hit the ceiling and said I was being sassy. He said I would hear about it the next day but finally agreed to keep what I had brought. I was apologetic to the group and said that I hoped there would be no confusion next time. The man didn't give me a tip that night, and the next morning he called me to his room and cussed me out for almost an hour. He called me just about everything I had ever heard over and over. The cussing didn't offend me, as I guess I was beginning to learn it makes little difference what one damn fool says. I just stood there and told the fellow that I had meant no offense. He finally told me to get out. A few minutes later he called me to come back in. His tone had changed completely, and seldom have I seen such an apologetic white man. He said that his father had taught him to respect Negroes and to never mistreat them. He emphasized that I shouldn't take it as a racial matter. He thanked me for my apology to the group and ended up walking over, shaking hands and giving me a good tip. I came to like this old fool, but I really felt sorry for him as much as anything. He had to put on a big show in front of others but was always nice to me in private. I tolerated him during his loudmouthing and enjoyed him when we were alone.

I was coming to realize there was no pat formula for working my way out of these situations. Miss Shelby and others had given me good information on how to avoid trouble and make gains at the same time, but I never knew what I might encounter. I came to realize that it was better to work constantly just at the very limit or boundary of the system, because in the forties, a Negro seldom crossed over the line without serious repercussions. So I met each incident, expecting at any minute to find a new approach or to re-treat. I was constantly aware that a white man could walk up and shoot me dead for little or no reason, and nothing would be said or done. At that time, a white man had never been convicted of a capital crime against a Negro in the state of Mississippi.

What irritated me the most while I was at the Cotton Boll was the fre-quency with which white men asked me to find them Negro girls. There were no Negro girls at the motor court and no names and addresses that I could furnish. But the white men always acted like I was holding out and then would ask a lot of personal questions about my own sex life. Usually they would get me to call a white girl, but a few would get angry and leave because I couldn't give them a Negro girl's name.

One middle-aged man whose mouth was always half-open had asked me numerous times to get him a colored girl. I had always been polite when I told him that I didn't know any Negro prostitutes. He usually went away pleasantly and would return in a week or so and ask me again. One night I said to him, "I've told you that we just don't have any Negro girls' telephone numbers, so why don't you just take the number of one of these white girls?" "You know white women ain't no fun," he said. I answered, "No, man, I don't know." "You mean you never had a white girl?" I told him that was right. He didn't say anything at first but just stood there staring at me with that mouth half-open. I think he might have had a hairlip at one time but had had an operation to improve it. Then he began grinning and said, "Lis-ten, boy, next time I come to town I'm bringing you one. Are you going to act right?" "Sure," I told him.

Several weeks later, the fellow came to the Cotton Boll and checked in during the afternoon before I came to work. When I started, I always looked down the list to see if I knew any of the guests. I saw his name and noticed that he had taken a room with two double beds, and naturally wondered why. He must have seen me come in, because I looked up and there he stood—leaning over the desk and grinning with that crooked mouth that never quite covered his yellow teeth. "Come here, boy," he motioned, "I got something for you down in my room."

"Is that so?" I said and figured that he had a white girl down there. I didn't think it would be too dangerous just to go with him and see what sort of arrangements he had made. So we went to his room, and he opened the door and led me in.

"See what I promised you? Ain't they something?" He was grinning bigger than ever and pointing to two very young white girls—both naked and in the same bed. They were sitting there looking at me and giggling. The man said to me, "Okay, now, you said you were going to act right."

"Damn right, I'll act right! I'm getting the hell out of here." And I wasted no time getting back to the desk. There was something so perverted about the whole thing, but it was no joke to the man who had made the arrangement. He really thought that he had set us up in style—one for him and one for me, all right there in the same room and maybe even in the same bed. Of course, if I had gone through with it—and lived—he would have expected me to get him Negro girls whenever he wanted them. On the other hand, there is no telling what could have happened to me if I had gone into the room. I could have lost my life just by being in there without actually touching either of the girls. I could have been castrated or killed—or maybe I could have had a good time and that would have been the end of it. The man was never unfriendly after that, but it was actually hard to tell, since he always had that half-grin on his face.

On many occasions a guy would order beer or whiskey or food and I would go to his door to deliver it. He would call for me to come in when I knocked, and I would see that he was engaged in sexual intercourse. Without ever stopping, the man would tell me to put the order on the table. I would do so and leave. It happened often enough that standard procedure was to make the delivery and return later for the money. I was never able to understand the irony of the white man not objecting to me, a Negro, viewing his woman as naked as the day she was born, furiously engaged in sexual intercourse, while he would have tried to kill me if I looked too long at her, fully clothed, on the street.

White people have always expressed dismay and disgust at the alleged immorality of the Negro community, but the things I saw at the Cotton Boll, done without shame between white men and women, convinced me we were amateurs at immorality. As an eighteen-year-old who had been raised in the black community, I saw forms of perversion that I had never known existed. The big difference between the moral reputations of the races was partially because we usually didn't have a hotel or tourist court to go to for seclusion. We had to use turnrows or a parked car. We were frequently arrested in cars, open pastures, barns, or cotton houses—popular places for sex where we were caught by the local police, followed by stories across the front pages of the local newspaper. Frequently and to the delight of many, the situations where we were caught engaging in sex could be treated humorously, and it appeared that Negroes were the ones indulging in sexual promiscuity. And only a few of us, such as black bellboys, were brought face to face with white immorality and learned the depths of perversion to which whites could sink. At the same time the whole white community knew about Negro transgressions.

Before I worked as a bellboy, I had believed that few if any white people would engage in the sexual activities I witnessed. My ultimate strong belief in equality between blacks and whites grew partly from those changed images from days at the motel.

My parents actually put a lot of strength in the traditional morals and sex taboos. They objected strongly to people living together who were not married. During my boyhood my father used to say, "If you think enough of a girl to be with her and if you get a baby by her, you are going to marry her. If you don't think enough of her to marry her, then stay away from her."

There was a typical scandal in my family over an illegitimate birth, but I was not told about it until later. Clora and Buddy Brown were my cousins. They lived in Clarksdale with our grandmother, and we all went to school together. One year, Clora wasn't at Grandmother's, and I was told she was not coming back. Later we learned Clora had gotten pregnant and was living with relatives in another town. Everyone was told it was Clora's mother's baby. The mother took care of the child, and Clora returned to school the following year. When word of the illegitimate birth got out, Clora was not in good standing with the rest of the family—only bad girls had illegitimate children. These were not unusual standards, and I found that my friends had gotten the same word—an emphatic *"don't"* when it came to sexual activity.

My own social life in those years still centered around the church. We had box suppers and fish fries and toe-touchings. This was when a bunch of girls would get behind a sheet and expose only their feet. The boys would choose their partners for the evening by their feet, and the boy had to stay with his choice the entire evening, and whatever she had in her food basket was his supper. There was usually some chicanery during the toe-touching, however, because a boy would work out something with a girl so that she would hold her toes in a certain position that he would recognize.

At one toe-touching, I had made arrangements with a girl I liked to have her little toe spread away from her foot. Well, when they put the sheet up and I made my choice, there were two sets of feet with a little toe poking off to the side. I was in a jam. The recreational supervisor was standing there to insure against talking or whispering. I made my choice, and it was the wrong girl, but the one I chose was good-looking and she had two fried chickens in her basket, and it turned out even better—her daddy raised chickens.

Another activity that I enjoyed was coaching the Myrtle Hall basketball team. When I got off work at the Cotton Boll at seven in the morning, I would sleep several hours and then go across the street to the school. I coached both the boys' and girls' teams, since the regular coach was in the service. I was not paid, but I enjoyed it, and we played a good schedule. Saturday was a big social night for many of us, young and old. But hardly a Saturday night passed without Negroes being beaten or shot by the police. There was a curfew imposed on Negroes in Clarksdale, but I had one of my own. My parents made it clear that Saturday night was not a good time for me to go downtown. They made me stay home, unless there was a special occasion. I understood the danger and usually listened to the radio, ironed my clothes, or did chores for Mother.

Negro preachers in Mississippi during this era were a mixed blessing. They did most good for the spirit but not much for the problems on earth. Some of them aroused their congregations to a fever pitch where they jumped and shouted, and then would announce that it was time for the collection, that everybody should give all they could to God, and even poor people would dump into the plates the money they needed so badly for other things. Ministries were a way of earning a living, and the pitch was the same as a salesman who waited until just the right moment to make his pitch for money.

The problem was not as acute in the Methodist Church, because the salaries of our preachers were supplemented by the national church. Nor did we ever have a lot of whooping and hollering at Haven Methodist. At other churches I have seen people lose all self-control and roll on the ground moaning. As I saw it, one main problem was that there were simply too many Negro churches. A group of deacons would fall out with a minister and then go start another church. On at least one occasion, a handful of deacons disagreed with the preacher on the number of hymns to be sung at each service. They took the members who agreed on their number and went and set up a new church in a barn while they built a new one. Everything was spread too thin, and thus few of the churches were strong.

Ministers and schoolteachers were the leaders in our community, but they were usually unsuccessful in getting concessions from whites. Teachers had some excuse because they were getting their salaries from white county and state officials. But there was no excuse for the Negro preachers—they were among the few who were not tied to the system. They were hired by Negroes and paid with our money. Still, it seemed that preachers were always borrowing money or getting into situations where they were beholden to the white community. And most disgusting to me were the Negro preachers who frequently considered it their duty to assure whites that Negroes were happy living on the white man's terms.

Many Negroes took the position that colored people just weren't supposed to have things as good as white people had them, and by accepting the master-servant relationship that made them less equal, they were able to get whites to go along with at least some of their requests.

But our teachers and preachers were reasonably successful in developing among us a sense of responsibility to family and race. They encouraged education, running our own homes and trying to take care of ourselves, and above all to try and be "somebody." In a way it is a miracle that these leaders were able to accomplish as much as they did, considering that they, too, were products of the system. They, too, shared the heritage of mythical white supremacy and racial inferiority, so we all stumbled and fumbled and fell and got up and went along together.

White loan sharks were one of the greatest evils that plagued our community. My family was always wary of them and never once got taken for a ride. But a family that lived near us lost all of their savings to a white man claiming to represent an insurance/loan company. This family had one member in his mid-nineties, and the loan representative went to a younger family member, pointing out that the old fellow didn't have much longer to live and that it would be wise to take out some life insurance on him. The white man explained that there was no use worrying the old fellow about it—that he would want the family to get what it could after he died.

Under the agreement the family was to pay about fifteen dollars a week for the life insurance, which could accumulate to five thousand dollars upon his death. But the man offered a deal where the family need only pay five dollars a week and the man would pay the other ten. Then when the man died, the agreement stipulated the company would keep what it had loaned the family as well as the interest due on the weekly loan.

The longer the old man lived, the more money the family paid the company and the more they "borrowed." Thus, the longer the old man lived, the more money the loan shark made. The family never knew the amount of interest being charged. The old man lived for almost ten years. The family had paid the white man around one thousand dollars and had "borrowed" almost seven thousand dollars from the company plus interest. So, the amount of interest increased steadily, and the white man came every week to collect whatever he could. If the family balked at payment, the crook would return with a fast-talking fellow in a black silk suit who would intimidate the Negro into paying whatever he had. When the old man died and the family tried to collect the five thousand dollars, they learned that before they could collect they had to pay the six thousand seven hundred and sixty dollars, plus interest over which they had had no control. And there was no way that he could ever get out of debt, until perhaps another white man came along and offered to "consolidate" his financial worries. If perchance the white loan sharks had also tried to take some whites for a ride, we might have had some recourse, since the courts would take the word of a white man but would never take ours.

And then there were ruthless Negroes, usually from the North, who would exploit our community in the same way. Normally we were less wary of people of our own race, but of course he could steal as much money as a white man. Usually, the Negro sharks would only stay in town long enough to take what they could before moving on to another community. The

Negro crook wouldn't be able to use the pressure of intimidation that would insure a profitable long-range scheme.

And so in the early forties, I perceived the continuation of a system in Clarksdale that depressed me. Few of the streets in the Negro section were paved, and streetlights for us were considered a luxury. There was no such thing as equal pay for equal work. Usually there were three Negroes working with one white man watching them, and the white man would get more pay than the three Negroes combined—true for jobs with the city or with private enterprise. The schools remained nowhere near equal in facilities, and whenever welfare was available it always went to the poor whites first. There were no public rest rooms for Negroes, and few private establishments provided them. When Negroes relieved themselves in back alleys or maybe when a child urinated in a street gutter with his mother holding his hand, they were sometimes arrested, and the incident was used as an instance of our depravity. The only thing administered to blacks generously was discrimination.

Chapter 5

The Lie of "Separate but Equal"

I was drafted into the army in 1943, and it was a fortunate thing. I was becoming more and more vocal in my dissatisfaction with the system but had not quite stepped too far over the line. I was straining at the bit, not knowing where to put my energies. I was still in the good graces of white men like Mr. Kyle who respected my devotion to a good education and my willingness to do more than any job called for. But some whites, particularly on Mr. Kyle's plantation, called me "uppity," and they had a good case. My background had pushed me in an "uppity" direction, but I was also good at avoiding trouble. Many white people in Clarksdale can't believe that I lived and worked here all my early life, because they had never seen nor heard of me until after the war. None of the police ever knew me, and the first time I appeared in a courtroom was in 1946 when I walked into the Coahoma County Courthouse and became the first Negro to ever register to vote in the Democratic primary.

Three years in the army taught me that racial segregation and discrimination were not unique to Mississippi but confirmed my feeling that the situation was worse in my home state. I also saw the overt racism in the army itself, at Camp Shelby, Mississippi, when I was inducted in 1943. Charles Hill, a friend of mine from Clarksdale, and I received our orders to report at the same time, and were together constantly until the end of the war.

The moment we got to Camp Shelby, the whites were sent to one part of the camp, the Negroes to another. The only thing not segregated were the men in charge—they were always white, and "in charge" was the operative word. We stayed at Camp Shelby for several days and were taught the fundamentals of military life and some drill operations. Then they shipped us to Fort McClellan, a large army installation just outside of Anniston, Alabama. I was there several weeks and trained with the 381st Infantry Division.

I had my twenty-first birthday just before I was inducted, and everything had been in such turmoil that my family had overlooked it. I didn't hear from home until I got to Fort McClellan and got my first piece of mail. It was a "Happy Birthday" letter from my parents with two dollars enclosed for spending money. The letter said several more of my friends had been drafted and all the parents were concerned over where we would be sent. Charles and I just knew that we didn't want to go to Guam or Iwo Jima, based on the stories we had heard about jungles and the fierceness of the battles.

After six sweltering weeks in Alabama, we were told that we were being sent to Camp Roberts, California. I was going to see a part of the country I had only heard about, and it beat the hell out of going to one of those dangerous hot spots. I had looked forward to a train ride all of my life. I would have been tickled to death to go by train from Clarksdale to Mound Bayou, and here I was going three thousand miles to California, about the longest train ride in the U.S.

After breakfast the morning of our departure, they called a formation and yelled out a car number for everybody, with certain cars for colored and others for whites only. Charles and I were assigned to the same car. It was hot on the train that morning we started across Alabama, but I was so excited I hardly noticed. It was so much more comfortable than a bus, because you could get up and move around, and there was even a water cooler.

It was a three-and-a-half day trip, and when we left Alabama and Mississippi my eyes started popping. I had never seen mountains before, and the Ozarks in Arkansas left me completely bewildered. I had heard about mountains and I had seen pictures of them, but the real thing was so different. On the train with the soldiers, there was plenty of company, but I had this feeling of isolation as the train ground up a mountain, winding through underpasses and crossing overpasses. I sat there with my face against the window and could see for miles until the view blended into the haze, and then my eyes tingled as they focused on a wall of sheer rock just several feet from my nose. Perhaps the absolute fascination with the views brought the notion of isolation, but I believe it was my feeling that one single train, no matter how many cars or men on it, was pretty insignificant in face of the magnificence through the windows.

The next day we entered the Great Plains. This wasn't quite as bewildering, because in some spots I was reminded of the Mississippi Delta—except for no cotton. And while, in the Delta, you can usually strain your eyes and see all the way to the end of a cotton field, in the plains you could strain your eyes and see all the way to nothing. It was dry and there were few trees, but it didn't appear that they had been cut down as in the Delta. It looked like trees had never been there. I couldn't understand how anything could live in that white vastness, and the little towns along the way looked like they were there only because the trains ran by and might stop.

Then we got to New Mexico, and I got my first glimpse of the Rocky Mountains. From a distance they looked something like the Japanese silk paintings I had seen in a gift shop at home, with a lake or river in the foreground and a snow-capped mountain in the background. The Rockies were even more impressive than the Ozarks, but that first shock was in Arkansas.

Then California—the greatest conglomeration of new sights I had ever beheld at one time. There were trees twice the size of any black walnut trees in the Delta, and they called them eucalyptus and redwoods. But the peak experience of the entire trip was when I saw the Pacific Ocean. I had never really believed that "Columbus sailed the Ocean blue," until I saw that Pacific water—as beautiful a blue as I had ever seen or imagined. I had looked at that mud-colored Mississippi for so long I couldn't believe my eyes, but there I was on top of a high cliff, with blue water lapping at a stone wall just beneath me. It was afternoon and the sun was setting on the horizon, and silhouetted against it about three hundred yards out was a hulking and jagged mound of stone shooting straight up out of the blue and looking black against the sun. My only comparison was the late afternoon in the Delta when I was walking across a cotton field into the sun and saw a brown and beaten tenant house on the horizon. The hot white earth ran clean up to the front of the dark image of the house and stopped abruptly. Then the hot white earth began again on the other side and ran on out of sight, just like the blue water I watched rippling away as far as I could see and blending into the sun. And even the waves splashing against the edge of dark rocks appeared at a distance like tall grass fluttering in the winds beside a tenant house. But I was a long way from Mississippi, and everything was so fascinating that I was feeling pretty good towards the U.S. Army, even if it was segregated.

At Camp Roberts, I was given advanced training in the quartermaster branch and assigned to a trucking division. Most Negroes were given this assignment, since we were not supposed to hold up well in the infantry division. Charles and I were soon sent to Hawaii, and during the voyage I saw enough blue water to last me for a long time. Aboard the ship, all facilities were segregated. Barracks were assigned by race, and whites and blacks ate at different times. There was a movie theater on the ship, and whites went one night and blacks the next. A good many of us resented this, so we organized the colored troops to protest the segregated movies. On the night we were supposed to see a movie, none of us went. The ship's announcer repeated over and over, "You colored soldiers, come on down and see the movie." None of us went, but nothing changed, except that there were some situations that could have flared into violence if we hadn't all been new soldiers and half scared of the famous army discipline. It took us a week to reach Hawaii, and we were glad to get there.

Several weeks after we arrived, Charles and I decided to go into Honolulu for some fun. Again, everything I saw was something I had never seen before, and it was fun to go to town even if we didn't spend any money. We walked all over the city and went to night places that admitted Negroes. Perhaps there was little or no segregation there before the U.S. Army moved in, but the place was pretty well segregated by 1944, and I saw more than one Negro soldier get tossed out of a place. It was late when we started back to camp. We were walking, and, as we approached the bridge that connected Oahu and Sand Island, we heard a moaning in the bushes along the road. We ran over and discovered a boy from our battalion. We knew him by the patch on his sleeve, because he was too drunk to even give his name. He was a white boy, and we looked him over to make sure he was just drunk and hadn't been injured. Charles and I decided to take him in, and we picked him up, although he was like a dead animal that you have just shot—not a quiver or movement. Charles was on one side and I was on the other, and each of us had one of the white boy's arms around our necks. We were walking him across the bridge when he regained consciousness for a moment. He raised his head, stared at Charles for a moment and then looked at me. His head flopped back down, but just before losing consciousness again, he mumbled, "I'll be goddamned, two niggers got me." Immediately Charles dropped his side, and I lowered the boy to the floor of the bridge. "That son-of-a-bitch!" Charles yelled. "Let's drop this white bastard over the bridge."

"Please don't murder the man," I begged, but Charles was furious that the solder had called him a nigger. We argued, and I maintained that we should at least carry him to the end of the bridge and leave him on the side of the road. Charles was adamant. "Come on, Aaron, we're gonna drop this son-of-a-bitch into the river. Man, I'm not carrying him another step—calling me nigger while I'm trying to help him." He was enraged, but I finally told him to go on and leave the white man with me and that I would get him across. The fellow was pretty big, and I had a hard time. Charles watched me and then said he would help if we could take the fellow by his feet and pull him across that way. So we did that, and I guess his head bumped all the way across that bridge. He probably woke up thinking that he had a dream about being in the arms of two niggers. Charles was satisfied in hoping that he had contributed a bad headache to the man's hangover.

Some of us worked hard to get Negro soldiers to chapel on Sunday mornings. Several of us were in the choir, and one Sunday I got twenty-five or so Negroes from my barracks to come. They were all sitting in the rear of the church listening to the white chaplain's sermon, when he made a reference to a day back home when it "rained pitchforks and nigger babies." Most of us got up and left and slammed the door behind us. The preacher realized what he had said and tried to make an apology, but nobody was in the mood to listen to him. From then on, not many Negroes went to chapel, and I didn't have the heart to ask them to return. The chaplain came around and made personal apologies, but we paid him no attention. I stopped going for a while myself, but I started back again because I enjoyed singing in the choir, and hearing the term "nigger" was nothing new to me.

The trucking company where I was assigned was placed in an integrated unit and was one of the army's first experiments with integration. There were four trucking companies stationed on Sand Island. One was composed of Negroes and the other three of whites, and we were all in the same battalion. We used the same PX, the same mess halls and the same recreational facilities. Some individual conflicts came up between the races, but they were usually broken up by officers.

On one occasion right before I left Hawaii there was a near disaster. The white boys were playing football and the Negroes were playing baseball—all on the same field. It was a big field, but several of us Negroes accidentally ran into the white football game. There was some bodily contact, and a fist-fight ensued and spread rapidly. Soon the whole field was engaged in a brawl, white against black. Soldiers, both black and white, headed for their barracks to get their weapons and settle the question once and for all. Fortunately, the run for the barracks gave cooler heads some time, and by the time the men reached the barracks, the doors were barred and officers took charge.

The concept of "separate but equal" was more real in the service than anything I had seen previously. Facilities were strictly separate, but for the most part, they were equal. But the experience allowed me to see that "separate but equal," even in its purest form, was still a sham. No matter how equal the facilities, the idea of white superiority and Negro inferiority remained, and we knew it was incongruous with the American idea of democracy that we were fighting for.

I soon found that there were NAACP chapters near every base where I was stationed. I always affiliated with these chapters, and many times it was helpful in working out racial disputes on the base. While individual Negro soldiers might be hesitant to speak up to a commanding officer about injustices, they were willing to allow an NAACP representative to speak for them. The NAACP officials were always available and made it their business to mediate. Negro soldiers who had never dreamed of joining the NAACP became enthusiastic members and started chapters when they returned home.

When I got back to Clarksdale in 1946, conditions were about the same, but I sensed undercurrents rising to the surface. A Progressive Voters' League had been formed to work for the implementation of the 1944 Supreme Court decision abolishing the "white primary." I was keenly interested in the decision and the fact that the Mississippi legislature had exempted returning veterans from paying the poll tax. Under existing poll tax laws a person had to have paid his poll tax for two years prior to the time that he voted.

As soon as I got home I began trying to get Negroes to go down to the courthouse to register to vote. Several had tried but with no success. There were about seventy five veterans returning to Clarksdale, and most of them were whites. The whites were having no trouble registering, but thus far no Negro had been able to do so. The first time I went to the circuit clerk's office to register, he told me he knew nothing about poll tax exemption for veterans. He was very nice but insisted that I was confused. I left his office and found some white veterans who told me that they had encountered no trouble at all. They had simply said that they wanted to register under the poll tax exemption law. The clerk allowed them to register and gave them a certificate showing that they were exempt from the poll tax. I borrowed one of the certificates and went back and tried to register again. I got the same innocent ignorance of any knowledge about poll tax exemption until I pulled out the certificate. When the clerk saw the certificate, he told me politely that I would still have to pass various tests to show that I was qualified to vote. I read several sections of the state constitution and went through more rigmarole satisfactorily. Then he registered me to vote. After it was all over, he said to me, "You know, Aaron, when you get out of college, you ought to come back to Clarksdale and help your people." "I'll do just that," I told him.

After that, Mr. Smith registered many Negroes, and he behaved like a gentleman. Later, while I was in college, I wrote Mr. Smith a letter and told him that, although he had done no more than duty required, I realized that when it came to me, he didn't really have to do that duty. I thanked him, and I understand that he showed that letter around quite a bit.

Soon after we registered, there was a mayor's election in Clarksdale, and those of us who were registered began to talk. Naturally, we were apprehensive—it was something new to be voting in a city election. The morning of election day I went down to the courthouse, and there were a good many Negroes standing around, talking and laughing. Many of them had registered to vote—some were veterans, but most were older men who had paid their poll tax and registered. I asked why they were standing around, why weren't they voting, and they said that they were waiting to let the veterans have the honor of voting first. Actually, I believe they were waiting to see what would happen to the first Negro who tried. I walked on into the voting place, signed my name, took my ballot, and voted. There was no reaction from the whites, and the other Negroes began to file in and vote. I was the first Negro in Coahoma County to vote in a Democratic primary.

Before going into the service, I had been saving my money to go to Alcorn A & M at Lorman, Mississippi, but when I returned I had decided to go to pharmacy school. I was eligible for the GI bill of rights, and I decided to enroll in the pharmacy school at Xavier University in New Orleans. I started in the fall of 1946, and my first revelation was that I had not learned much at the agricultural high school. What chemistry I had learned was of little value, and I had to begin all over. I had enough money from the GI bill—a lifesaver because I didn't have to work. I had to study so much, I could never have held down a job on the side. I was too busy with my studies to take an active role in the New Orleans NAACP, but I was elated in 1947 when I read that a motion had been filed in the courts to abolish segregation in public schools. I was not very optimistic about the success of the suit, and I was content to live for a while with things as they were and work the best I could for my individual improvement.

Some of us from Xavier did stay in contact with the few right-minded white students from Tulane and Loyola, mostly through the United States National Student Association (NSA). NSA was a national confederation of student governments founded in 1947 by returning veterans, and I even went as a delegate from Xavier to one of the very early national congresses in the midwest. That is where I met Al Lowenstein, who later helped us with 1964 Freedom Summer.

During my junior year at Xavier each student in my class was required to serve an apprenticeship in a New Orleans drugstore. I had been looking forward to this, especially since I wanted to know my way around an actual store. I was accepted by a Negro family, Mr. and Mrs. W. R. Lopez, who owned a drugstore on Congress Street. My relationship with the Lopezes turned out to be much more than just business, and after a while I was living with them almost as a son. Mrs. Lopez had graduated from the college of

Lie of "Separate but Equal" 65

pharmacy at Xavier and was interested in hearing about school. Since I enjoyed talking, we got along fine, and I was never allowed to pay rent—sleeping and eating there for a year and a half. I tried to repay them by helping with household chores.

I worked in the store afternoons after school and on weekends and learned how to fill prescriptions and how to run a drugstore. I also placed and received stock orders and sold general merchandise. It was my first experience at selling, and I found it interesting and enjoyable. My big moment came one summer when Mr. Lopez told me that he and his wife were going on a trip for several days and that they were leaving me in charge of the store. I learned a lot and everything went smoothly, unlike my experience back in Webb when my father left me alone in the shoe shop.

The Lopez Pharmacy was located in the middle of a housing project for low-income whites, and I became further convinced that poor whites are not unwilling to get along with blacks, and that poverty is a more common tie than race. I thought I had seen poverty in Mississippi, but on Congress Street in New Orleans, I saw the poorest people—black and white—that I had ever seen in my life. Most of the poor whites in the projects patronized the Lopez Pharmacy, and we prepared their medicines and gave them credit. Some paid, some promised to pay, and others we never saw again. The fact that the Lopezes were Negro never seemed to make any difference, except on rare occasions when rowdies would break a window and call us "niggers."

There was a small room at the drugstore that was kept particularly as a study room, with reference books, some children's books, and several study tables. A pencil sharpener was on the wall, probably the only one in the neighborhood. Younger children would bring their money in to buy a pencil, and we would keep an eye on them to be sure they didn't trim their new pencil down to nothing. The study room provided a place for the children when their own homes were too noisy or inadequate.

Part of my job was to spend time each day helping these children with their studies. Mr. and Mrs. Lopez did this also when they had spare time. It seemed perfectly natural that white youngsters from impoverished homes would come daily for assistance from Negroes who were better off educationally and economically.

Graduation day at Xavier was scheduled for June 1950, but I had a problem. The date was the same as the Mississippi State Pharmaceutical Board Test being given at the University of Mississippi in Oxford. I had to take and pass that test before I could get my license to operate a drugstore and fill prescriptions. The nuns at Xavier told me that nobody had ever graduated from there without attending the actual ceremony. They explained that each student had to march up, receive his degree, then kiss the bishop's ring. The nuns seemed offended that I was trying to figure out a way not to march and said, "You are going to have to march, son, to get your degree from here." They would not waive this strict rule, even if it meant that I would miss taking my state board exam.

My friend Joe was in the same pickle. We studied the board exam schedule carefully and finally figured how we might be able to work it. We had been talking about how expensive it would be to go up to Ole Miss for the exam, so we had been saving our money. We had to fly up to Memphis, drive to Oxford and take one part of the exam, then fly back to New Orleans in time to march that night. The next morning we had to fly and drive to Oxford and complete the second part of the exam. John Duddy of the Ellis Bagwell Drug Company, my old friend from the Cotton Boll Court, met Joe and me at the Memphis airport on our first trip and drove us down to Oxford. We got to Ole Miss the night before the exam and called the dean, who had made arrangements for us to stay with a Negro family off campus.

The next morning we went to the pharmacy building where the test was being given. There were about two hundred and fifty students from all over the South taking the test. There was one other Negro student besides Joe and myself. John Leslie of Leslie's Drug Store in Oxford met the three of us when we arrived on campus and made sure that we were extended every courtesy. At lunch he went out and got sandwiches for us and himself. To me that was a kind gesture, and it didn't seem to bother any of his white friends.

Several months before the exam, Joe and I had bought a paperback book called *Your State Board and Mine*. It was a refresher and review to help you do well on the board test. It had sample questions, and Joe and I learned the thing backwards and forwards. Luckily for us, it appeared that Mississippi had copied its board test verbatim from that study book. The oral test was given first, and that's where I made my mark. I like talking, and whenever the man would ask me a question, I had studied so much that I started talking and elaborating until he had to tell me to stop. Then we took the first part of the written exam. That afternoon we flew back to New Orleans for graduation and returned the next day to complete the exam. I wasn't apprehensive about going to Ole Miss to take the test. We sat anywhere we pleased, and at no time was there evidence of discrimination. Possibly it might have been worse if John Leslie hadn't been there. A month later I was pleased to learn that I scored the third-highest grade on the examination, and I thought they should have named that little study book *Your State Board and Mine* and *Mississippi's*.

I returned to Clarksdale in 1950. That was a good year for me. I married Noelle and went into my own pharmacy business. Dr. O. G. Smith was the only Negro physician in Clarksdale, and there were no Negro pharmacists. Before graduating from Xavier, I had discussed my opening a drugstore with Dr. Smith—it was normal procedure to try and line up a physician who would assure you of support and send patients to you for service. He was doing business with Palace Drug Store, which was owned and operated by a white native Mississippian, K. W. Walker. Dr. Smith suggested that Walker and I try to get together so that he could support us both. I approached Mr. Walker and suggested that we go into business together, and we got along well from the first. As it turned out, John Duddy, my old friend from the Cotton Boll Court, sold drugs and pharmaceutical supplies to Mr. Walker, and he helped our association along. We corresponded until I came home, and the fact of my being black and his being white never had any bearing on our partnership.

When I returned after graduation, Walker had already rented a building and partially stocked it. It was located on the corner of Ashton and Fourth streets, and we called it the Fourth Street Drug Store. We were in a predominantly Negro section of town, but there were other white storekeepers besides Walker, and most of them hired Negro help and were friendly to their Negro customers. Maybe it was partly just good business, but George Ellis next door to us had blacks as personal friends, and I am sure there were others. Our drugstore was to become the gathering place and the hub for political and civil rights planning for three decades.

Walker and I got along well from the start and understood each other on a man-to-man basis. I realized that there were certain things he could not do, and some that I could not do. I respected the customs, if I thought a violation would bring hardship to Walker. I accepted that we might be close friends but could not eat together in public. We often sat in the back of the store and talked about our lives like any two friends. Our friendship grew, and it got to the point that I would visit him in his home, and he would come to see me at mine—but usually only in an emergency situation. Our children and wives occasionally saw each other at the store, but our friendship never extended to our families.

We needed a third man around the store to take care of stock and clean up, so we hired Morris Bailey, a Negro man who had worked at Haggard's Drug Store since he was ten years old. He was about twenty-five when he came to work for us. Although he had never had any formal training, he knew about operating a drugstore. Mr. Haggard, who was white, had given Morris a job at ten and seemed to have a deep affection for him, but not deep enough to see that Morris ever got an education so that someday he might earn a decent living himself. Mr. Haggard would tell other whites how he loved Morris like his own son. Morris drove his boss around Clarksdale in a big Buick—considered a top-line job for a teenage Negro boy. Mr. Haggard would point to Morris and say, "I raised that boy and I love him," but as usual it was the kind of love that made Mr. Haggard feel responsible for Morris's immediate needs such as food and medical bills. It was the kind of love that the system permitted and even admired, and it left Morris in a position of inferiority that required him to depend on the white man. Had Morris been white, this love would have brought him education and encouragement toward prosperity and citizenship for himself.

During the early fifties, I was friends with only a few whites in Clarksdale. The reason for this was that so few whites took seriously our claims about achieving equality. Washington was far away, and few whites were concerned about the NAACP suit demanding an end to segregated schools. Most whites that I considered friends seemed willing to accept me on an equal basis simply because I was a businessman making about the same amount of money as they were. Few were motivated by any feelings of humanitarianism or social justice.

In retrospect, one very unusual situation seemed perfectly normal at the time. The Clarksdale Civic Music Association was a group that each year brought in concerts and artists. Mrs. Rosemarie Clark, whose husband came from a founding family of Clarksdale, was the chair of the association, which included fifty or so Negroes and maybe five hundred whites who bought memberships at the beginning of the season. A central committee met to discuss what artists to bring and to schedule the performances. Four or five of us were members and we had meetings from house to house. Several times, we had luncheon meetings at Mrs. Clark's home, one of the finest in the city. There was no segregation in these committee meetings, and I never heard of any objection. We would all sit around the same table and talk and nibble on snacks or sandwiches. People like the Clarks were immune to the law inside their own homes, but then out in public where we had the concerts, we found ourselves in the poorer, segregated seating enforced by law. And the association was disbanded in 1955, I believe in the wake of the storm caused by the 1954 Supreme Court decision on school desegregation.

The racial situation seemed about the same as before I went to Xavier, but awareness of the lie of "separate but equal" was spreading in the black community. Hundreds of Negroes had spent half of the last decade travelling around the world and were ready to demand equality. Ex-soldiers told their friends and families things that they had seen in their travels and the word had spread that conditions in Coahoma County had not been ordained by God. In a sense, the broader views gained through the war were our greatest single morale booster in those years.

The situation was ripe for leadership, and someone was needed whose livelihood was not dependent on the white community. Four years earlier when I had been the first Negro to vote in the Democratic primary, there had been a considerable amount of publicity in the local newspaper. As I mentioned earlier, there had been some hesitation on the part of Negroes who were registered and wanted to vote, and I had been the one to step up and cast the first black vote. When I got home from Xavier, I was thrust directly into civil rights activity and the work of the Progressive Voters' League.

Clarksdale's population was twenty thousand in 1950, half white and half Negro. The racial imbalance was in the county, where Negroes greatly outnumbered whites. The city and county policemen were all white, and white people completely controlled politics, finances, and employment. They held a tight grip, and we knew that our fight for equality was going to be long and difficult. Most adult Negroes were employed on a day-to-day basis. A large number of ex-sharecroppers lived in the city, and they did the same work that they had always done, but on a daily shift. When they had work in the fields, they boarded the buses and trucks at sunrise and returned in the evening. Farm mechanization had begun on a small scale, but there was almost no industry, and Clarksdale remained primarily an agricultural community.

The most glaring of the inequities was in the public schools. Whites in control didn't even make an effort to pretend that facilities were equal. Not only were the physical plants of the white schools far superior to those of the black school, but also the difference in curriculum and teachers was staggering. The number of pupils per teacher was much greater in the Negro school, and more liberal arts courses and even trade education were available in the white schools. We all knew of these inequities and were determined to do something about them.

In 1951 an incident occurred that required the Negro community to assert itself on the issue of law enforcement. Two Negro girls, aged seventeen and nineteen, were raped by two white men who picked them up at pistol point and threatened them into submission. One of the girls was the sister of a close friend of mine, and I took a personal interest in the matter.

The two white men approached the girls on a Saturday night in the Negro section of town and forced them into the car. They drove to a heavily wooded section northeast of Clarksdale known as the "Park" and threatened them, raped them, and left them there. The girls' parents became anxious and began to search for them. Meanwhile the girls had walked all the way home, and told their parents. The police were notified, and the rapists were arrested.

The following Tuesday the two men were found not guilty and freed by a justice of the peace court. The white men testified that they had had sexual relations with the girls, but that it had been with the girls' willing consent. The girls testified that they had been threatened at pistol point, but it made no difference to the court. The outcome was normal for similar cases throughout the state and generally accepted as part of the system.

The night after the justice of the peace exonerated the white rapists, the Progressive Voters' League met to discuss the possibility of getting the case to a grand jury. Several of our most prominent members of the Negro community were infuriated and demanded that we pool our funds and hire a lawyer to serve as special prosecutor. We felt the need to express our outrage, or it would amount to just another case of white men raping Negro women and getting away with it. We also felt that nothing would come of our efforts.

The rape victims were at the meeting with their parents, and they seemed to want to let the matter drop. The father of one of the girls worked at the compress and was afraid that he would lose his job if the case went to trial. It was almost more than I could bear when he told us, "We don't want any trouble. Nothing we can do can change what has been done to my child— might as well drop the whole thing."

I got the floor and said as politely as I could, "You say you don't want any trouble—well, you are already in trouble. If you were my father and this had happened to me and you stood there and talked about trouble, I would disown you. The fact that it was these two girls was only chance. It could have been any two Negro girls or women in Clarksdale, and it's time we tried to put a stop to it. If we don't protest, this type of thing will continue forever, and the time has come for us to be heard."

We finally persuaded the families to let the league look for legal assistance. Only one lawyer in the city, George Maynard, was willing to take the case. He was one of the most liberal whites in Clarksdale and asked for a fee of two thousand dollars, a staggering amount of money for us to raise, but we were determined.

Maynard got the two white men indicted by the grand jury, and this was a significant achievement, more than we had expected. When the case came to trial two months later, the judge cleared the courtroom for the argument. There was no conviction. Many questions were left in our minds, but we were not surprised. No white man had ever been convicted in Mississippi for committing a capital crime against a Negro. We worked hard but were only able to pay Maynard about twelve hundred dollars.

We were disappointed in the outcome of this case, but it had become clear that Negroes in Clarksdale needed broader legal protection, and, at the next meeting of the Progressive Voters' League, we decided to organize an NAACP branch in Clarksdale— with an eye to their history of legal protection. W. A. Higgins, the principal of the Negro high school, made the suggestion. He and most of the schoolteachers were already members. This was before the 1954 Supreme Court decision, and most whites did not consider the NAACP as a great threat, since they advocated working within the framework of the law. Higgins corresponded with the NAACP national headquarters and called me one day to say the response was encouraging and that we should organize a local branch. He said that he did not have enough time for the necessary work and asked me to handle it.

I did not run into much opposition in the Negro community, and there was no comment in the white community. If they knew what was going on, they weren't concerned—so sure were they of the entrenchment of the system of segregation. R. L. Drew, H. Y. Hackett, Leola Guest, and several other black citizens supported the plan, and we invited NAACP southeastern regional director Ruby Hurley from Atlanta and Reverend Amos Holmes, statewide NAACP president, to come to Clarksdale for the organizational meeting. It was held at the Haven Methodist Church and drew two hundred charter members. The visitors assured us that we would have the NAACP's legal support in all cases pertaining to civil rights. I was elected president of the local branch at the organizational meeting. My concept of our role was at long last to get legal assistance when we needed it and perhaps remedy the frequent abuses our people suffered at the hands of whites. But the existence of the branch opened our eyes to other civil rights issues. Speakers came to our meetings and made statements that seemed unbelievable to us. Thurgood Marshall came shortly after we had organized and promised that Ole Miss would be open to Negro students in the foreseeable future.

One of our strongest members was a young man named Medgar Evers. I had met Medgar in 1950 at Mound Bayou while he was working with the Magnolia Mutual Life Insurance Company, a predominantly Negro group. Medgar had heard Thurgood Marshall speak and in 1953 answered a call for a volunteer to attempt to desegregate Ole Miss. He applied for their law school, and the next year the NAACP national office asked him to become their first field secretary in Mississippi.

Immediately after the rape cases in 1951, the Denzill Turner killing took place. Turner was an epileptic who had been receiving treatment since childhood. He and his father were at the bus station awaiting the arrival of his brother. Denzill had a seizure which caused him to flounder around on the pavement outside the station. Several white onlookers, not understanding the young man's condition, went inside and reported to the manager that there was a drunk Negro in front of the terminal. The manager rushed outside, and found that Turner's seizure had passed and that he was normal again. But the manager asked Turner why he was at the station and where he was going. Turner replied, "None of your business . . . I ain't asked you for no ticket and why do you want to know where I'm going." The manager was furious and called the police to report there was a drunken Negro at the station grabbing white women as they got off the bus. Turner's father tried to explain to the manager that the boy was an epileptic and that he would take him home. But the police were so angry over the manager's report of the alleged happenings that they stopped the two about a block from the station. The father tried to explain that the boy was sick and that he was taking him home as fast as he could, but the police said that they had to arrest him, jerked him from his father's arms, and tried to put him in the police car. Young Turner was as strong as a bull and began to fight them. He got away and began running, but one of the three policemen caught him and pinned his arms behind him. Another policeman grabbed one arm and as the two held him, the third policeman put a bullet through Turner's head. He was in his twenties when he was killed.

As expected, the justice of the peace court exonerated the policeman who had killed Turner. None of the three policemen were even suspended during the investigation. The court ruled that it was justifiable homicide. I became part of a group organized to protest the Turner killing. Mayor Kinchen O'Keefe had been out of town at the time of the killing and trial, and we felt that he would have handled it differently. We met with him when he came home, along with four or five other whites, including the chief of police.

I argued that it had been a racial killing, pure and simple, where the police had shown wanton disregard for human life. The police had never been in danger of losing their lives and could not legitimately claim self-defense. I said it was a sorry state of affairs when three city policeman were so ineffectual and physically weak they could not subdue one unarmed man. Instead of answering my charge, Mayor O'Keefe said that police didn't have to be in danger of losing their lives before taking serious action. They only had to think they were in such danger. This led me to point out that someone had poor judgment to hire policemen who were so stupid that they were unable to tell when they were in real danger. I also said that police should be intelligent enough to discern between drunkenness and an uncontrollable disease such as epilepsy. I didn't get many answers, but one of the whites said that I spoke as though I had been trained to refute arguments. I didn't know whether I had received a compliment or not. It was only later that I understood the ominous significance of the remark.

The meeting ended and the chief of police said that he was sorry about the killing and that he would do his best to see that it didn't happen again. But he still refused to suspend the three policemen.

During the time I was trying to get answers about the killing, several city officials approached my partner, Walker, and asked him to get me to keep quiet. They came right in the store to talk to Walker for the better part of an hour. Then Walker called me over to join them. Deputy Sheriff Black began to quiz me about why I wasn't satisfied with the way things were. They said that I was wrong in speaking out about the killing and that I had better keep my mouth shut.

"This was a useless, wanton killing—outright murder showing overt racial prejudice," I told them. The police didn't like my remarks and looked to Walker for support. Walker had been listening to the conversation and said, "I think you have discussed this long enough. I want you to know that I think Henry is right, and personally I would go to hell for him." This was an unusual position for a white man to take in the presence of local law enforcement officers, but as Walker told me later, "It wasn't a matter of black and white, it was a matter of right and wrong."

Three days after my meeting with the mayor, I learned the significance of the "trained to argue" comment from the white man. About noon the

Clarksdale police invaded our store and asked for me. Morris Bailey was there and told them that I was at home eating lunch and he would telephone me if they liked. They said they would wait, and, when I started back to the store, I saw seven or eight police cars on the block. I parked the car, and, as I approached the store, I saw Sheriff Greek Rice crouched behind a building. He was looking very intense, so I didn't stop to speak to him—he was evidently onto something big. I walked into the store and was immediately stopped by the chief of the finger-printing division of the Clarksdale police force.

About the same time, a man I had never seen before said, "Are you Aaron Henry?" I said I was, and he showed me his identification from the Federal Bureau of Investigation. "I'd like to talk to you," he said, and we walked to the back of the store. The FBI agent asked me where I had been the last ten years. It hit me that I was still unknown to many whites, although I had grown up in Clarksdale. I told him that I had gone into the service, gone to college, and come back home. The agent told me the bureau was trying to track down ten communists who had jumped bail and that they had reports that one of them was in Clarksdale.

I asked if he was talking about the Ben Davis crowd that I had been reading about in the paper. The agent asked if I knew them, and when I said no, he wanted to take my fingerprints. It was a big deal, and all the Clarksdale police were still gathered round. The agent told me to get an ink pad, and as I opened the safe to get it, one of the policemen held his hand on his pistol. They took a print, and the agent looked at some other prints, smiled, and then announced that mine didn't match any of the communists', and that I was cleared. Everybody laughed, including the Clarksdale police. They had thought or maybe hoped they had cornered one of the FBI's most wanted. Somebody at the mayor's meeting had decided that I refuted arguments like a communist and had started the whole investigation.

For many years, I was grateful for this incident. When a man is charged with being a communist, questions linger in people's minds, regardless of whether there is ever evidence to back up the charges. But I had been cleared by the FBI itself and with a considerable flourish at that. The entire police force was there, people were peeping out of their windows, and evidently I had been the one person who had not had a clue about what was happening.

After this confrontation ended in laughter, people later hesitated to raise the communist charges. The whole time the police were claiming that his partner might be a communist, old Walker was standing in the back of the store laughing. Before I had arrived, they had shared their suspicions, and Walker had told them, "Well, y'all are crazy. Aaron ain't never seen a communist; he ain't never been north of Memphis." After that, for a long time he called me "Red." I told him, "It's hell enough being black without being black and red at the same time."

Chapter 6

People Get Ready

As protest began to stir among local Negroes in the early fifties, it became more acceptable to express dissatisfaction with the status quo. This change was significant, because so many Negroes had been willing to accept conditions rather than question them and gamble with reprisals. White Mississippians usually look back at this period prior to 1954 and point to the splendid race relations that existed. What they were really saying, I believe, is that civil rights activity had not gained much momentum, and even if some Negroes were no longer happy in their place, most of them were willing to stay there and wait for someone else to take the initiative. There was very little true communication between the races. Also during this period of "good" race relations, the killings and lynchings and beatings continued as they had in the past, but they were considered part of the system and did not mar the concept of those "good" relations.

Most physical reprisals against Negroes continued for the same old reasons—sassing whites, looking at a white woman, and so on—not for civil rights activities. Then there were always the cases of whites simply taking the law into their hands to punish a black for a crime which he did not commit. But there were also the few "uppity niggers" scattered over the state who had worked themselves into an economic situation that made them totally independent of the white community. White society seldom heard about the vigorous protests of these Negro rebels, since the radio and press rarely gave coverage to the meetings where the protests were aired.

Communication continued in the traditional master-servant relationship. On our part, the Negro would lie to his white boss when the boss asked if he was happy with the status quo—he knew he needed to say what the white man wanted to hear. I suspect that every Negro maid in Mississippi has been asked at some point how she felt, and most of them obligingly told the white lady boss that they were as happy as could be. Then at the white ladies' tea party they were all happy to hear that the maids of all had said the same thing. Many Negroes thought the segregation laws were perpetual and could not be changed. Some believed that there was actually a basic difference between the races that made segregation necessarily and unalterably the law of the land. A majority of both races accepted segregation as a way of life that was going to be with us forever. Until people outside the system—or independent of it—helped fashion new ideas and a fresh spirit of hope, there was little effective agitation for change. But once there was hope, then came the bright vision and the swelling tides for change.

When I returned to Clarksdale in 1950 and began my pharmaceutical practice, one of my first efforts was to establish good relations with every medical doctor in the area. This endeavor took me to Mound Bayou, an all-Negro community located about thirty miles south of Clarksdale. I met the people at the Taborian Hospital and Friendship Clinic, including Dr. T. R. M. Howard, one of the best-known Negro physicians in the state. Before I met Dr. Howard, I had read an article about him in the *Saturday Evening Post*, in which he was advocating using a capital "N" in "Negro" and which told about how he was making great strides in improving the conditions of his race. So I already had a great deal of respect for the man. When we did meet, I told Dr. Howard how much I admired him, that we were fortunate to have a man like him in our community, and that I would like to help promote his ideas. A close friendship developed from our meeting, and the prescriptions that he wrote for our store gave a good boost to our young business.

Soon after we met, Dr. Howard told me that a statewide civil rights organization could be effective in Mississippi. He proposed the formation of a group to be called the Regional Council of Negro Leadership (RCNL), which he hoped could be an organization to parallel the Delta Council, a white group providing a combined voice on the economic interests of the

Delta. The Delta Council, which had thousands of members, might best be described as an oversized chamber of commerce.

Someone alerted the Delta Council that Dr. Howard was telling people that the council was supporting the idea of the RCNL as a "separate but equal" arrangement. At one of our first meetings, however, a representative of the Delta Council came and announced that they neither supported nor opposed our formation, and any talk of their support was misinformation. This angered many of us, because we felt they were meddling in our attempts to organize.

In the beginning, Dr. Howard did not conceive of our council as a civil rights group. Rather, the purpose was to give some organized voice to the Negro economic and social interests throughout the Delta. It was almost like a local NAACP. But with the strife with the Delta Council, we emerged as an organization opposed to the established system. At our first official meeting, I was elected secretary of the board, and Medgar Evers was elected program director.

The RCNL functioned mainly through committee work and public rallies. Its headquarters remained in Mound Bayou, but the semiannual meetings were held all over the state. We would switch our meeting sites, hoping to involve as many Negroes as possible, and sometimes as many as ten thousand came to our huge circus tents that seated acres of people. We always tried to have a prominent speaker, and Congressmen Dawson and Diggs and Thurgood Marshall himself came down.

Money was a problem at first, but then funds came from dues and public appeals and passing the hat at meetings. After the group was well established and publicized, we were able to rely on contributions from all over the country.

The general attitude of whites toward the council was that we were sort of a homegrown NAACP that opposed the status quo. But whites were also slowly becoming aware that the NAACP was making progress through the courts, and they began to view the council with suspicious eyes. Their agitation was mostly through threatening phone calls to our officers and a clear message that Dr. Howard and his cohorts were considered to be rabble-rousers. However, no steps were taken to declare us illegal until 1954 when the Supreme Court decision put us and the NAACP into total disrepute.

At its inception, the regional council established a committee to try to make real the "separate but equal" guarantees of the federal government, and I was made chair of the committee. We were trying to get an equal share of every dollar spent on the state and federal level. We said we would settle for nothing less than a "dollar-for-dollar, brick-for-brick distribution of revenues" among Negro and white. The articulation of this position brought the matter into open discussion and consideration in the black community.

Our most successful program was probably the 1953 boycott of gas stations that refused to allow us to use the rest rooms. Our slogan for the campaign appeared on bumper stickers all over the state: "DON'T BUY GAS WHERE YOU CAN'T USE THE WASHROOM." The boycott was Dr. Howard's idea, and he had fifty thousand bumper stickers printed. Later, we found that the slogan might be violating the law, so we changed the wording, and the second fifty thousand said, "WE DON'T BUY GAS WHERE WE CAN'T USE THE WASHROOM." All over the state, Negroes were driving up to service stations and asking in the same breath for gas and to use the washroom. They would drive off when told that there were no washrooms available for Negroes. Most service stations were finally forced to add rest rooms to accommodate us, and we considered this a valuable improvement.

Voter registration was the chief concern of the regional council. We had an educational program to teach Negroes the basic procedures for registering, since most of them had never even been in contact with a Negro who had registered or voted. We tried to teach them how to pass the voter qualification tests. While this might seem the wrong approach for real improvement, it was the only way to go about it. So we got copies of the state constitution and into the hands of potential voters who could learn enough to satisfy the registrar. We got the copies from Heber Ladner, Mississippi's secretary of state, until he found out how they were being used and put a quick stop to it.

At first, white opposition to our registration drives was disorganized and generally ineffectual. They did not believe white supremacy was in danger, and usually the registrar was able to hold the line without the aid of the Citizens' Council or the Ku Klux Klan. Neither group was active in the Delta at that time.

The number of people who tried to register varied markedly from county to county, because the registrars themselves were so different, and they were the sole judges of who could register. In areas where there was a history of Black and Tan Republicanism—where Negroes had always been able to vote in national elections—a substantial number of people tried to register. They knew how to go about it and were less afraid. Where there had been no previous political participation and few knowledgeable people to help others, a pervading fear shrouded the notion of going down to the courthouse and asking to register.

Similarly, the amount of harassment varied sharply from county to county. In areas such as Clarksdale, where Negroes had been more vocal in their protests for a long time, the whites accepted our demand for the vote as just another complaint. But where whites had never contended with Negro protest, attempts to register caused quite a stir. Where there was the most progress, there was less intimidation and harassment, and the opposite for other communities, so the better got better and the worse became worse.

The regional council had testimonial meetings where people would relate their experiences in trying to register and reprisals they had encountered—usually a matter of losing jobs but sometimes cases of being beaten or shot. A number of Negroes were killed for trying to register during this period. The testimonials were usually given when we had visitors like Congressman Diggs or national NAACP officials. We needed to impress them with the reality of the hardships surrounding our attempts to register.

Then, during the 1954 session of the state legislature, new voting requirements were established to sharpen the powers of the local registrar in deciding who was qualified to vote. Prior to 1954, qualification laws necessitated reading *or* interpreting some part of the state constitution. Under the new requirements, an applicant was required to read *and* interpret and write (copy) any of the 285 sections of the constitution and to answer 23 questions that were meant to cause confusion. And, of course, the registrar didn't have to answer to anyone unless a suit was brought in federal court, a step that smacked of suicide, as far as most of us were concerned.

Other legislative activity in Jackson that year included a two-headed package of laws designed to circumvent the pending Supreme Court decision on school desegregation. That decision would trigger which of the two laws would go into effect. Anticipation of the ruling had begun in a special session of the legislature in late 1953 when an "equalization" program was passed for the public schools. This was the first time the legislature had made any attempt to fulfill the "separate but equal" requirement of the federal government. The equalization program called for equal salaries for white and Negro teachers, equal transportation facilities, and so on. Equalization would go into effect only if the Supreme Court ruled favorably on the state's position of continued separation by race. A few months later when the regular 1954 session convened, the legislators, to show the court their good will, passed the equalization program. Then, anticipating an "unfavorable" decision by the court, the legislature appropriated only enough money to operate the public schools for one year. So, the state was trying to influence the court for the "favorable" decision to maintain "separate but equal," while simultaneously making plans to circumvent an "unfavorable" decision requiring school desegregation.

There were no outright black segregationists in the membership of the regional council. We had the Separate but Equal Committee, but that was strictly an effort to push as far as we could within the realm of the law. We had spent years trying everything we could to get the "separate but equal" doctrine to work, but had been met only with noncooperation, beatings, and even death. In a very impressive way, the whites had proved to us that there could never be a "separate but equal" society.

There was only one man on the council's board with leanings toward segregationist sentiments, and he didn't last long. Percy Greene was the editor of the *Jackson Advocate*, and he came out editorially in opposition to the national NAACP position on school desegregation. Percy said that the NAACP should concentrate on voter registration instead of integration activities. When Dr. Howard called Percy on the carpet at a board meeting and asked him why he took this stand, the editor became furious, cursed the council, and stormed out of the meeting.

Through these times and even in the early sixties, I don't think we had a great desire to integrate just for the sake of being with white people. We wanted integration to better our position. We knew that separate but equal could never work, and only in an integrated society would we be accorded the advantages that white Americans already had. Because the whites were able to keep the Negroes in a semi-illiterate state, ignorant of how other people lived, they prevented us from believing that change was possible. To a large degree, it was outside forces that brought the change—we had so few tools to do it ourselves. Some learned to scratch where he didn't itch, to pull off his hat when addressed by whites. We acquiesced to the Uncle Tom philosophy in order to survive—playing to the ego of whites. Some of us may have been assuring white bosses that they wanted no part of the integration business, but how many men with ten children and a forty-dollar weekly pay check can afford to lose their jobs over a principle? But we knew changes were coming. We felt them and watched for them and hoped and prayed that the day would come soon.

Chapter 7

An Empty Box

Our day—or we thought it was our day—came on May 17, 1954, bringing with it the most turbulent years in this country's recent domestic history. We had been upset and outraged over the deprivations, beatings, and lynchings of the past, but now we were to be faced with an escalation of deadly injustices that would go unchecked by local, state, and federal authorities. We were elated when we heard about the Supreme Court decision—a second emancipation. Few of us dreamed we were setting out to battle with no weapons and no protection. The relatively quiet years of the early fifties were only the calm before the storm. The Supreme Court had given us a beautifully wrapped gift, but when we removed the shiny wrappings, the box was empty.

In the immediate jubilation that followed the *Brown* decision, Mississippi Negroes placed too much faith in the good will and decency of the white officials who were supposed to implement the new law. Many of us were naive enough to believe that people would obey a ruling that was the law of the land, whether they liked it or not. Negroes who felt this way were willing to allow the whites time to prepare for the changes that would be demanded. We were seriously mistaken in our generosity. A few Negro leaders, like Leroy Chappel in Greenville, did argue strongly that a lull in our political activities would mean a hardening of defiance and a strengthening of white defenses. He insisted that we waste no time in planning for implementation of the court decision, but I was sympathetic with the position that we ought to give the whites time to come around to obeying the law.

The prevailing opinion—to give a little time—turned out to be poor judgment and misplaced confidence. In retrospect, it is difficult to understand how we could have been so naive. Chappel was proven right when the white community used the time to fan the fires of a reaction that would stave off compliance for years.

I truly believed that it was the start of real freedom, but with a long and difficult road still ahead to absolute equality. My mother and father, who always had tried to maintain as much dignity and self-respect as they could under the circumstances, were overjoyed. The abolition of segregated schools was something that they had hardly considered in their wildest dreams. Now here it was in their lifetime.

There were still a few Negroes scattered around, such as editor Percy Greene, now well on his way to becoming the official "Negro" of the state of Mississippi, who claimed that integration of the public schools was wrong. They claimed that equality could be attained at the polls, which was the same argument that the "liberal segregationists" endorsed. No doubt, some of these Negroes saw this stance as a means of gaining a form of respect within the white community. I have never considered their position to have any validity and saw them being used by white segregationists who quoted them by the mouthful as proof that the Negro *really* wants segregation, too.

The most disgusting reaction among some Negroes to the new law came from the fear that had been instilled in them during generations of oppression. These people declared, "I don't want my children going to school with whites, because whites are nasty and they stink." This foolishness, of course, was the same thing that the whites said about Negroes. Some Negroes used this childish approach to cover basic fears of taking the steps to enroll their children in the white school. Rather than admit fear, they said they were against integration anyway and explained it by degrading whites.

Most of the white people that I talked to in the beginning regarded the decision as a law that would have to be obeyed, but they were not happy about it. Customers at the drugstore, deliverymen, and whites that I saw casually in Clarksdale all expressed intentions of compliance. One driver who brought our drugs and supplies said to me, "They're raising a whole lot of hell about white and colored children going to school together, but why get up in the air about it? My children are going to have to go to school with Negroes and we might as well go along with the law."

This attitude of resignation reinforced our feeling that time should be given for the white community to adjust, and, if there had been some state leadership in the right direction, countless problems could have been avoided. Instead, within several months, whites mobilized against compliance, and most of them were advocating outright disobedience to the law.

In June of 1954, the Clarksdale and Coahoma County school boards jointly called together a biracial meeting. Several Negroes—Marian Reid, Dr. O. G. Smith, W. W. Nelson, and I—were invited to discuss improvements needed in the local Negro schools. The context was the old "separate but equal" idea, and here we were meeting on the heels of a Supreme Court decision that had just outlawed that doctrine. The whites, of course, were trying to get the Negro community to willingly continue a segregated system. They were now offering us improvements and conditions that had been guaranteed under the "separate but equal" law but that had never been effected. They understood the new decision well but knew it would be implemented only if local Negroes agitated for it. If they could placate us, there would be no integration. Similar meetings were held all over the state, and reactions varied from place to place, depending on the strength of our political activities just prior to the decision. Most of us were insulted by such an obvious buyoff.

At our Clarksdale meeting, I didn't say a word until they called on me, and then I started explaining that all of the problems under discussion came from maintaining a segregated school system. One point was the fact that Negro children had to get up so early in the morning to catch the school bus, since the bus had to make several trips to get all of them to school on time. It was the same in the evening when some children didn't get home until seven or eight. I pointed out that if they used all of the buses to carry all of the children, the problem would vanish.

We also discussed feeding children who were too poor to eat in the school cafeteria, and the board politely asked our consent to use leftover food to feed them. I argued that if we had all of the children in one school, food management would also be easier.

I made it clear that segregation was the cause of all our problems and that I could no longer go along with it. I told them that I intended to devote all of my energies to implementing the Supreme Court decision. For most of the whites at the meeting, it was the first time they had had a face-to-face confrontation with a Negro advocating total desegregation. I knew that it was easier for me, since I was in no way dependent on the white community for my livelihood and was not subject to serious economic reprisals. I had to take a strong stand.

My old friend Mr. Kyle, the owner of the Cotton Boll Court, who had befriended me in my younger days, was on the county school board. My statement appeared to be very upsetting to him. I had been negotiating a loan from him so that I could buy Walker's share in the Fourth Street Drug Store, since Walker was purchasing the Walgreen Agency. Several days after the meeting, Mr. Kyle told me that he couldn't lend me money if I was going to push for the desegregation of public schools. We went on a long drive one night and talked over the matter. He explained that if I continued to push and that if it was known that he had helped me financially, it would mean ostracism for him and his family. He didn't tell me a lot of tales, simply that I should try to understand and that I could borrow money without paying interest if I would be content with "separate but equal" and stop agitating for desegregation. I had put him in a tight position where he was being asked to identify himself with a Negro who was directly involved in the civil rights struggle. I was committed to work for the total destruction of the system that Mr. Kyle believed in and valued, and I never held it against him that he was unwilling to associate with me financially or in any other way.

So, I had worked myself into a pretty bad position for borrowing money, and word spread rapidly about my stand at the school board meeting. I was satisfied with what I had done, and, from then on, no one had to speculate on where I stood. About a month after the meeting an incident occurred that established once and for all the position of Negro leaders on the question of implementation of school desegregation. It began when Walter Sillers, speaker of the state house of representatives and spokesman for Governor Hugh White, called for a statewide meeting of Negro leaders. The purpose of this first statewide interracial meeting since Reconstruction was to get the approval of state Negro leaders for a voluntary segregation plan. In return, the Negro leaders would be promised a massive effort by the state to equalize white and Negro schools. Dr. Howard, who was serving as our spokesman, insisted that the leaders' group be expanded to get better representation. Governor White agreed and asked that Dr. Howard and Negro segregationist Percy Greene supply other names of Negro attenders. From the names on these lists, one hundred Negroes were invited to meet in Jackson on July 30, 1954.

Emmett Stringer, the state NAACP president, felt it was imperative that we have a private meeting the day before the meeting with the governor to gain unity and arrive at a majority opinion. We didn't know all the people invited by the governor, but we contacted about seventy and met at the Farish Street Baptist Church in Jackson. We met at six in the evening and broke up about midnight. E. W. Banks of the Peoples Funeral Home opened the meeting and suggested that we take a strong stand against segregation and for implementation of the Supreme Court decision. Percy Greene disagreed and said that we were foolish to want to abolish segregation. Percy wanted us to concentrate our energies on voter registration and felt that we should neither oppose nor endorse the decision. That was the last of those sentiments that night. The liberal forces began to speak, and, before long, the group was almost unanimously in support of implementation. The pattern was set, and we were ready for the governor's meeting the next day.

A slight shadow hovered over the meeting because our chief spokesman, Dr. Howard, was on bad terms with Governor White. Shortly before, Dr. Howard had issued a statement saying that if Hugh White said that Negroes in Mississippi were satisfied with existing conditions, then he was the damnedest liar God ever made. Some of the governor's supporters had asked Dr. Howard to retract his statement, and Howard reiterated: "If the governor said that we are satisfied, he *is* the damnedest liar that God ever made." It was decided that Howard would not make our opening statement.

We put E. W. Banks near the microphone so he could get the jump on everyone else and make sure the first statement read was in support of the court decision. Then the rest of us would speak in support of Banks. Walter Sillers opened the meeting and meandered along about the years of splendid relations between the races in Mississippi. Banks was sitting there like a cat ready to spring, and every time old Sillers would slow down, cough, or clear his throat, Banks's hand would shoot up and wave frantically. Banks was such a nuisance that Sillers interrupted his speech and said he would recognize Banks when the time came. Banks hollered back, "Well, all right then."

Sillers appeared a little rattled as he finished his remarks, recognized Banks, and gave him the floor. Banks hopped up and read our statement that we were "unalterably opposed to any efforts of either white or Negro citizens to circumvent the decision of the Supreme Court of the United States outlawing segregation in the public schools!"

The place exploded. People were on their feet, yelling, "FREEDOM! FREEDOM!" There was shouting and screaming. Then came enthusiastic applause. When that died down, Sillers began to recognize individuals who he hoped would support him, but one after another we stood and spoke against segregation. It didn't look as if Sillers was going to find a segregationist in the crowd. Then Professor Alvin Jones from Union County took the floor. He was a sad-looking fellow and spoke in a slow, quiet voice. Without looking up, he began to speak. "Don't let us be fools now. White folks have been good to us all our lives. Let's not kick them in the face. I don't want my children to go to school with white children and here's why. Suppose my little boy and Governor White's little boy get in a fight and I whupped 'em both. Mrs. White's boy goes home and tells her that I whupped him, and she's gonna come looking for me with a shotgun." He got more and more enthusiastic as he bumbled around making his point. He finally sat down, and a murmur slowly swept the room. We were disgusted but amused that he had brought in Governor White's wife—not a smart thing to do.

Mrs. Ruby Stutts Lyells—got the floor after Jones and said, "I could see in your faces while Mr. Jones spoke that many of you were sorry. But I am glad he spoke because he is an outstanding example of what we must be rid of—folks like him whose minds have been warped by segregation." As she talked, Mrs. Lyells walked up and down the aisles and pointed to Jones, who just kept sinking lower and lower in his chair.

Percy Greene got up and made a speech which nobody remembers, except that he talked about peace and harmony and that we should all try to live together. The meeting was keyed up by then, and, when Percy sat down, almost everyone's hand went up. Mr. Sillers looked around the room carefully and spotted the Reverend H.H. Humes. Sillers knew Humes, thought him a trustworthy ally, and called on him.

Reverend Humes stood up and waited until everything was completely quiet. Then he looked up at Sillers. "Mr. Sillers, there ain't no use in y'all being mad with us over this thing. It wasn't us that made that decision. It was nine white men that made that decision. The trouble is that for too long y'all been giving us schools where we could study the earth through the floor and the stars through the roof."

The room became electric. Sillers said, "This meeting is over." He knew if he had lost Humes, he had lost us all. Of the one hundred of us in attendance, only one had endorsed the governor's program. Governor White issued a statement to the press: "I am stunned. I have believed that the vast majority of Negroes would go along. Now I am definitely of the opinion you can't put faith in any of them on this proposition."

I was really proud to be a Mississippi Negro and to have stood with my people. The press gave it big play. "NEGROES STAND NINETY-NINE TO ONE AGAINST SEGREGATION: HOWARD VINDICATED."

At the same time we thought we were making progress, the forces of reaction geared up to make progress of their own. Robert "Tut" Patterson, a Clarksdale native, read Judge Tom Brady's book, *Black Monday*, laying out the sordid results of integration and mongrelization of the white race. He went to work to save the South. He met with several like-minded men in Indianola and formed the first Citizens' Council, established to prevent integration in any phase of Mississippi life. Their goals were to make it impossible for any Negro in favor of desegregation to find or keep a job, to cut off his credit or mortgage renewal, and to discourage Negro voting. It was also clear that whites who were sympathetic to civil rights would suffer the same reprisals.

From a small beginning, the Citizens' Council would grow to a membership exceeding thirty thousand during the next few years, and what little interracial cooperation we had developed was doomed to die. Any white person suggesting that interracial communication might soothe the strife was ostracized, at minimum. The council slammed those doors, and white moderates were silenced quickly. Negro groups such as the Regional Council of Negro Leadership and the Progressive Voters' League were forced underground or nearly out of business during the reign of the Citizens' Council. And the NAACP, identified in whites' minds with the Supreme Court ruling, became the most hated organization in the South, and particularly in Mississippi. The council's plan was to quash every move made by Negroes to take advantage of the desegregation decision. They hoped that economic pressure would make Negroes cooperate and that social and political pressure would work against recalcitrant whites.

By November, only four months after the Citizens' Council's formation, state NAACP president Emmett Stringer announced that one local NAACP president had been forced to resign. "As for me," he told the *New York Times*, "I can't get credit anywhere in Mississippi and I'm just getting started." In late May 1955, the Supreme Court rendered its "implementation decision," and immediately the NAACP filed petitions for desegregation of the public schools in Vicksburg, Natchez, Jackson, Yazoo City, and Clarksdale. Our local chapter filed the Clarksdale petition.

We started the process at a public meeting. The petition had been prepared by the NAACP legal department and called upon the local school board to implement the Supreme Court decision immediately. We posted the petitions in churches and businesses, and they remained there for a month. When we collected them and took count, we had more than four hundred signatures of heads of families. We sent the completed petitions by registered mail to the school board in September 1955.

The next thing we knew, the names and addresses of all of the petition signers appeared in the local newspaper—the school board's first step. The accompanying story said that this was to alert the community that "these people are the agitators and trouble-makers." Reprisals came swiftly, and we realized that perhaps we had made a serious mistake by using so many names of people who were not prepared to handle the intimidation. We should have only used the names of people already known to be in the movement. We had used four hundred and fifty names in hopes of showing the real desire for integration, and we thought this would lessen the harassment of a smaller number. But large numbers had no effect on the oppression of the Citizens' Council and other racist groups. Some of the signers were forced to flee the state, others could not buy even basic staples, and carpenters and plumbers in the building trades were no longer hired by whites. Wholesale houses refused to sell Negro trade workers materials that they needed. Whites looked at the petition list, and if your name was on it, you just caught hell.

The Citizens' Council was sweeping the state and picking up momentum steadily. An air of fanaticism prevailed, and it almost seemed as if the whites had gone insane. Soon, even white people who had been willing initially to accept the decision hardened their positions. Some whites who joined the council did say that they did so to keep the radical element under control. The names of people who signed school petitions across the state were given to banks and other credit agencies with the suggestion that credit be denied to signers. Intimidation and job loss soon reached such proportions that many signers removed their names. The council was not subtle in its approach and announced frequently in newspapers that they would continue dealing with us through economic reprisals: "Not the lash, not the rope, we'll starve 'em out."

The harassment affected voter registration as well, and by 1955, Attorney General J. P. Coleman announced that Negro registration had fallen by ten thousand since 1952. The Citizens' Councils in some towns were more vicious, and reprisals more brutal. For example, in Belzoni, the council was determined to get Gus Courts and Reverend George Lee removed from the voting roles. Both were staunch members of the Regional Council of Negro Leadership and the NAACP. They refused to budge, asserting that they had a right to vote and pointing out that they had passed the test before pressure became so great. In March 1955, Courts was evicted from his grocery store after pressure was brought on the building owner. A member of the council showed Courts a list of the ninety-five Negroes who were registered in Humphreys County and said that all on the list who didn't remove their names would lose their jobs.

Two months later, Reverend George Lee, who also refused to remove his name, was returning from a regional council meeting at Mound Bayou. When he reached Belzoni, he was shot to death in his car. A coroner's jury ruled that Lee had died of "causes unknown." But Sheriff Ike Shelton conducted an investigation and said he had trouble determining whether the pellets found in Lee's head were bullets or fillings in his teeth. Shelton's final report said that Lee had been shot by another Negro because of an argument over a woman, not over his voting activities.

We had a memorial service for Mr. Lee in Belzoni, and the NAACP, to no avail, asked the FBI for protection. We felt we needed protection because the past had taught us that when one Negro is killed, stay out of town if your skin is black. And here we were having a memorial service right in the middle of town. For one of the first times, no protection was needed—there wasn't a white man on the streets the day of the service, except for the press. There was a great turnout of Negroes for the funeral. This large presence of Negroes and absence of whites marked a turning point.

At the service, the state NAACP president, Dr. A. H. McCoy, told the crowd, "I directly blame the Citizens' Council for Lee's murder." Roy Wilkins spoke and said that violence would not deter us from our goal: "Where they kill one of us today, a thousand will stand tomorrow." But the secretary of the local Citizens' Council took exception to the accusation of the murder, saying that "The council had nothing to do with Lee's death, because violence is against our constitution and bylaws." No one was ever brought to trial for the murder.

Election year 1955 was pretty rowdy for Mississippi, and the candidates just screamed "NIGGER!" back and forth and took almost the same stands on everything. The campaigns were purely negative, damning Negroes, our voting and our school desegregation efforts, and the five candidates for governor were all supported by the Citizens' Council. The state Democratic Party chairman, Bidwell Adams, rallied to the cause and said, "Negroes may be national Democrats, but they are not Mississippi Democrats . . . We don't intend to have Negroes voting in this primary." The truth of the matter was that had we been able to vote, we wouldn't have voted for either of the Democratic candidates who battled it out in the runoff—J. P. Coleman and Paul Johnson.

For the second primary in August, Gus Courts and twenty-two other Negroes tried to vote in Belzoni, were challenged under new registration laws, and had their ballots thrown out. Across the state the same thing happened—Negroes able to vote in the past had their ballots tossed out. J. P.

Coleman won the governorship and gave a solemn pledge that there would be no public school integration while he was governor.

During that August, in McComb, Lamar Smith, active in voter registration, was shot down and killed in the middle of the day in front of the Pike County courthouse. Three white men were indicted for murder, but never brought to trial. Judge Tom Brady, author of the white supremacist tract *Black Monday*, was the circuit judge. Brady explained that it was impossible in Mississippi to get a white man to testify against another white man for a crime against a Negro.

Three weeks later I learned that Emmett Till, a fourteen-year-old Negro boy from Chicago, had disappeared. He was visiting his granduncle for the summer in Leflore County, and the newspaper said that two white men had been arrested for kidnapping Till, but it was undetermined what had become of him. The men were Roy Bryant and his half-brother, J. W. Milam, and it was rumored that young Till had whistled at one of their wives. Several days later a fisherman found Till's body in the Tallahatchie River. A heavy gin fan was tied around the boy's neck.

Rumors circulated that a person in Drew had seen Till in the back of a pickup truck early one morning and that someone had also seen two men steal the gin that had been found around Till's neck. I drove over to Mound Bayou to tell Dr. Howard, who went to Sheriff Sandy Smith of Leflore County, where the men were being held on the kidnapping charges. We were asking, in light of new and still-developing evidence, that the trial be postponed for several days. Sheriff Smith and Attorney Stanley Sanders refused and said that the trial would proceed as scheduled.

Dr. Howard called a press conference, and the reporters included Clark Portious, a Scripps Howard reporter from Memphis, and Simeon Booker, a Negro reporter from *Ebony*. Sheriff Smith and Attorney Sanders were also present. Howard said that additional evidence had been found in the Till case—that several people in Drew were potential witnesses—and that he had asked authorities for a one-day postponement. Smith and Sanders realized the reporters would make a big story out of it, so they agreed to put off the trial for one day.

That night several of us went to Attorney Sanders's office in Drew and told him that we planned to comb the area. He told us that we were on our own if we were going to go looking for witnesses and that if we got shot, it was our business.

We had heard that a cotton worker named Mamie Smith knew something, so Ruby Hurley, NAACP regional director from Atlanta, put on an old dress the next morning and went into the fields to pick cotton. We hoped she could get the story without being noticed. Mamie had seen two Negro boys on the back of a truck driven by Milam and Bryant, and the boys were holding something under a canvas. The boys' names were Collins and Loggins. We talked to several other people who had witnessed Milam and Bryant transporting Till and got them to appear at the trial. They told what they had seen, but the trial was not taken seriously by the defendants or the jury, and the two men were freed. The day after the trial we drove Mamie and several other people up to Memphis and put them on a bus going north.

Later it was revealed that the two white men had gotten the two Negro boys to assist them in the slaying. After they were exonerated, Milam and Bryant sold the story of what actually happened to a national magazine. A few days after the trial, we got word that Collins wanted to talk. Considerable preparation was made for the meeting, and Alex Wilson of the Chicago *Defender* came down to get Collins out of the state if he wanted to go. We went to a restaurant in Tutwiler to meet the boy. He was frightened to death and said that he didn't know a thing about the slaying of Emmett Till. We insisted that he had been a participant and that perhaps he felt his life was in danger if he talked. Collins continued to insist that he didn't know anything. Alex Wilson told him he would take him out of Mississippi if he would talk. Collins finally said he would let us know something later on. That night at supper at my house a knock came on the door. It was Collins with a grip, saying he was ready to go to Chicago then and there. Alex put Collins in the car that night. The boy's story in full—everything he had seen and done—later appeared in the *Defender*, but Milam and Bryant were already free.

Louis Lomax, a prominent black journalist, came down about a month later looking for Loggins, the other Negro boy who had participated in the kidnapping and murder of Emmett Till. Lomax found the boy and told me that he appeared to be on the verge of a mental breakdown and kept saying,

"Please, please, don't ask me any questions. Don't make me tell you anything." While Lomax was there, Loggins disappeared and was never heard from again—no body or any trace of him.

By this time, Gus Courts, who was still refusing to remove his name from the voting books, had gotten situated in a new store in Belzoni. In late November 1955, someone drove up to the front of the store and started firing a gun. Courts was critically wounded. He insisted that he be taken to the Negro hospital in Mound Bayou. He later recovered but never reopened his store and decided to move to Chicago. In the hearing on the shooting, Mrs. Savannah Luton, who testified that Courts's assailant had been a white man, was immediately taken off the welfare rolls.

Two years later Courts testified for civil rights legislation in Washington and the *New York Times* quoted him as saying: "My wife and I and thousands of Mississippians have had to run away . . . We had to flee in the night. We are the American refugees from the terror in the South, all because we want to vote. Not only are they killing colored people who want to vote and be citizens, but they are squeezing them out of business, foreclosing their mortgages, refusing them credit from the banks to operate their farms."

With Lee dead and Courts in Chicago, Humphreys County and Belzoni were left with only one Negro on the registration book, T. V. Johnson. He was an undertaker, and his intimidation at the hands of the Citizens' Council was severe. Negroes who patronized him were also intimidated and the council effected a boycott of his business. Although Johnson never removed his name, the harassment was so fierce that he was afraid to go the polls.

Also, soon after the Emmett Till case, Elmer Kimball, a good friend of the men who had murdered Till, killed Clinton Melton, a Negro service station attendant in Glendora. The white service station owner and several other white witnesses said that there had been no provocation, and the killing was outright murder. But Kimball called it self-defense, and the jury believed him.

So the bloody and death-pocked year of 1955 ended with at least four Negroes dead at the hands of whites, all of whom were exonerated. It was sad that fine men like Gus Courts had to leave the state, but for many Negroes it wasn't comfortable in the mid-fifties to stay where it was no crime for a white man to kill a Negro. We were losing in the struggle to vote and go to better schools. The state legislature enacted laws which further restricted our voting and other rights, and gradually most white people in the state, voluntarily or under pressure, shut their eyes and minds and claimed their seat in the "closed society." Whites who remained sympathetic were dubbed "nigger-lovers" and "race mixers," with severe reprisals levelled against them as well.

On the national level, few persons of authority seemed to care what happened to a Mississippi Negro who asked for his rights of citizenship, and the morale of our movement was dwindling. Making the gesture to vote was not worth the sure reprisals. Slowly, the old submissiveness crept back as the best way to avoid violence or intimidation. The whites had won a big round, and, for several years after early 1956, there was no extreme violence, because it was not necessary. The threat of it was enough. We all knew we moved under a cloud, and we moved cautiously.

Prior to the 1954 Supreme Court decision, most whites, if they had even heard of the NAACP, usually didn't feel one way or the other about it, and there were no reprisals for membership. But after the ruling, white Mississippi was convinced the NAACP was largely responsible for that contemptible Washington decision, and they set about to destroy it using any means. Where the means were not legal, the legislature made them legal. If the means were too ridiculous for the legislature to endorse, the Citizens' Councils and their allies awaited.

In March 1956, the legislature passed a declaration of "interposition," which was intended to interpose certain rights of the state of Mississippi between the national government and its state citizens. The legislators did this against the advice of Governor Coleman, who called the idea of interposition "legal poppycock." (Governor Ross Barnett later suggested interposition as a legal means of keeping James Meredith out of the University of Mississippi in 1961.)

The legislature, bathing in delusions of interposition, then established the State Sovereignty Commission, with its stated purpose being "to protect the sovereignty of Mississippi from encroachment thereon by the federal government." This group included an investigative division, which was authorized to pay informers who would provide information on persons aiding in the encroachment by the federal government. It often seemed to us the primary function of the State Sovereignty Commission was to frustrate efforts of the NAACP. In retrospect, it appears that they were dedicated to frustrating any attempt at implementing the law of the land. They made it their business to know the names and occupations of all people in the state who were known for lack of dedication to the hallowed "southern way of life."

But legal maneuvers were not enough for the 1956 legislature. They were proud of their interposition doctrine and the establishment of the State Sovereignty Commission, which actually later channeled state funds to the Citizens' Council. Continuing under the guidance of their aged speaker, Sillers, faithful in his incompetence, the body passed a law that made "stirring up litigation" a crime. Then, to help preserve their way of life, the legislature repealed the state's compulsory school attendance law.

Pressures against the NAACP escalated, and it became hazardous to hold membership. Dr. Howard, our longtime spokesman, declared that the Citizens' Council had made it impossible for him to continue living in the state, and he went to Chicago; we lost an effective leader. The pattern was followed all over the state as Negroes were harassed into getting out of the NAACP. Almost all of the chapters became inactive and in some cases were completely abandoned. In Indianola, Clinton Battle, head of the NAACP, was also forced to leave the state. He had asked the FBI to investigate, but, as Battle said, "They sent a white man born and raised in Mississippi to investigate. He told me I should tell the sheriff. When I saw that the federal government wasn't going to do anything about the violation of my civil rights, I knew that I might as well move out of state."

Our feelings of neglect and abandonment by the federal government deepened rapidly, with no reason to feel otherwise. The Supreme Court had ruled it was our right to put our names on school petitions. We did it, and we paid with jobs and lives, while the federal government, guardian of the Constitution, sat and watched. This was the Constitution, parts of which our schoolchildren memorized, that assured us of our right to vote. So we had no support in our quest, and we weren't sure who was to blame. We later came to attribute this sad state of affairs to the weak and ineffective domestic leadership of President Eisenhower.

In 1957, it appeared the situation might improve. Congress was debating a civil rights bill that year—the first since 1875. One main point would give the Department of Justice the authority to bring suits on behalf of Negroes deprived of their voting rights. The NAACP was keenly interested that this be included in the bill and cited the flagrant disregard for Negro voting rights in Mississippi. We believed that Congress would pass a much stronger civil rights bill if they could be convinced of the dire situation in Mississippi and other Deep South states.

But official Mississippi reacted with indignation to suggestions of voting rights deprivation. Governor Coleman told reporters on February 7, 1957, "There is no intimidation of Negroes in Mississippi." Medgar Evers replied: "It is true that this bill may be late for Emmett Till of Chicago, Illinois, Lamar Smith of Brookhaven, the Reverend George W. Lee and Gus Courts of Belzoni, and Clinton Melton of Glendora, but it will not be too late for Negroes in the state who cannot get justice in the courts, and where white people take the law into their own hands. We deplore the statement that Negroes are not intimidated when teachers had to sign an oath that they were not members of the NAACP . . ."

Medgar Evers and I were close during these years. C. R. Darden was the NAACP state conference president, and Medgar was the field secretary, the only full-time paid employee. Since there were seldom any official investigations of crimes committed against Negroes, one of Medgar's duties was to travel to the locality, look into the crime, and file a report with the NAACP state president. Usually, Darden would go with Medgar, but when Darden's job took him out of state, Medgar asked me to go along.

Most incidents we investigated were cases of brutality, but denial of voting rights and other cases of discrimination began to come to our attention. The president of the Amite County chapter of the NAACP, E. W. Steptoe, called us in 1956 to investigate a case of county authorities actively trying to suppress the local chapter. During a night meeting, the police had barged in and dispersed the meeting, and demanded that all minutes and membership rolls be turned over to them. To Medgar and me this was clearly an invasion of privacy as well as denial of the right to peaceful assembly, and we filed appropriate charges against the county.

By 1957, Darden, who was very conservative, often clashed with activist Medgar Evers. Several board members encouraged me to run for state president. I had been vice president for several years, secretary before that, and I had been president of the local chapter in Clarksdale, so I knew many people in the organization. I ran against Darden in 1957 and lost to him by a vote of 316 to 305. Two years later I ran again and won.

In 1957, I also began my association with the Southern Christian Leadership Conference, based in Atlanta and headed by Martin Luther King, Jr. King had led the successful bus boycott in Montgomery, and I had attended an SCLC meeting in Memphis. Later the SCLC board met in Clarksdale, and R. L. Drew and I agreed to be the SCLC board members for Mississippi. The SCLC program and philosophy advocated nonviolence and appealing to the moral conscience of the community to do right for the sake of doing right. They wanted to "love hell out of Mississippi." This philosophy was a major factor in the success of the movement, but it was difficult to endorse fully on a personal basis—I just never quite got there.

The Mississippi legislature of 1958 began where its predecessor had left off. Not content with an array of existing legal conflicts and paradoxes, they set about to deepen the complications. Their purpose was to frustrate the Supreme Court decision further and render the NAACP totally impotent in Mississippi. Two bills authorizing legislative investigation of the NAACP were passed. Other bills gave the governor the right to close any school threatened with integration. The Sovereignty Commission was given further support, and the attorney general was armed with greater powers in fighting integration suits.

My election as NAACP state conference president came in 1959, and, in keeping with tradition, I resigned as president of the Coahoma County branch. John Melchor, who had been harassed into removing his name from a school desegregation petition, was elected president of our local chapter, but the intimidation resumed, and he resigned. His wife was still teaching school and did not want to risk being fired. The local chapter asked me to come back as president, and I did.

Soon after my election as state president, Medgar and I went to New York for the fifty-year celebration convention of the NAACP. He and I made the annual report on Mississippi, and it was clear that we were in dire need of assistance. As part of the convention, all delegates were expected to visit Washington and call on their congressmen, but ours refused to see Medgar and me. Mississippi was the only state whose congressmen refused to see NAACP delegates, and this fact was reported to the convention. The floor was filled with congressmen when the announcement was made, and several of them expressed their disgust and offered to give whatever assistance they could. They invited us to regard them as our own congressmen. This group of sympathetic legislators grew steadily until it numbered twenty-five representatives and seven or eight senators who were always willing to listen to our problems and try to help us. A collect telephone call made them available to us anytime we needed them.

The trip to Washington was my first lobbying excursion, and there would be many more. A weak civil rights bill was passed in 1960, and we stepped up lobbying efforts. Medgar and I made numerous trips to Washington, going from office to office and talking to congressmen about our problems and giving them our views on proposed legislation. Many of them were keenly interested, and most were appalled that we had to appeal to senators and representatives from states other than our own. We continued to call on our own, who continued to refuse to receive us. Their secretaries always told us, "He is out."

During the Eisenhower administration a bright spot appeared but soon faded. Several Justice Department representatives actually came to Mississippi to ask about conditions. But the same representative never came twice, and it seemed each new one knew nothing that we had told his predecessor. We would have to start from scratch with our reports, and it became clear that the department was simply going through the motions. It was a waste of their time and of ours.

But we couldn't forget that the Supreme Court's implementation decision of 1955 told the South to proceed with school desegregation "with all deliberate speed." It was plain that we could expect no help from local, state, or federal authorities, and those of us who were in the fight were in it all the way. We had to hang on, hoping that a man more sympathetic to our cause and more committed to upholding the laws of the land would be elected to the presidency in 1960.

Chapter 8

Mr. Doar's Promise

The new decade of the sixties ushered in two public officials who would play significant roles in the struggle for Mississippi justice. Ironically, they stood in direct opposition to each other. Governor Ross R. Barnett was inaugurated amid a flourish of promises to lead the state down a path of progress and return her to governmental concepts of one hundred years earlier. President John F. Kennedy stated his firm resolve that every American citizen would enjoy his or her basic constitutional and human rights, and, within a month after his inauguration, steps were taken to accomplish this.

Our first evidence of President Kennedy's dedication to equal rights was the arrival of Justice Department representatives John Doar and Robert Owens. I was a little skeptical when they came to the Fourth Street Drug Store and said they would like to meet with several of our local Negro activists. R. L. Drew, John Melchor, H. Y. Hackett, Mrs. Vera Pigee, Rev. J. D. Rayford, and I met with them in a room over the drugstore.

Before Doar and Owens stated their business, I explained to them that we had no reason to have any confidence in them—that their kind would usually come and talk to us for hours, take elaborate notes, then go off, leave their notes on the table, and never be heard from again. I added that we were tired of this kind of foolishness. Doar said he realized that there was some justification for our feelings but assured us that things were going to change. We had little reason to be optimistic, but we gave them a full report on our problems with voter registration, saying that those who had nerve enough to try failed to pass the tests and that many of those involved in the efforts lost their jobs and were fortunate if that was all they lost. We explained that the masses were afraid to take any stand at all or even to express their desire to vote because of the fear of reprisals. Our contention was that this intimidation and the fears associated with the exercise of basic rights were grounds enough for steps by the federal government.

Doar explained to us, honestly and convincingly, that no existing laws permitted the government's taking steps to eliminate fear. He agreed that the government couldn't close the stable door until the horse was stolen and pointed out that only a federal police force could deal with the problem. But he promised to do all that he could to help us, and I can say wholeheartedly that Mr. Doar kept his promise.

From the time of Doar's first visit, the situation began to improve. The Justice Department encouraged people to take a stand when denied the right to register and vote and supported such efforts through court action. Once John Doar and the Justice Department made it clear that they wanted to know about every case of discrimination that occurred, Medgar and I spent as much time as we could putting them in touch with people who had been denied the right to vote. It was not difficult to find these people, but it was terribly hard to find a person who was willing to become part of a federal suit and thus run the risk of sacrificing everything. Medgar and I canvassed the Delta counties, and, with help from men like Robert Miles of Batesville, we found several people willing to tell their story to Doar. When he had accumulated enough firsthand information, the Justice Department filed a motion at Batesville which was heard before a federal grand jury in Oxford. Medgar and I were not permitted in the courtroom during the hearing, but we stood outside with those who had come to testify to reassure them of our support. We realized the sacrifice they were making and wanted them to know we were willing to subject ourselves to any threats or violence along with them. The court proceedings were long, but, even with several years of legal entanglements, this suit was finally successful.

Tallahatchie County was also a stronghold against Negro voting. Even with a substantial number trying to register, not a single Negro had been successful since Reconstruction. Some leaders contacted Medgar and me for an investigation. We talked with Mrs. Birdie Kagler and Richard West and wired President Kennedy requesting his aid. We received a telegram saying the Justice Department was looking into the problems, and we believed him—a far cry from a meaningless response during the Eisenhower administration.

Doar and Owens arrived in the state soon after, and we put them in touch with leaders in Tallahatchie County willing to go public with the treatment they were receiving from voting officials. They talked with people who had been threatened or intimidated and, after several weeks of investigation, filed a motion against the county. Doar argued the case before a federal court in Clarksdale and was able to get the court to invalidate the law requiring the test on constitutional interpretation in Tallahatchie County. An injunction was brought against the registrar on the basis that he was discriminatory in his decisions on who was eligible to vote. It was not legally possible to enjoin registrars in all eighty-two Mississippi counties, so we worked to get separate injunctions in as many counties as possible but concentrated in the Delta where there was a heavy Negro population. Medgar and I systematically searched every county for people to explain their problems to the men from the Justice Department—assuring them that this was the only way they would ever get the right to vote. Once people were prepared to talk, the department sent in several men to follow the cases through to the courts.

Medgar and I also investigated cases of racial brutality or murder and tried to obtain affidavits from witnesses. For example, in 1960 a Negro prisoner died in the Clarksdale jail after a severe beating by the police. The authorities told us that the prisoner, Louis Stapleton, had died of a heat stroke, but it seemed more likely that the beating caused the stroke. We called in federal authorities, who attempted to get an indictment against the responsible persons in the sheriff's department, contending that the beating and death would not have occurred if Louis Stapleton had been white. The case was never resolved.

In another investigation, Medgar and I learned that Bessie Turner of Clarksdale had been arrested and jailed for "rolling" a city employee. The facts leading up to the incident were never clear, but it was certain that twenty-two-year-old Bessie had been beaten in the Clarksdale jail. The police said they were trying to get her to tell what she had done with seventy-nine dollars that she had allegedly stolen from a Negro city employee while on a trip with him. While searching her at the jail, three white men made her take off her clothes and lie on the floor completely naked. They turned her on her stomach and beat her across the buttocks with a leather strap. Then they rolled her on her back and beat her about the genitals. Medgar and I tried unsuccessfully to get an indictment for police brutality from a federal grand jury in Oxford. In testimony later, in 1965, Bessie connected the entire incident to her attempts to register to vote.

In most of these cases, we were not able to get punishment for guilty parties, but at least we got them into court and into the spotlight of public attention. Soon, Negroes across the state recognized the sympathy of the Kennedy administration with our problems. It was a great morale booster and stimulant for action. Civil rights activity began increasing back up to the 1955 level when wanton brutality by lawless whites had us stymied. We knew this new wave of action would move us along, but we also knew it would follow the patterns of history and lead to severe reaction and reprisals.

In 1960, Medgar and I went to Los Angeles as guests of the West Coast region of the NAACP and visited a building which housed all the Jewish organizations that were involved in social action. The B'nai B'rith, the Anti-Defamation League, and the Jewish Women's Association were there, and we were impressed with their unity of concerns. We saw no indication of strife among the groups, and they seemed to be working together so effectively. At that time, the NAACP was the dominant civil rights group in Mississippi, and there was no strife between it and several other smaller groups (Southern Christian Leadership Conference, Congress of Racial Equality, Student Nonviolent Coordinating Committee, and the Progressive Voters' League). Usually there was a casual overlapping of the membership of the organizations with the goal of equal rights as the common bond. But after seeing the unity of the Jewish groups in California, Medgar and I were convinced that the Mississippi movement could be made more potent by drawing all of the groups under a common umbrella while each maintained its own identity.

Several months later we organized the Coahoma County Council of Federated Organizations, which included several local civil rights groups. The new thrust was successful in spearheading voter registration and in attacking other racial problems in the county, and it was good to try it out just on a county level.

In late May 1961, the first freedom riders began arriving in Mississippi. Most whites laughed when the editor of the *Jackson Daily News*, James M. Ward, started making jokes about the impending "invasion" of the state by northerners using interstate transportation facilities. The purpose of the riders was to test the ruling by the Interstate Commerce Commission which required that all public interstate transportation facilities be desegregated immediately. The riders were promptly arrested when they tried to use rest rooms and waiting rooms at Jackson's bus depots. They were charged with breach of the peace and resisting arrest. Most of the fines for the first freedom riders were reasonable, but they all chose to go to jail to serve their sentences. They were placed in the Hinds County jail but soon were moved to the State Penitentiary at Parchman. Riders continued to pour into Jackson during the rest of the summer, and officials continued to arrest them and jail them when they refused to pay their fines.

Our NAACP felt it was important to support the freedom rides to show it was not just a bunch of "outsiders." I came down from Clarksdale and joined the riders at the Greyhound Bus Station. We asked for some orange juice. Then the police came, told us to leave or we'd be arrested, then put us in the paddy wagon and we ended up in Parchman State Penitentiary. They made us take off our clothes—Stokely Carmichael and Jim Forman were with us and they helped to lift our spirits. Black and white men were together and the same for women, so we were only segregated by sex. We refused to post bond because we didn't want the state to get all that money, and while many could have paid their fines and been released, they chose to remain in jail to dramatize the injustice of the original arrests for attempting to use public facilities. By the end of the summer over three-hundred had been arrested and most of them were lodged at Parchman. While many could have paid their fines and been released, they chose to remain in jail to dramatize the injustice of the original arrests for their attempts to use public facilities.

Soon after the first arrests, Medgar and I, along with several others, set about to arrange a meeting with Governor Barnett to ask him to release the people who were being held. Our basic contention was that they were arrested illegally to begin with and that the governor should pardon them. But five years of Citizens' Council diatribes had given the NAACP such a bad name that Barnett refused to meet with us. It seemed that it would have been as politically expedient for him to meet with a group to discuss organizing a Communist Party in Mississippi.

Realizing that we had to meet with him under some auspices other than the NAACP, we turned to the idea of forming a statewide organization modeled after the Coahoma County Council of Federated Organizations. We expanded to include nearly all of the state's Negro leaders, and, since the Citizens' Council was not yet on to us, Barnett was willing to meet with us. We had become so accustomed to the oddities and inconsistencies of the Barnett administration that we ignored his willingness to meet with the same NAACP people as long as we came under a different name.

Our meeting with Barnett accomplished nothing at all. First, he tried to sell us on supporting separate but equal in Mississippi, which we could not do. We talked to him about the arithmetics of welfare and how the state could afford more to help the plight of the poor, but he wouldn't hear it. We asked that he pardon the freedom riders being held at Parchman, since there was no legal basis for their arrest in the first place. We explained that if he were to release them, it would help the image of Mississippi in the eyes of the nation. Although he did not say it, it was plain that such a release would be a sharp blow to his administration. It would amount to an admission of wrongdoing in the beginning. But he simply told us that the freedom riders had been arrested for breach of the peace and other violations not related to civil rights. He made it clear that the riders would remain in prison and serve their terms if they chose not to pay their fines.

We had not expected a favorable meeting with Governor Barnett, so we weren't disappointed with the outcome. But we were happy with the establishment of the statewide COFO. We were convinced that COFO would increase our effectiveness in civil rights work all over the state, and at last the federal government had its eyes on Mississippi.

Chapter 9

The Diabolical Plot

The years immediately prior to the 1954 Supreme Court decision had indeed been the calm before the storm. The storm came in with four known deaths related to civil rights and hundreds of beatings and economic reprisals. Local activity waned for a short while, but courageous people from the outside, including the federal government, convinced us that they were with us in the quest. The years from 1956 to 1961, although relatively calm, marked significant advancement for us. We continued to believe that even better days were to come. We did not know that those five years were another easy calm before a violent storm.

The arrival of Robert Moses in early 1961 marked a high point in the Mississippi civil rights movement. Moses grew up in New York's Harlem, had a master's degree, and had taught math for several years before coming south. A member of the Student Nonviolent Coordinating Committee, Moses was a powerful catalyst in stimulating interest and enthusiasm all over the state. His quiet command of any group with which he was dealing gave him a respect that soon was legendary. Several years later when his renown became too great for him, he quietly changed his name and went away. He was an enigma to many people, and, while blacks revered him, whites were wary.

Moses went first to McComb in Pike County, one of the toughest areas in the state, at the request of C. C. Bryant, a local NAACP leader. Bryant had read an article about Moses in *Jet* Magazine, and had gotten in touch with him and explained how bad conditions were in his part of the state. Within several months after his arrival, Moses had organized schools to teach Negroes how to meet voter registration requirements. One of his first disciples was Herbert Lee, a relatively prosperous Negro farmer in Amite County, who owned his own land and had a large family. Lee was respected in both the black and white communities. Moses influenced him to become active in voter registration, and Lee began to lead the way for local Negroes. Moses and Lee understood the important difference between an outsider and a local person who will advocate and act for change. For several months Lee worked constantly, convincing local Negroes to participate in the voter registration schools.

Then, on September 25, Lee was shot and killed by E. H. Hurst, a member of the Mississippi legislature. Witnesses said that Lee was murdered without provocation as he sat in his truck at a cotton gin in Amite County. Hurst claimed self-defense and was exonerated. Herbert Lee was the first of the SNCC forces to be murdered, and it was an enormous blow to their staff and for the local people.

Medgar and I had a brief meeting with President Kennedy in August 1961, when the NAACP convention was held in Philadelphia. The national board members and several others traveled down to Washington on a "freedom train" for the meeting. Medgar and I, although not members of the board, were included so we could give a firsthand report of the terrible conditions in Mississippi. For many years the Mississippi NAACP delegation had been given preferential treatment at the conventions because of the severity of our problems. President Kennedy listened to us intently, was very cordial, and gave us a tour of the White House.

A few months after our meeting with the president, the mayor of Clarksdale told the chamber of commerce that there would be no Negro participation in the local Christmas parade. The announcement triggered our first major confrontation since 1955. Our community had become accustomed to seeing our band at the end of the parade, followed by our floats. Negro children spent weeks preparing the floats and learning the music, and adults took pride because our band always outstepped and outplayed everyone else.

We were affronted by the mayor's edict. We had joined in the parade for years, and there seemed to be no reason for the decision. Apparently he resented the progress we were making all over the state. His announcement came in late November, just as merchants were making their big push for Christmas sales. The chamber of commerce was supporting the mayor, and we decided the most appropriate and effective response would be economic pressure against all merchants who were chamber members. The NAACP called for a boycott of downtown stores, and the slogan was: "If we can't parade downtown, we won't trade downtown." We printed handbills and sent out newsletters asking that all Negroes join in the boycott. The merchants felt the pressure from the beginning.

I had a telephone call from county attorney Thomas H.(Babe) Pearson one afternoon, asking that I discuss the boycott with him. I was pleased that Babe had let on that the boycott was effective and told him it would be my pleasure to meet with him at any time. We met at his office at seven-thirty the next morning. He told me he knew I was leading the effort, and he wanted to advise me that it was illegal. He read something from a law book but did not explain how it was related to the boycott, and I told him our lawyers had advised us that we were not violating the law, unless we used threats, force, or intimidation to try and make people participate. He finally told me he would put me in jail if I didn't use my influence to call off the boycott. He gave no explanation of the legal process involved in such an arrest and was clearly relying on his ability to put a Negro in jail anytime he wished. I told him he would have to do just that because I had no intention of calling it off.

Babe looked offended and bellowed for Clarksdale police chief Ben Collins, who immediately appeared from a side room. Without looking at me, Babe said to Ben: "Take this nigger to jail." I knew that the arrest was illegal, since no warrant had been issued and I was not committing a crime in their presence, but I knew even better not to argue with an armed policeman. And I didn't mind going to jail, since I believed it would result in an intensification of the boycott.

The incident took on comical proportions when we got to the jail. They were uncertain whether or not to book me, and none of them knew what charge to make. They went off and had a conference and left me standing in the lobby. I was there quite a while but felt confident nothing would happen to me as long as I didn't try to run. Then I looked up and saw them bringing in five men and two women—all leaders in the boycott and other civil rights activity. The group was composed of the best of our leadership in Clarksdale. We spoke to each other, and there was some laughing and joking. I think it was mainly because we were talking so much that they herded us into the general lockup area, away from the business section of the jail. No charges had been made against any of us, and we assumed that they were trying to contrive some.

While we were in lockup, a policeman came in and told us they were in the process of arresting twenty-five more of us, but before any more came in, Coahoma county sheriff L. A. Ross arrived and stopped everything. He actually seemed offended by our detention and genuinely outraged at the entire situation. We were enjoying thinking of the healthy effect the incident would have on the boycott, felt in no immediate danger, and relished what followed.

Sheriff Ross was talking to us through the bars, and Babe Pearson came in. Ross turned on him and demanded that he explain why he had locked us up. Babe didn't answer at first, but, after shuffling his feet, he said they had locked us up on account of the boycott and that the boycott was illegal. We knew Ross didn't like what was going on and felt privileged to have ringside seats. Babe tried to explain how we were violating the law and made several inane remarks. Ross lashed into him: "Babe, don't you know you have locked up some of the best citizens of Clarksdale? The Negro community makes up about half of this town, and these people are the leaders. Here you are putting them in jail and don't even know why. You have no charges against them, and there's no chance of solving our problems as long as people like you act this way."

Ross demanded to know why he hadn't been told that we were being locked up and ordered that any more arrests should stop at once. Two hours later, we were all charged with restraint of trade and released on our own recognizance.

After this, the boycott reached its peak. Merchants were feeling the pinch and had to reckon with the fact that we were one-half of the population and had money to spend. Several days after our release, Sheriff Ross telephoned me and said that Babe Pearson was insisting that we be put under tangible bond for our appearance in court. Ross was very reasonable, said he would prepare the papers and that he would appreciate my coming over to get them. He asked me to get the papers signed and return them to him, and each of us who had been arrested was placed under a two-thousand-dollar property bond, promising our appearance in court.

Initially we were brought to trial in a justice of the peace court and found guilty of restraint of trade. County court upheld the conviction, and we appealed to the circuit court, which ruled that the petition should be amended, or we would be freed. But there was no amendment, and we were neither acquitted nor found guilty, and the bond money was held. We were out of jail but unsure of our legal status.

The boycott lasted, with decreasing effectiveness, for three years. Because of transportation problems in trading elsewhere, it became more and more difficult to boycott downtown merchants. We finally voted to call it off after the passage of the 1964 Civil Rights Act. By that time, we had gotten to the point where more people were disregarding the boycott than supporting it, and the passage of the bill gave us a dramatic way of ending it. We simply announced that there was no need to continue since the federal government had aligned itself with the problems of Negro citizenship in Mississippi.

By 1962, a strong movement was under way across the state. The Citizens' Council had seen its best days, and Governor Barnett was bumbling along making promises that neither helped his position of white supremacy nor harmed our goal of equal rights. The federal government was actively supporting our efforts, and most Mississippi Negroes believed there was a chance of eventually attaining equal rights and no longer questioned whether it was right or wrong to desire them. But now the issues were clearer, and most of us understood that it was up to us individually to do our share in the struggle.

Our greatest progress was limited to areas where there were strong concentrations of outside workers along with local Negroes independent enough to stand up against the white community. In south Mississippi and other rural sections, little progress was being made, and we knew we had to spread the movement to these parts. The solution might lie with the statewide Council of Federated Organizations.

In January 1962, Bob Moses and I met with Medgar Evers in his Jackson office to discuss the best way to revitalize COFO, which had been dormant since our meeting with Governor Barnett the previous spring. We wanted to organize the group so we could join forces and launch a broad attack on the problems we were facing throughout the state. The unified efforts of the four major civil rights groups would mean greater efficiency, and we would have the advantage of working with the head personnel of four main groups to develop new ideas and approaches based on the pool of experience and knowledge. It would enable us to establish small cadres in remote areas and to stimulate and promote civil rights activities on the part of local Negroes.

Our primary aim was to register voters. We met and explained to the boards of the four national organizations (CORE, SNCC, NAACP, and SCLC) our belief that voter registration was the most effective way to work in Mississippi. We made it clear that each group would retain its identity but that a unified effort was necessary.

SNCC was enthusiastic from the beginning, and their workers played the largest role in COFO operations. Their dedication was largely due to Bob Moses, who had already gained a fine reputation as SNCC grew. Although he was not the type of person to take over the official leadership of a group, his ideas usually became SNCC policy in short order. Bob Moses was COFO's program director, and Dave Dennis of CORE was assistant director.

Once we had the backing of the national organizations, we set about organizing across the state. I was elected president of COFO and Carsie Hall, a Jackson attorney, was elected secretary. We had decided that the presidency would be rotated from group to group, but over the months no one else seemed interested and I stayed on. One of the healthiest things about COFO was that petty political disagreements never stood in the way of our major objectives.

Until 1962, most of the harassment and intimidation of my family and me had been relatively minor. Threats consisted mostly of anonymous telephone calls and occasional verbal abuse on the streets. I was convinced that the best policy was to ignore such incidents or simply laugh them off. I have never lost sight of my father's efforts to shield his family from knowledge of injustices and indignities he suffered on our behalf, and I have tried to spare my wife and daughter in the same manner.

But things were tightening up on me in Clarksdale, and the white segregationists seemed aware that I had missed my share of reprisals. I doubt if they realized that they had never even asked me to resign from the NAACP, as they had all of the other leaders. And I am proud that the people in Clarksdale who had known me the longest could testify that from the very beginning I had been an "uppity nigger." I simply cannot account for why reprisals against me had never been more serious than several hours in jail for my participation in the boycott. I suspect that it was because I had been able to remain totally without obligation to any member of the white community. And I had friends within the white community—friends on a man-to-man basis, not a Negro-to-white basis. Also, I believe that my strong stand from the early fifties made most whites realize that they couldn't make me back off. Since our meeting with the county school board in 1955 when I spoke for desegregation rather than equalization of separate facilities, the whites knew that I would make known to anyone exactly where I stood. They also knew that less fortunate people who did not own their own business and were not independent could be intimidated and coerced.

In any case, I had very little trouble until the spring of 1962, and then it was at the hands of police chief Ben Collins and county attorney Babe Pearson, the two who had instigated the slapstick drama of arresting us for the economic boycott and then were not sure what charges to file against us. The two were comically ignorant, and it was a shame that they were in charge of law enforcement in Clarksdale.

Saturday, March 3, 1962, seemed to be another normal day. I usually saw some people at the store on Saturdays that I didn't get to see during the week. On this particular morning, Noelle drove me to the drugstore, dropped me off, and went to do some grocery shopping. She came back about ten o'clock, and I drove her home. On the way back I left the car at the Delta Burial, a funeral establishment where several of the employees made extra money by washing cars in their spare time. I talked with some people for a few minutes and then walked back to the store. Clifton Smith, my other pharmacist, was there, and we spent the rest of the morning talking and waiting on customers. At twelve-thirty Clifton left on his long afternoon break, to return at five and work until seven.

I talked to customers and friends all afternoon, and when Clifton came back, I walked to the Delta Burial to pick up my car. These were still boycott days, and a small group had assembled at the Delta Burial to discuss the pros and cons of continuing the effort to force white merchants into employing Negroes in jobs above the menial level. I jumped into the argument and said that this was not the time to end the boycott, since the whites were just beginning to feel the real pressure—that we should not stop until we had accomplished our goal. Others argued that we had set an impossible goal. The debate lasted only a few minutes, and then I drove home.

I got home about five-thirty. *Dance Party*, which my daughter, Rebecca, always watched, was just going off the TV. It seems this program had become an essential part of our family's life, and supper was never served until it was over. Rebecca had been teaching me to dance the twist, and, just as I came in the door, a twist tune was playing. Rebecca jumped up, and we wiggled around for a few minutes before the program ended.

Noelle was teaching in the county schools at the time, and a student teacher named Julie Turner was spending the weekend with us. Julie's boyfriend, Sidney Wallace, was there also, and I talked to the two of them before having my dinner. I went to bed immediately after, as usual, for a two-or-three hour rest.

Rebecca came rushing into my bedroom about six thirty and frantically told me that there were lights flashing outside in the driveway. The telephone threats had increased greatly since we had begun the boycott, and I think Rebecca and Noelle were more keyed up than usual. Most of the calls came at night, and I tried to get the phone as quickly as possible, but when I didn't, or if I was out of town, my wife and daughter bore the brunt of the threats and obscenities.

Before I was thoroughly awake, someone was knocking at the door, and Noelle answered. She came back and told me that Ben Collins wanted to talk to me. My first thought, innocently, was that a friend was in trouble and had asked to see me. Then I realized that this was unlikely and knew that Ben had personal business with me. I put on my robe and went to the door. Ben was standing there, almost, but not quite, inside the door. "What do you want?"

"Aaron, I've got a warrant for your arrest." He rustled the paper he held in his hand. I asked him the charge, and he mumbled something about misconduct in Mound Bayou, the all-Negro community thirty miles south in another county.

I asked to see the warrant, and Ben showed it to me. It was signed by Sterling Lee Eilert, and I noted the name because it was such an odd one. Ben told me that the trouble had occurred earlier that day in Mound Bayou and that I would have to go with him to jail. I was aware of the irregularity of his taking me to the Clarksdale jail for a crime that allegedly was committed in Bolivar County, but I told him to wait for me to get dressed. My main concern was to keep the talk of the arrest to a minimum in front of my family. I knew that I had not even been in Mound Bayou and had not committed a crime. I was gullible enough to think it was a matter of mistaken identity, and I didn't want Noelle and Rebecca to suffer undue worry.

Ben followed me to the bedroom and watched me take off my pajamas and get dressed. I telephoned John Melchor and told him that I was being arrested and taken to city hall. I told him I didn't know what charges had been made but that someone had taken out a warrant for my arrest. He assured me that he would come to city hall immediately.

Ben was not in a hostile mood during our drive, and we talked about odds and ends. We discussed the boycott, and he admitted that the merchants were feeling it and complaining to city officials. There were several police cars parked in front of city hall when we arrived, but there weren't many people inside the building. I wasn't booked, and, as far as I knew, not charged with any crime. Ben just took me straight to a cell and locked me up. At no time had he mistreated me, and I was amazed at the irregularity of the entire matter, but I was still sleepy, so I lay down on the bunk and went back to sleep.

About an hour later, Ben rattled the bars of the cell and woke me up. Still without hostility, he called my name and told me to get up. He unlocked the cell door and led me into a room where about a dozen white men were seated around a conference table. The only thing I knew for sure was that Ben had said that the crime took place in the all-Negro Mound Bayou, so I was rather expecting a Negro accuser. I still thought it would amount to a case of mistaken identity. The only people I knew at the table were Babe Pearson and Clarksdale's mayor, W. S. Kincade. I was still sleepy and didn't pay too much attention to the others.

As Ben and I entered the room, one of the men snapped, "Get him out of here. We aren't ready for him yet." Ben took me into an adjoining room and I waited for thirty or forty minutes. When Ben finally came back and took me into the conference room, the only men there were Babe Pearson, Mayor Kincade, a few Clarksdale policemen and two men that I didn't know. I later learned that they were police officers from Bolivar County, where Mound Bayou is located.

Babe handed me the microphone of a tape recorder and told me to account for my activities that day. I knew that I could prove that I had not left Clarksdale but was beginning to wonder if it would make any difference. I recorded all of my activities and was as cooperative as possible. For the first time, the atmosphere in the room moved from quiet tension to unspoken hostility. The men listened almost with boredom to my account, and there were no questions when I finished. I didn't know if this was an official interrogation, but it seemed to me that they should have had some questions.

As soon as I finished, Babe switched off the tape recorder, and everybody started getting up. The two Bolivar County officers told me that I had to come with them. Again, I was struck with the irregularity, especially in view of the unquestioned testimony I had just given on my whereabouts of the day. I also knew it wasn't customary for police officers of one county to make an arrest in another county. It was becoming quite clear that nothing about the matter was following any established legal procedures. I turned and asked Ben if I had to go with the Bolivar County policemen, and he nodded. I then asked him why, and for the first time, hostility bubbled through his red face. "You'll find out." I told him I guessed I would soon enough and resigned myself to going with the Bolivar County officers.

I waited a few minutes in the conference room alone, and then the Bolivar policemen returned with an elaborate set of chains. They made me stand up, wrapped a piece of chain around my waist, and chained my hands behind my back. It was a tight arrangement, and I could do nothing more than walk. I then realized that they could beat me around the head or do anything that they pleased, and I wouldn't be able to fight back. I told them that I didn't like being chained like that—that I was perfectly willing to go with them quietly. But there were no smiles and my protest was received as a smart remark. One of the officers glared, and I thought for a moment that he was going to hit me. Then I asked them if they thought I had robbed a bank or something, and they told me to just start walking. I followed them outside and got into the backseat of a police car.

Three men were in the front seat, and I didn't know whether one of them was Sterling Lee Eilert, the man whose name was on the arrest warrant. My question on where we were going went unanswered. I figured we were going to Cleveland, the county seat of Bolivar County, where the main jail was located. But we stopped halfway to Cleveland, in Shelby, and they took me into the jail there. They left me standing in the hall, still handcuffed and chained, while they went into the office and had another conference. Then they came out and went upstairs, leaving me unattended in the hallway. When they came back, one of them said that were taking me on down to the Cleveland jail. In retrospect, the whole thing was a little amusing because all of the officers acted like they were on a television detective story show— but, as hard as they tried, they just didn't fit the roles.

They led me back to the police car and made me get in the backseat. As before, I rode and looked at the back of the same three heads, not certain who they were. They didn't say much during the drive, and, when we passed through Mound Bayou, I commented that I thought I was charged with some sort of misconduct there. No response was made, and there was silence during the ten miles before we arrived in Cleveland. The hostility I had noted in Clarksdale had settled to a silent somberness, and it was beginning to be a little frightening. When you can get a man to talk to you, it doesn't take long to learn where he stands, but when he won't say a word, your imagination can do cartwheels. I didn't know what was about to happen, but I was glad that John Melchor had told me that he would meet me at city hall in Clarksdale. I assumed they had told him that he couldn't see me, and I knew he was doing all he could to help me. On the other hand, I realized that I was being shuffled from place to place and that without the cooperation of the authorities, which seemed unlikely, Melchor would not be able to find out where they had taken me.

When we got to the Cleveland jail, they led me in and again I stood in the hall. I asked an officer if I could make a telephone call, and he told me I could wait and make the call in the morning. I asked if he could tell me the charges, and he said that I would find out soon enough.

They told me to start walking up the stairs, and the somberness turned again to hostility. As I was mounting the steps, I heard one of them behind me say, "Since this son-of-a-bitch likes white women so much, let's put him in the cell with them." I knew that the man was talking death talk and had no idea what was about to happen. When I got to the top of the stairs, I saw a door that said "White Ladies" on it, and it struck me as a peculiar thing to see in a jailhouse. While I was standing shackled to the hilt, wondering what sort of "ladies" came to the Cleveland jail, one of the men stepped in front of me and unlocked the door. Another man behind me told me roughly to get into the room. I thought to myself, "It's going to be hell now," but I didn't hesitate as I walked into the white ladies' cell. I didn't know if there would be a white woman in there or what, but by that time I was thinking that maybe they were fixing it to look like I had tried to rape a white woman. I knew that if they did this, they wouldn't even have to bother with a trial to get rid of me.

But the cell was clean, and there were no white ladies present. It had a private lavatory, and I must say that the accommodations were much better than they had been in Clarksdale. I was so relieved to be alone that I lay down and went back to sleep.

While I slept peacefully in the Bolivar County jail, my friends and family were trying desperately to learn where I was being held. The authorities at the Clarksdale city hall said they had not seen me and had no knowledge of my whereabouts. The Clarksdale police department denied that they had arrested me and said that they didn't know who had taken me in.

This caused considerable alarm, and R. L. Drew telephoned Attorney General Robert Kennedy. He told Kennedy that the Clarksdale police chief had arrested me and taken me in but that now the police department was denying any knowledge. Kennedy got in touch with the Coahoma County sheriff, L. A. Ross, a man I respected, and told him that the U.S. government was holding him responsible for my safety. Sheriff Ross got busy, found out where I was being held, and notified my family.

At noon the next day I was still asleep, and the door began to rattle. The jailer told me to get up, there were some people to see me. I still didn't know if anyone knew where I was, but when the jailer led me down the steps from the white ladies' room, there in the hall were Jess Brown, Medgar Evers, R. L. Drew and fifteen or twenty others. They had come to pay my bond of two thousand dollars.

Jess Brown asked the jailer what I was charged with, and he said he didn't know. But by this time, having listened to officers and other Negro prisoners talking, I had been able to gather the essence of the charges. I was accused of picking up a young white hitchhiker near Mound Bayou and asking him to find me a white woman. When the boy said he couldn't do that, the conversation had allegedly moved to other forms of sex. I was supposed to have told the boy that he would have to play the role of substitute if he couldn't find a white woman for me. I told this to Jess, who asked the jailer about the charges again, but he repeated that he had heard nothing.

Jess then asked who had signed the warrant for my arrest, and the jailer said that a justice of the peace named Rowe had signed the papers. Jess telephoned Mr. Rowe to ask him about the charges, and Rowe said that he didn't know anything about my arrest and had never signed a warrant. Jess was able to learn that I had been booked on a general charge of misconduct, but no one could explain the nature of the misconduct. I was released on the two-thousand-dollar bond, and my friends took me back to Clarksdale.

A justice of the peace hearing was held on March 14, 1962, at Shelby, halfway between Clarksdale and Cleveland. All of the people who had been involved in the arrest were at this hearing, including Sterling Lee Eilert. There was an air of smugness about the place. Sterling Lee Eilert testified that he had been hitchhiking south from Clarksdale and that I had picked him up in my car. He said that we had started talking about sex and that I had asked him to find me a white woman. He said that when he had refused I had said he would have to serve as a substitute. Then, according to the boy's testimony, I reached over and grabbed his penis, at which point Eilert had jumped from the car and fled. He said that he was able to get the last three digits of my license number as I sped away and that he walked to Shelby and reported the incident to the police. There happened to be a Clarksdale policeman at the Shelby station that day, and he heard the description that Eilert gave of me and my car. The Clarksdale officer identified the person as being me, and on this basis a warrant was taken out for my arrest.

A warrant was produced at the justice of the peace hearing, but it was unclear who had signed it and why the Clarksdale police were able to serve it. Just after the hearing, however, the justice of the peace who had issued the original warrant told several people that the warrant used as evidence was not the same one that he had originally issued for use in the arrest. But the contradictions made no difference, and I was fined five hundred dollars and given six months in jail.

A few days later, Mrs. Vera Pigee, one of our most active civil rights workers in Clarksdale, told me that an anonymous phone caller whispered to her that I was fortunate to be alive, that the only reason I was living was that he had failed to follow through on his part of an arrangement. Mrs. Pigee asked him about the arrangement, and he explained that he was supposed to have hanged me in the Clarksdale jail, with an official explanation following that I was so disgraced over the arrest on morals charges that I had committed suicide. We had no way of knowing if this was true or why he had failed to come through with his end of the bargain.

The day after my release from the Cleveland jail, Medgar called me to say that John Doar was in Jackson and that I should come down and discuss the incident with him. Doar and I had an appointment for eleven o'clock that night. I drove down to Jackson and took a couple of hours to tell him the full story.

I had begun to feel that Ben Collins and Babe Pearson were behind the whole thing, and indications to support my feelings were falling into place in my mind. Ben Collins had arrested me with no legal justification for an arrest outside of his jurisdiction. Coahoma County's Sheriff Ross, encouraged no doubt by the pressure from Robert Kennedy, had jumped in immediately, learned my whereabouts, and made it clear he would deal severely with anyone who harmed me. Ross kept telling everyone that he had nothing to do with the arrest, and it seemed to me that, without cooking his own goose, he avowed as much as he could that the responsibility for the whole incident lay elsewhere.

It was also improper that my only interrogation was by Clarksdale officials, rather than in the county where the crime was supposedly committed. Then the fact that I was jailed without being made aware of the charges and held without the privilege of contacting friends or relatives caused me further suspicion. I felt that Babe Pearson and Ben Collins were clearly capable of being parties to almost any plan to get rid of me, but the way they went about this caper enraged me.

At one point, not long after my release from jail, I made a statement in public: "There's not a soul involved in this except that goddam Ben Collins and that chickenshit Babe Pearson." I later was sorry that I had used such vulgar terms to express my disgust, but I was as angry as hell at the time, and, regrettably, the terms were apt descriptions of the two men. I was convinced that they were trying to destroy my effectiveness in a movement in which most of the participants at the time were men. I felt that the arrest was an attempt to prevent people, particularly the young men who were so very important to us, from participating in a movement where they might be accused of homosexuality. I had never had any respect for Collins or Pearson, but I was appalled that they could contrive such a putrid fabrication. It was easy to say that my being found not guilty made no difference, because few people believed there was any truth to the matter anyway. But it made a difference to me. It didn't matter if *nobody* believed the charges. My anger was over the deviousness of the plot—intended not only to render me completely ineffectual, but also to assassinate the character of the entire movement.

On the other hand, it marked an interesting point in the history of intimidation of civil rights workers. No longer were bigoted officials satisfied with trying to brand us as communist. That charge, along with the claim that our goal was to put a Negro in every white woman's bed, had lost its punch. Standard charges were getting old, and even those who screamed them the loudest were beginning to feel foolish. So they picked a new charge—one detested equally by whites and Negroes—homosexuality.

The night after I talked to John Doar in Jackson, John Herbers of United Press International called me and said that I had been seen leaving the federal building well after midnight and asked what was going on. We talked generally, but I was hesitant until I had talked to my lawyer. Jess Brown said that I should tell the world about the case and basically wasn't worried about the possibility of libel suits. He was used to working under the assumption that Negroes didn't stand a chance in a Mississippi court and that efforts should be directed toward getting into a federal court. In some cases, if the lower state courts were too ludicrous in their verdicts, the state supreme court would reverse them rather than have them thrown into the national spotlight.

When Herbers got in touch with me again, I told him everything that had happened and almost everything I suspected. I did say that I believed Collins and Pearson were conspirators behind the incident and that they had gotten Sterling Lee Eilert to make the charges against me. I am not sure if I used the phrase "diabolical plot," or whether Herbers suggested it. I think it was probably the latter, because, before then, the phrase was not familiar to me. Wherever it came from, that phrase was the basis of the libel suits the two of them filed against me.

Soon after I got back to Clarksdale, I realized that I had stirred up a hornet's nest. Babe Pearson phoned me and said, "Look here, nigger, I just got through reading in the paper where you have been talking about me. Listen, goddammit, I'm gonna stop you from talking about me." I bid him good night and hung up. Several days later I read in the paper that Babe had filed a twenty-five-thousand-dollar libel suit against me for the statements that I had made to the press about his participation in the so-called "diabolical plot." Ben Collins never said a word to me. He just quietly filed a libel suit for fifteen thousand dollars, based on the same allegations. It didn't make much difference to me if they sued, since I felt confident that I wouldn't have to pay the money in the long run. Also, I hoped that during the hearings I would have a chance to bring out the things that I had witnessed while in their charge. I did feel a little slighted that they were only asking for forty thousand dollars between them. Over in Alabama two civil rights leaders were being sued for one million dollars.

The two cases were handled separately, but the testimony was the same. The entire proceedings smacked again of the slapstick comedy that often accompanied Mississippi justice. Most of the records in the case had been lost or destroyed, with each official testifying that he couldn't imagine what had happened to a certain record or that some bit of information had slipped his recollection.

They were able to produce an arrest warrant, but it was an entirely new one—a third one—different from the one presented at the justice of the peace court when I first was tried and from the one that had been drawn up originally. There was some discussion among the officials as to where this one had come from, since nobody could identify the writing on the warrant, and nobody would admit to knowing where it came from. It remained as evidence in the hearing.

Babe's lawyer was Charlie Sullivan, who later ran an unsuccessful campaign for governor. He contended that I had libeled county attorney Pearson by making untrue remarks about him with the intent to defame him. Sullivan told the all-white jury in his summation, "Ladies and gentlemen, a few years ago, if Aaron Henry had made those kinds of statements against a white man, the man would have killed him. But today we are asking you for only twenty-five-thousand dollars as a substitute." When Sullivan represented Collins, the next week, he repeated the same comparison, asking only fifteen thousand dollars as a substitute. It was interesting to think about Sullivan's point that a large sum of money could accomplish the same thing as my death. I wondered if Sullivan considered this a mark of progress.

The juries awarded both Pearson and Collins full damages, and my attorneys appealed the cases. The state supreme court sustained the decisions, and we appealed to the U.S. Supreme Court. In 1965, the Supreme Court reversed the decisions and said that my statements were no more than fair comment and criticism of public officials. Right before the reversal, I ran into Ben Collins one day when I was posting bond for someone in jail. Ben stopped me and said, "Say, fellow, when you gonna pay me?" "When am I gonna pay you?" I said. "Ain't you heard what the court said? You are gonna have to pay me."

Ben looked perplexed for a second and then said, "Is that right," and shrugged his shoulders. "Well, I sure ain't got it." I guess he later learned that I was teasing him. About this time, the question of my life insurance became a joke with Ben, and I never really minded. When we would see each other at civil rights demonstrations, he would ask how much life insurance I was carrying, indicating that he hoped it was enough to pay his fifteen thousand if I died or was killed.

The morals charge was appealed from the justice of the peace court to the circuit court that was sitting in Cleveland. Robert Carter, my attorney, took the same approach that Jess Brown had used, but I had little chance of acquittal in a Mississippi court. It was important that everything be handled properly on our side, so that we could appeal to the federal courts. At the Circuit Court trial, there was the same problem of misplaced records and the warrant that nobody had seen before. We were encouraged, however, when the jury stayed out for two hours and thought there might be a chance for acquittal, but they, too, finally returned with a verdict of guilty.

The judge did not give the sentence in open court but called me back into his chamber. He said to me, "Son, I see what they are doing to you, but I have got to sentence you because the jury found you guilty. You understand that, don't you?" I told him that I understood, and then he asked if anyone wished to make a statement before the sentencing. District attorney Hoke Stoke stood up and said he thought I should get the maximum sentence—that I had been found guilty of a very serious crime and that any leniency would encourage this sort of thing.

My lawyer told the judge that the case hadn't been proved—that there were circumstances which warranted leniency. The judge asked me what sentence I had been given in the lower court, and I told him that I had been sentenced to six months and fined five hundred dollars. The judge said, "Well, now you have two months and a two-hundred-dollar fine. How's that?" It was kind of the judge to be so lenient, but difficult for me to appreciate it when I shouldn't have been given anything at all. Carter thought the leniency would strengthen our position when we went to federal court.

The case was appealed to the state supreme court on the grounds that pertinent records were not produced during the trial and, in fact, were missing by the state's admission. We also claimed that the evidence produced was improperly secured. We pointed out that the authorities did not search me or the car until they had placed me in jail, and we showed the irregularities of the arrest and interrogation procedures.

The state supreme court reversed the decision of the lower courts. We were surprised and pleased at the favorable outcome, but our pleasure was short-lived. A week later the court reversed itself and said that the decision of the lower courts should stand. We believed this was the result of political pressure. Attorney General Joe Patterson was up for reelection at the time, and he could not afford to lose to me. His opponent would gain an extraordinarily effective platform piece by Mississippi standards—that Patterson couldn't even convict the president of the NAACP.

We weren't discouraged—we were just back to the starting line again. We appealed the case to the U.S. Supreme Court, the conviction was reversed, and the case was remanded to the state supreme court.*

*While it appears that the 1962 charge was trumped up and a case of harassment, Aaron Henry's bisexuality was later assumed by his friends and associates. The essence of their interview comments was: "We all knew it, it made no difference to us, and it had no impact on his political life nor on his contributions to the freedom movement."

Chapter 10

"Father, Forgive Them"

As 1962 progressed and COFO became increasingly effective in the civil rights struggle across the state, we were running into a big problem—we were overextended. Whites were reacting to our progress, and many of the local Negroes who followed COFO workers and tried to register to vote met with severe reprisals. Naturally, the civil rights groups felt an obligation to stand by the people who had lost their jobs or been dealt with more severely, and fulfilling our obligations became increasingly difficult. In rural areas, particularly on plantations, almost every Negro had his hawkeyed keeper who was aware of his every move, and, if there were reprisals, COFO would send as many workers as possible for support. As this began to happen all over the state, we couldn't respond effectively.

A good example of this was the case of Fannie Lou Hamer, later to become revered for her movement work and role at our challenge to the Democratic Party in Atlantic City in 1964. Mrs. Hamer was severely intimidated by white citizens of Ruleville, in Sunflower County, after she had tried to register to vote. She had spent most of her life as a sharecropper on a large cotton plantation, and she probably never even thought about voting. But she heard some of the COFO people talking about everyone trying to register, and, after she had been to the courthouse, the plantation owner came around and told her to get off the place and not to return until she had removed her name from the registration book. She told him that she was registering for herself, not for him, and that she had no intention of having her name removed. The owner told her to be off the place by nightfall.

Mrs. Hamer left her home and family and went to live with friends in

Ruleville for the time being. Ten days later, sixteen bullets were fired into the house where she was staying. No one was injured. Although she had had only a minor role previously in the movement, an attempted murder had taken place in Senator James Eastland's home county.

This was one of many cases where we felt compelled to help people who were following COFO's programs. Soon after, we began a program of economic aid to people who had been displaced, and Mrs. Hamer was one of the earliest recipients. While experiences like Mrs. Hamer's frequently hampered the movement, at the same time they bolstered our fervor and determination.

The summer of 1962 was earmarked for a massive voter registration campaign, particularly in the Delta counties where the heavy Negro population made our efforts more effective and the results more immediate. The Taconic and Field foundations gave grants to be administered through the Voter Education Project (VEP), a new program sponsored by the Southern Regional Council in Atlanta.

Voter registration activity had been going on all summer in Coahoma and Leflore counties and several others without the aid of VEP. The project's plan was to establish several headquarters from which to launch a massive campaign. The headquarters were to be called citizenship schools, and the basic text would be the Mississippi state constitution. At that time, in order to register, one had to be prepared to interpret to the satisfaction of the circuit clerk any one of the 286 articles of the state constitution. Of course, we often wondered if the legislators themselves understood the voting amendments they had passed, and the circuit clerks were unfamiliar with the articles. So we faced a difficult problem.

The citizenship schools would also teach encouraging others to go down and register. Students would go from door to door asking people to register and passing out handbills and putting up posters in public buildings and churches. People were encouraged to participate in picketing to protest voting discrimination.

In August, we held an organizational meeting for the Voter Education Project in Clarksdale. But while the meeting was in progress, the Clarksdale police department, under Ben Collins, surrounded the building. When the meeting was over and people began leaving, the police stopped each person,

questioned why they had gone to the meeting, and took names and addresses. No one was arrested, but later, as they were leaving town, six of
our influential leaders were apprehended. James Farmer and Dave Dennis
of CORE and Bob Moses, Landy McNair, Willie Peacock, and Sam Block of
SNCC were arrested and charged with loitering, even though several of
them were in moving cars.

The Justice Department was alerted that civil rights workers had been arrested because of their involvement with a legitimate voter registration program. Federal attorneys were promised immediately, but, while they were
on their way, the city officials dropped the charges against everyone except
Dave Dennis, who had to pay a fine.

But this was only the beginning. Ben Collins and Babe Pearson didn't
like the idea of a citizenship school operating in their town, and they set
about closing it with their usual bumbling enthusiasm. Even when there
was a legitimate violation of some city ordinance, it was seldom that Babe
and Ben were able to apply the appropriate charges to the violation.

Miss Willie Griffin was one of the few paid employees of the local branch
of the NAACP, and her job was to encourage Negroes to try and register to
vote. In September 1962, while our boycott was still in effect, Willie was
downtown trying to get people to go to the courthouse with her. One of Ben
Collins's officers walked up to her and arrested her for "restraint of trade," a
charge that had been used against some of the boycott leaders earlier. She
was taken to jail, booked, and placed in a cell without a bed or chair. She
pulled some padding off the wall and made a seat on the floor, sat down, and
waited until an officer came back and told her that they had discovered some
profane literature in her pocketbook. The literature was a printed card
which included a picture of a well-dressed white man and a shabbily dressed
Negro. The caption was: "The NAACP has sent me to segregate you trashy
bastards." Then the officer noticed she had taken the padding off the walls
and promptly added several more charges, including resisting arrest and destroying public property, to the charge of possession of profane literature.

Another example of police harassment in Clarksdale occurred when
COFO workers Charles McLaurin and James Jones were taking people to the
courthouse to register. Charles stopped the car to pick up an elderly lady,

and an officer arrested him for blocking traffic. Jones asked the officer why he was arresting Charles and was promptly arrested himself for interfering with an officer. They were taken to jail and told me later that Charles was slapped around while they were booking him.

A voter registration campaign was launched in Leflore County that same summer, and resistance was strong. COFO sent in a large group of workers, and the Greenwood area became the most active area in the state. Many Negroes went to the citizenship schools and then down to try to register, and white retaliation was proportionate, including standard reprisals of loss of employment, eviction from homes, denial of credit, and general intimidation. Many of the displaced people turned to the federal surplus food program, and it was clear that many would have starved without this assistance. But it was also very clear to Leflore County officials, and in October they halted the food program, with an immediate effect on twenty-two thousand residents who were dependent on the surplus food. They were either going to starve to death or capitulate to the pressures of the white community.

We had to do something. These people were suffering because they had followed our advice—we had a moral responsibility as well as the question of our intentions as organizers. We had always assured local people that we would stick with them through thick and thin in the quest for equality. Our immediate move was to solicit food and clothes from Negroes in the Delta who were not facing starvation, but not many families were well off enough themselves to spare food and clothing. Then we appealed to the national offices of the NAACP, CORE, SCLC, and SNCC for assistance, and they responded as best they could under their own tight budgets. The NAACP was the best equipped financially, but it was paying out huge amounts to maintain its legal forces in the South during a period when quick legal counsel was the most necessary.

We then decided to launch a nationwide appeal under the auspices of COFO to let the nation know that there were people starving in Leflore County, Mississippi, because officials had voted to cut off federal surplus food. We made the appeal through the national press and television, which at the time were giving excellent coverage to Mississippi activities.

The response was speedy and generous. Food and clothing and money began coming from all over the country. An added bonus was that the Leflore County officials' actions had been made into a national scandal, and letters from across the country expressed indignation over their inhumane behavior. As usual—as with most of our civil rights progress—the press had proved to be one of our most valuable allies. Newsmen reported what they saw, and it was the white Mississippian's fault if he was depicted as a shoddy character.

At first, it was impossible to secure a building in Leflore County for our movement headquarters. We needed a solid base and an actual site for food and clothing distribution and finally had to set up the operation fifty-five miles away in Clarksdale in the basement of the Haven United Methodist Church.

One of the earliest shipments of food and clothing came from a group of students who had conducted a drive at Michigan State University. A week before Christmas, 1962, Ivanhoe Donaldson and Ben Taylor, two Negro students, drove down from Michigan to Clarksdale with a truckload of supplies. We got word a few days later saying that there was a shipment of goods available in Louisville but no means of getting it to Mississippi. Donaldson and Taylor departed immediately for Louisville in their truck.

It was quite late when they got back several nights later, and they parked the truck in front of the Fourth Street Drug Store, locked it, and went to sleep. Several policemen appeared and began banging on the windows and doors with nightsticks and flashing their lights into the truck. Donaldson and Taylor were arrested for vagrancy and taken to jail.

When I got to the drugstore the next morning I noticed the truck parked in front and assumed the boys had found a place to spend the night and would be along shortly. But as the morning passed, there was no sign of them, and I was hesitant to begin unloading the truck without them. For all I knew, someone could have gotten a truck like theirs, gotten Michigan license plates, filled it with supplies, and parked it at my door. And then when I started unloading it, the police might swoop down and charge me with burglarizing the truck. Such was the way our minds had to work.

About noon, a friend came into the store and handed me a note from Donaldson saying that they were in jail and for me to please do something. The friend said that Donaldson had smuggled the note out of the jail and that the police were not allowing them to make any phone calls. I went to the jail immediately, and the officer in charge reluctantly told me that the two were being held but gave no details and refused to let me see them. He said the police were still investigating. Back at the store, I telephoned an NAACP lawyer in Jackson who drove up immediately. The police allowed the attorney to see the boys, but that was not the end—the truckload of supplies that Donaldson and Taylor had left in the truck had been confiscated by the Clarksdale police department. During the "investigation" the police had searched the truck and discovered a supply of medicine samples that several doctors in Louisville had sent to me to be distributed by prescription, but without charge. One of the doctors in Clarksdale, L. W. McCaskill, had agreed to help as well, and he was to send me patients in need of free medicine. Most of the samples were vitamins and food supplements and relatively harmless medications. But there were some samples of Butisol, a barbiturate, and Donaldson and Taylor were charged with illegal possession of narcotics and each held under a fifteen-thousand-dollar bond. We couldn't raise the money immediately, and the two boys stayed in jail about ten days. The narcotics charges were dropped, and I suspected that it was due to the national publicity we had mustered. After their release, Donaldson made twelve more trips carrying supplies from Michigan to Mississippi.

So our national appeal was a great success. The impoverished Negroes of Mississippi had come to realize that their struggle was an American one. From then on, assistance of every sort increased, and expressions of genuine concern came from everywhere. Once again, unsavory efforts by white Mississippi officials worked to their own detriment. After federal food supplies were cut off and trucks started rolling in, many rural Mississippi Negroes were eating better and were clothed better than ever before in their lives. They saw they were not utterly dependent on a white-controlled system, and they realized that civil rights groups could do more than just talk about freedom and voting.

This bolstered confidence in the movement, and we recruited hundreds of Negroes who had never seen a civil rights worker until they received food from him. Of course, as they gave out the supplies, workers talked about voter registration and movement activities, and registration increased tremendously. Particularly in Greenwood and Leflore County, Negroes were passing the voting test in such numbers that Greenwood became one of our strongholds in the Delta.

In 1962, I met Clyde Kennard and became aware of one of the most tragic cases in Mississippi freedom movement history. Medgar took me up to Parchman where Kennard was imprisoned. Kennard's mistreatment at the hands of top officials in Mississippi was not as dramatic as some, and not much has been written about it. He wasn't shot down in the streets nor blown into a thousand pieces when he turned on his car ignition switch, but he died after years of illegal detention in Mississippi jails and prisons.

Kennard was a thirty-year-old black veteran who was determined to go to Mississippi Southern College [now the University of Southern Mississippi] in his hometown of Hattiesburg. Clyde had more faith in white people than was good for him. Against Medgar's advice, Kennard insisted that he did not need any aid from the NAACP. He appreciated Medgar's offer to help but felt that he could gain admittance on his own. At some earlier point, Kennard had been personally advised by Governor Coleman that it would be better if he did not try to enroll. Kennard explained that he wanted to go to school in his hometown and wanted to go to a place that would suit his own educational goals. Governor Coleman said that the state would pay for Kennard's education elsewhere, but the young man, in his honesty and innocence, insisted on sticking to his original intention.

In September 1959, when Kennard went to the campus to see about enrolling, he returned to his car and found three policemen waiting to arrest him on the charge of possession of liquor. Kennard explained that he did not drink and could produce witnesses who would testify to this, but the officers told him that most bootleggers did not drink. The charges were not even pressed, so the planting of the liquor and the arrest were meant as a clear threat. But Clyde continued his efforts to enroll, and a year later he was arrested and placed in jail for stealing five sacks of chicken feed. The police had entered his home one night without a warrant. Kennard had not objected, since he was certain there was no chicken feed on the premises. The officers found the feed stacked neatly in the backyard and produced a teenage Negro boy who testified that Clyde had paid him to steal it from a local store. Kennard was charged with burglary.

In cases of burglary, bond is discretionary, and in Kennard's case the judge would not allow it. Consequently, during the year that his case was in the courts, Clyde had to remain in jail. At the first trial when Kennard was convicted, Medgar stood up and blasted the court and the officials and the governor and everyone who he thought had a hand in this "mockery of justice." He was charged with contempt of court, and there was no question of Medgar's contempt that day. Kennard remained in jail and the state supreme court sustained the conviction. The United States Supreme Court left the decision standing, and Kennard started serving seven years in the State Penitentiary at Parchman for a conviction of stealing five sacks of chicken feed.

Clyde started feeling ill soon after he entered the prison, was diagnosed with suffering from an ulcer, and was told that he needed to go frequently to the university hospital for treatment. But the prison officials would not allow him to make the trips, and finally Clyde's "ulcer" was properly diagnosed as cancer.

At the annual meeting of the NAACP in Jackson in 1962, while Clyde was still in prison, Medgar presented awards to outstanding workers in the movement. One of the awards was given to Clyde's mother, and, as he read the citation, Medgar broke down crying. I was standing with him and tried to get him to let me finish, but he insisted on continuing, cleared his throat, coughed, and made his way through it.

Negro comedian Dick Gregory became interested in Clyde's case and appealed to every governor in the country to use his influence to get Governor Barnett to pardon Kennard. Finally, Barnett ordered his release in the spring of 1963, and Clyde went to Chicago, where Gregory paid for his surgery and medical bills at the university hospital. Clyde died a few months later at age thirty-six.

My dealings with James H. Meredith, the first Negro to graduate from the University of Mississippi, were on a more personal basis. I first met him in 1961 when he was a student at Jackson State College and called upon the NAACP to assist him in gaining admission to Ole Miss in 1962. We were convinced that he had a legitimate desire to get an education at the best institution in the state, and I felt that Meredith had the nerve to stick through all of the problems that would come. As chairman of our state board, I supported him in his bid for our assistance, and we voted to place our resources at his disposal. From then on it was in the hands of the attorneys.

About two months after Meredith's stormy admission and enrollment, I telephoned him to see how things were going. He said that he was doing relatively well except that he got terribly lonely and spent most of his weekends either in Memphis or Jackson. He asked me to come visit him, so I alerted the marshals on campus and paid him a call. We talked a few hours, and he told me he was wrapped up in writing an article for *Look* magazine. We discussed the article, but mostly I listened. I visited him several times later that year.

Meredith was an unusual person, but then no ordinary person could have stood up under the immense pressures that he faced that year. He had some peculiar ideas, but that was just the way God made him. He always felt that he was right and seldom thought anyone else was. This characteristic is not an asset under normal circumstances, but I believe it helped him accomplish what he did.

By the end of 1962, few reasonable people thought that the civil rights movement in Mississippi could be stopped. With the exception of Barnett and Citizens' Council supporters, who were still screaming "Never," most white Mississippians simply hoped to impede the movement's momentum. Most Negroes were convinced that they were fighting for the right, and the people of America were behind them morally and financially. Civil rights groups in the state had developed a strong and close-knit organization in COFO with a structure far better than any of the white supremacy groups— with the possible exception of the state government.

The two factors chiefly responsible for the slowly turning tide were the abundance of assistance from the outside and the excellent news coverage provided by the national press. To a lesser degree, the negative, blundering, and reactionary course followed by state officials and white supremacy leaders had helped endear our cause to the American public.

Blood stained the year 1963, but with each murder, bombing, and shooting the feelings of black people intensified, growing into a thunderous demand for immediate and complete equality before every aspect of the law. Strong voter registration campaigns were launched across the state, and, as physical retaliation by whites escalated, their acts were shrouded in a new aura of anonymity. White officials in most areas refused to meet and discuss matters with black leaders they deemed "troublemakers," and the arbitrary rejection eliminated the possibility of reasonable negotiations between the conflicting sides. The almost total denial of black political expression—exacerbated by the refusal of a hearing before local officials—actually paved the way for an interracial slate of candidates in the gubernatorial race in the fall of 1963. Our statewide campaign for high offices was the germination of the Mississippi Freedom Democratic Party, a group which later would attempt to remove the state's elected congressmen from their seats, on the grounds that they had gained office through unconstitutional election procedures.

But the event most damaging to our cause in terms of lost leadership turned out to also be the catalyst that stirred the movement to a fever pitch, with the fervor necessary to break old ties with a white Mississippi. The tragedy was the June 1963 ambush murder of Medgar Evers, the man whom I regard as the greatest of all of those who have dedicated their lives to the struggle for freedom.

Early in 1963, the Voter Education Project had been firmly established in Greenwood, and local participation was increasing satisfactorily. The Negroes of Greenwood and Leflore County were facing the anticipated reprisals and intimidations, but general morale seemed to be holding up. Then on the night of February 28, as they drove out of Greenwood, Bob Moses and two coworkers noticed that they were being followed. Earlier, they had spotted a late-model Buick with no license plates parked in front of their headquarters and had seen several white men in it. Jim Travis, a local worker, was driving along with Moses and Randolph Blackwell, a representative of the Southern Regional Council in Atlanta. As they were talking about the trailing car, it pulled alongside of them, and thirteen .45 caliber bullets came shattering into their car. Two struck Travis in the shoulder and neck. The Buick sped away, and Moses, who was sitting in the middle, guided the car to a stop as Travis slumped down in the seat. Neither Moses nor Blackwell was hit.

The house in Webb, Miss. where the Henry family lived after leaving Flowers Plantation in 1927. Henry's father set up a cobbling shop, and Henry witnessed the great Mississippi River flood in the Delta that year. (Credit: Ann Curry, 1997)

Henry's family joined the Haven United Methodist Church when they moved to Clarksdale in 1927. The church was the site of movement planning and activity during the 1950s and 1960s and remains so today. (Credit: Ann Curry, 1997)

In the late 1950s, a NAACP strategy meeting was held in the Masonic Temple, W. M. Stringer Grand Lodge, in Clarksdale. Standing from left: Carsie Hall, Wade Walton, Henry, unidentified. Seated from left: John C. Melchor, Medgar Evers, Cleo Jackson, H. Y. Hackett. (Credit: Bennie Gooden Collection)

After graduation from pharmacy school, Henry opened the Fourth Street Drug Store in Clarksdale in 1950. It served as a gathering place for movement activists until it burned down in 1993. Posters, photographs, and signs reflected the political and civil rights issues of the times, as illustrated by the photographs of President Lyndon B. Johnson and Vice President Hubert Humphrey. (Credit: Milly Moorhead)

This sign was placed in the window of Henry's home after the firebombing on Easter weekend in 1963. Michigan Congressman Charles Diggs was a house guest at the time. (Credit: Newsweek Collection, Special Collections Department, Robert W. Woodruff Library, Emory University)

During the Freedom Vote campaign in the fall of 1964, Jackson NAACP activist I. S. Sander's car and home were bombed. Henry investigated the attack, along with other violent acts, during his long years as NAACP State Conference president. (Credit: Tougaloo College Archives)

At the Atlantic City Convention in 1964, delegates of the Freedom Democratic Party challenged the seating of the Mississippi Democratic all-white delegation. At a rally on the boardwalk outside of convention headquarters, Henry held a poster of murdered civil rights activist, Mickey Schwerner. Left of Henry, Fannie Lou Hamer, Mrs. Schwerner, and Mr. Schwerner. Behind Hamer, Reverend Ed King. (Credit: © 1976 George Ballis/Take Stock)

After the 1964 Freedom Summer, large posters were displayed in memory of slain civil rights activists, Andrew Goodman, James Chaney, and Mickey Schwerner, at the Fourth Street Drug Store. Henry had recruited Goodman at Queen's College, New York and brought his body home to his family. (Credit: Milly Moorhead)

Henry and others listened to Charles Evers at the 1971 state nominating convention in Jackson. The Democratic Party of Mississippi was integrated after Henry and the other loyalist delegates were seated at the 1968 convention in Chicago. (Credit: Doris A. Derby)

In the 1970s, Henry helped wage the battle to keep funds flowing into Mississippi from the Office of Economic Opportunity. Theodore Berry, from Washington OEO, traveled through Mississippi to assess needs for grants. Left to right: Unidentified, Theodore Berry, and Henry. (Credit: Tougaloo College Archives)

Mississippi children demonstrated for the continuation of OEO funding. (Credit: Tougaloo College Archives)

In the 1970s, Henry and Winson Hudson sang at a Health Care meeting. (Credit: *The Clarion-Ledger*, Jackson, Miss.)

Charles Evers, Myrlie Evers, Hubert Humphrey, and Henry. In the mid-1970s, Henry remained close to Humphrey because of political ties but also their mutual interest in pharmacy. (Credit: Tougaloo College Archives)

Daughter Rebecca, holding their
first grandson, Aaron McClinton,
with Noelle Michael Henry and
Henry, Clarksdale, 1978. (Credit:
Aaron Henry Collection)

President Jimmy Carter helped in the final settlement of
the suit against Jackson television station WLBT. He
also appointed Henry to the Federal Commission on
Aging and to the President's Council. (Credit: Aaron
Henry Collection)

Henry at the grave of Medgar Evers, Arlington Cemetery,
Washington, D.C., 1978. After meeting in 1950, Evers and Henry
became close friends. Evers's assassination in 1963 remained a catalyst for Henry's unwavering struggle for freedom. (Credit: Tougaloo
College Archives)

Henry was elected chairman of the board of WLBT in December of 1979. His office was located in one of the station's buildings, and the walls of one room carried photos of his friends and colleagues dedicated to the struggle. (Credit: Constance Curry)

Fences outside of Henry's office also displayed posters and photographs of musicians, activists, and politicians who were important to him. (Credit: Constance Curry)

In the yard behind his office was Aaron's Garden where he planted vegetables and put up signs for certain WLBT employees. In spite of suggestions from friends and colleagues, Henry, a man of little pretense, refused to remove his garden, posters, or tattered sign identifying WLBT. (Credit: Constance Curry)

"Mr. President, you can mess with me, and you can mess with my children, but don't mess with my Mama."

Henry served as chairman of the board of the National Caucus and Center for the Black Aged. This short quotation was directed toward President Reagan in Henry's 1980 testimony before the U.S. House Select Committee on Aging, as it moved to reduce Social Security, Medicare, and Medicaid benefits for the elderly. (Credit: Chea Prince)

Henry, grandsons Aaron and DeMon McClinton, and daughter Rebecca, Clarksdale, 1993. (Credit: Aaron Henry Collection)

Henry, Sargent Shriver, Booker T. Jones, President and CEO of MINACT, INC., in June of 1993 recognized the 30,000th graduate from the Job Corps Program at the Earle C. Clements Job Corps Center. Shriver served as first director of the Office of Economic Opportunity under President Lyndon Johnson from 1964 to 1968. Under Shriver's leadership, Job Corps was founded in 1964, along with VISTA, Head Start, and other programs to help the disadvantaged. The Earle C. Clements Job Corps Center in Morganfield, Kentucky serves the largest population of Job Corps students in the nation. It was formerly the Breckinridge Job Corps Center. (Credit: Tougaloo College Archives)

The Clarksdale headquarters for Henry's campaigns and work in the Mississippi State Legislature from 1979-96. (Credit: Ann Curry)

Moses called me later that night to tell what had happened. He said that Travis was seriously injured but that doctors at the Greenwood hospital expected him to recover. He was being transferred to the hospital in Jackson. Moses had alerted the local authorities, but the assailants' car, without plates, could only be given a general identification.

The day after the shooting, Wiley Branton, director of the Voter Education Project in Atlanta, made a statement to the press asking that all of the voter registration workers scattered across Mississippi converge on Greenwood and show the people that there would be no backing down. He noted that it was of paramount importance that no degree of violence cause the workers to lose their initiative. His statement concluded, "Leflore County, Mississippi, has selected itself as the testing ground for democracy, and we shall meet the challenge there."

Branton was a descendant of Greenwood Leflore, the French-Indian millionaire slavetrader for whom the county and town are named. The whites in Greenwood probably thought Branton's ultimatum was a foolish stand for a native Mississippi Negro to take, but the county did become a testing ground. Workers from SNCC, CORE, the NAACP, and SCLC flooded the town and county to the saturation point, and soon the area was bubbling with voter registration activities on every corner.

The patterns of action, reaction, and counterreaction continued, and a wave of violence swept Greenwood as the white response to the influx of civil rights workers. The most serious incident was the bombing of the building where the COFO office was located. Everything in the office was destroyed, including all voter registration records. Authorities said that there was no evidence of arson.

Another COFO car was blasted with a shotgun, but without injuries. Shotguns were fired into several homes, but again providence spared us injuries. These forms of intimidation and reprisals against local Negroes continued, then increased, and it was difficult to retain the following that had been established. Less than a month after the Travis shooting, Bob Moses led a voter march to the county courthouse. They were turned away with police dogs, cattle prods, and riot sticks.

While tension in Greenwood was at a high key, we held a mass meeting in Clarksdale to express our support of civil rights efforts in the neighboring town. We attracted a large gathering, including Dick Gregory, who had offered to help in any way possible. The police were watching our activities as always and had practically surrounded the church where we were meeting. It was primarily a rally, and we were singing and telling the stories of various atrocities going on in Greenwood. Suddenly a smoking canister came sailing through an open window and hurtled across to the opposite side of the room. It struck one of the women seated in a pew. Charles Newson, who was sitting nearby, lunged toward the bomb and threw it out of the window nearest him.

By that time, people were scrambling out of the church, especially those who had been sitting in the rear and had not seen Charles toss the bomb back out the window. They had only seen the smoking canister fly through the church, just as we were telling about the bombings and shootings that often accompanied voter registration activities. As people fled and ran into the street, Hudson Bell, the police commissioner, and several officers who were standing around a little grocery store across from the church, were laughing hilariously. The canister never exploded, and the commissioner and his officers made no secret of our reaction to someone's idea of a practical joke.

We got the meeting under way again, and a Negro man stood up and said that he had been offered ten dollars by several Clarksdale policemen to start a fight with four white boys who were in town to help with the voter registration program. He said that he had made some minor attempts to start fights with the boys, but he changed his mind when they explained that they were in town to help the local Negroes. This man had an extensive and relatively legitimate police record for every misdemeanor imaginable, and I was not surprised that the police had approached him with the offer. We doubted his reliability, but his claim reminded me of an incident that had occurred several days earlier. Four or five white boys had brought a load of food and clothing down from the University of Ohio. While they were unloading the goods, Samuel Benjamin, a Negro employee of the city, and several other local colored men tried to start a fight with them. The white youths would not respond to them, and nothing ever developed. I suspected that this was another case of city officials paying or even ordering Negroes that they controlled to stir up trouble with out-of-state white workers.

Before the meeting was over, a policeman entered the church and said that Commissioner Bell wanted to talk to Dick Gregory. Since Gregory was my houseguest, I went outside with him. As we approached, there was some snickering among several policemen near Bell. It died away when we got there. Bell asked Dick where he was staying in Clarksdale, and Dick refused to tell him, indicating that it was none of Bell's business. Bell told Gregory that he had better tell him if he wanted any police protection while he was in Clarksdale. Dick laughed in his face and said that he didn't want protection from anybody who would pay ten dollars to get white boys beaten up so that they could be jailed for fighting. It was clear that Bell resented this remark, but it was also obvious that Gregory was willing to stand there all night and match wits with him. Finally, looking a little befuddled, the commissioner pointed to an automobile across the street and said, "You think the FBI is going to protect you, but you're wrong. They are all sitting over there in that car drinking, and they won't be able to protect you." We turned and went back into the church.

Violence against local Negroes and civil rights workers became more frequent and severe as the spring progressed, and we became aware of the immediate need for federal protection. The Justice Department was continuing its work of handling court suits and legal matters, but this was not deterring the acts of wanton brutality against Negroes. We understood the position of the government and the difficulty federal authorities had in finding a legitimate entry into problems of intimidation, but we made constant appeals with the hope that they could find some way to help us.

In April we decided to get one of our "adopted" congressmen to come to Clarksdale, to see the situation firsthand and report back to President Kennedy. We had learned long before not to expect any cooperation from our own representative, who refused to even meet with us. Congressman Charles Diggs from Michigan, one of our oldest allies, agreed to come for an informal investigation. Diggs spoke at a mass meeting at the Jerusalem Baptist Church on April 11 and returned home with me to spend the night. Curtis Wilkie, a friend and reporter for the *Clarksdale Press Register*, joined us at my house to interview Diggs. The next day the paper carried a fairly prominent story about Diggs's being in town, explaining the nature of his visit and mentioning that he was staying in my home.

We spent that day touring Coahoma and neighboring counties so that Diggs could see what we were up against. We drove to Mound Bayou and over to Greenwood and inspected all of the civil rights centers. Several times, we were able to show him evidence of recent violence, never thinking that Diggs was going to get his own full-fledged, firsthand initiation later that night.

We were all sound asleep in my house when a sharp blast broke the early morning silence. I could hear glass shattering and a truck roaring away. I ran to the living room and found the window curtains blazing and the room quickly filling with smoke. My daughter Rebecca's room was nearest the point of explosion, and I rushed to get her out of the house. She was difficult to wake up, and, about the time I was rushing her past the flames toward the front door, another bomb exploded in the living room. I got her out of the house and went back to see about Noelle and Diggs. The entire front part of the house was illuminated with flames, and the smoke was getting worse. I met Noelle and Diggs in the hall, told Noelle to get out and take care of Rebecca and told Diggs to call the fire department. I had become frantic during the confusion, but Diggs and I started a water brigade from the kitchen to the living room, fearing every moment that another bomb would explode.

While we were fighting the fire, Noelle came to the door and yelled that there was another bomb sizzling underneath the car, and I told her that she would have to take care of that one. The fire department arrived twenty-five minutes after we had called them, and Diggs and I had already extinguished the fire. Noelle had backed the car away from the other bomb. The police came soon after the firemen, but they were apprehensive about beginning an investigation. We told them that two firebombs had exploded and there was a third one that might still be live. They stood around hesitating to get near the house. When things had settled down, I called Medgar in Jackson and told him what had happened. He reported it to the wire services. We didn't sleep anymore that night because of constant telephone calls.

The next day, the incident was in every major newspaper in the country, since Congressman Diggs was in the house when it was bombed. At least our problems were refreshed in the minds of people everywhere.

Early in the morning after the bombings, Chief Collins came to the house after I had gone to work. He told Noelle that there was supposed to be a third bomb and it could be dangerous if they didn't find it. He looked all around the house, and then Noelle told him about the bomb that had been under the car. Collins found something in the drive, and took it with him. It turned out to be the third bomb that the police couldn't find but knew was supposed to be there. There was no evidence for me to say that the Clarksdale police were in on the bombing, but it was clear that some of them knew that three bombs were supposed to have been thrown at the house. That day was Good Friday, and we put a sign in the shattered front window which said: "FATHER, FORGIVE THEM."

Later that day, Charles Diggs issued a statement that he would ask the House Judiciary Committee to hold a series of hearings in the Clarksdale area. He had seen evidence of discrimination in voter registration and general abuse against Negroes who tried to exercise their constitutional rights. He stated that the committee should have a firsthand look at the situation, which would provide a psychological impact that would be lost in a hearing room in Washington.

The Clarksdale police acted with admirable swiftness, and two men were arrested and charged with arson by noon of the next day. Ted Carr, a twenty-four-year-old college student, and Luther Audrey Cauthen, twenty-six, were arrested and each held on a ten-thousand-dollar bond. I had been acquainted with Cauthen for years, and while I knew he didn't approve of my progressive ideas, I was shocked that he would try to take my life.

According to the *Press Register*, both men admitted their guilt, and were reported as saying that they were only having fun and didn't know whose house they were bombing and didn't mean any harm. They insisted that they didn't even know Congressman Diggs was in town and that they didn't know if Negroes or whites lived in the house that they bombed. During their trials, a white service station attendant testified that he had seen them making the bombs and heard them say what they were going to do with them. The attendant also testified that when the men returned after the bombing, he heard one of them say, "Aaron Henry is a lucky son-of-a-bitch if he didn't get burned up."

The trials were held separately, and, when the first man was found not guilty by the all-white jury, charges were dropped against the other. This was not surprising, and it was heartening that they had been apprehended and charged and that at least one of them had been brought to trial. Most of the white community showed genuine indignation over the incident, mainly, I believe, because Congressman Diggs had been in the house at the time. But I am sure that there were whites who were against this sort of thing in general. The *Press Register* ran a front page editorial deploring the act.

Several days after the trial, my old acquaintance Cauthen stopped by the drugstore to see me. He said that he wanted to apologize for having a part in the bombing and that he would like to explain what really happened. I was cordial and said I would be glad to listen. He told me that he and Carr were just riding around having fun—all the same things that were in the newspaper—but here he had the audacity to tell me personally and with a straight face. But he added that he was only driving the truck and did not know Carr was going to throw the bombs. He was perfectly serious in saying that he hoped I wouldn't hold anything against him. I told him to forget the whole thing.

Our voter registration drive was still picking up steam, and increased intimidation seemed to have little detrimental effect. Then in early May the front of my drugstore was nearly blasted off by an explosion. It was a stormy Saturday evening, and I was having dinner in the store with a couple of clerks and several customers. We were sitting in the rear part of the customer area where the tables are located, and suddenly we saw a blinding blue flash and felt a concussion that I thought would bring the store down on our heads. A moment later we saw a gaping hole in the upper front part of the building just above the front door.

I phoned Sheriff Ross immediately, since he was usually more honest and competent than the police chief, Collins. When he arrived, the press was with him. They said that they had heard the blast on the other side of town. Sheriff Ross began his investigation, first saying that a hole had been cut in the roof of the store and that he was assuming a timebomb had been planted there. Later that night, he changed his mind and said he thought the explosion was a bolt of lightning. Several of us wanted to go with the police onto the roof to see what had happened, but they said it was too dangerous to allow anyone up there until the investigation was completed. The police kept saying that lightning must have caused the blast, because there was no bomb residue found around the place of the explosion. I don't know about the residue, but, assuming the explosion was as clean as the police claimed, it is likely that a bomb could have been made with nitroglycerine, a chemical that leaves no residue. Someone could have come onto the roof unnoticed from the rear, and planted the bomb. Or, since a timer was not found, the bomb could have been tossed from the rear of the roof to the front.

The FBI filed a preliminary report on the findings with the Clarksdale police, as was customary, but I never saw it. I understand that the report did say the explosion was the result of a bolt of lightning, and, to my knowledge, a final FBI report was never made.

We all knew that there was no way to predict what would happen from day to day. A short time after the store was bombed, I was in bed one night when I heard gunshots on the street in front of the house. Noelle and I then heard something that sounded like pellets striking the side of the house. I went out and investigated but couldn't see what had happened. The next morning, I saw that the front window had been shot out and that several spent slugs were lodged in the asbestos siding on the house. Fitz Farris, Sheriff Ross's chief deputy, conducted an investigation, but no arrests were made. It was another case of random violence, and there was little hope of apprehending the responsible people.

Another outrageous example of official manipulation of justice occurred shortly after this in Holmes County. Hartman Turnbow, leader of the voter registration campaign in the county, was asleep with his family one night when firebombs began exploding in the front of the house, and bullets ripped through several of the windows. No one was injured, and the police gave little indication that they were interested in finding the criminals. The day after the bombing, Bob Moses arrived to make an investigation. Bob himself was arrested and charged with impeding the official investigation of the fire. When the police completed their investigation, they arrested five civil rights leaders, including Turnbow and Moses, and jailed them on charges of setting fire to the house to create racial agitation.

With the heavy saturation of all brands of civil rights workers in the Delta counties, Medgar Evers had been spending most of his time in Jackson working towards the desegregation of public facilities. At that time, there was no federal law requiring that private businesses serve customers and hire employees on a nondiscriminatory basis, but the NAACP was trying to bring strong economic pressure against the uncooperative merchants and businessmen. And we were threatening citywide marches and demonstrations if the city officials would not meet to discuss the issue.

The NAACP state board met in Jackson on May 23 and passed a resolution demanding that Mayor Allen Thompson meet with a representative group. We asked that all forms of racial segregation be abolished in Jackson. In the statement we claimed that the Negro population of the city was great enough to support a boycott that would affect the entire city.

Mayor Thompson rejected our request. His announcement came at a conference he had called with seventy-five white business leaders. He said, "No biracial committee will be appointed in Jackson. . . . The only thing that can come from such an arrangement is compliance with the demands of racial agitators from the outside." He said that the "agitators" were the ones who would be on any such committee and that he would have nothing to do with them. Thompson claimed that he was always willing to talk to local Negroes—just as he would talk to any citizen—but that he would not talk to any Negro who was a "member of the NAACP or CORE, or any other racial agitator."

He also claimed that the majority of Jackson Negroes favored the city's position on segregation and that they were afraid to speak up because of their fear of the agitators. But later that month, as a result, I suspect, of the economic boycott that was getting under way, Mayor Thompson agreed to meet with a committee of fourteen who would be named by Negro leaders. However, ten of the fourteen we named for the committee did not suit the mayor, and he substituted names of Negroes who did.

On June 12, I went to Jackson to confer with Medgar on testimony that we were going to present to the House Judiciary Committee in Washington the next day. We had been asked to appear before the committee in support of civil rights legislation, and we wanted to make sure our testimonies were not repetitive. I was to fly to Houston, Texas, that night to speak to the Texas Pharmaceutical Association the next morning. Medgar and I planned to meet in Washington that afternoon.

Medgar and I went to a public meeting the night of June 12 at the Pearl Street AME Church and stayed at the church to discuss our testimony until about eleven-thirty. I left my car at the church, and Medgar drove me to the airport. We discussed the demonstrations that were going on in Jackson at the time, and Medgar said that he was being followed constantly by unidentified cars. The telephone harassment was worse than ever before, and his house had been bombed two weeks earlier, although there was no serious damage. He told me that he had alerted the FBI to all of this, but that he had not taken any new security precautions. He was still going about his business unescorted, and his home was unprotected at night. He was worried about his wife and three children.

Our ride to the airport was like a hundred others, and our conversation was about the immediate, with little reference to the past or future. Neither of us had any premonition that this would be our last ride together. Medgar left me at the airport. When he arrived at his house thirty minutes later, he was shot and killed in his driveway by a sniper with a high-powered rifle.

When I got to Houston that night, I went straight to my hotel and to bed. I was scheduled to make the speech at ten o'clock the next morning, and, while getting dressed, I turned on the television set to the *Today Show*. I had read in the paper that Lena Horne, who had been spending some time in Mississippi, was going to discuss what she had seen. When the picture came into focus, I saw Miss Horne sitting there, and beside her was Roy Wilkins, national executive director of the NAACP. My first reaction was that the program would be particularly interesting with Wilkins appearing as well, and then I saw a small inset photograph of Medgar at the top of the screen.

I wondered for a moment why they had the inset, and then the sound came on and the announcer said, "Due to the tragic death last night of Medgar Evers, we have asked Roy Wilkins to appear on *Today* with Lena

Horne." I would have that feeling only once again—six months later when John Kennedy was assassinated. [Aaron Henry had to amend this five years later when Martin Luther King, Jr., and Robert Kennedy were both assassinated.] My feeling was one of emptiness and helpless anguish, of absolute and total loss. Common fear always draws people closer, and Medgar and I had become so used to the feeling that "today might be my last" that we hardly noticed it anymore. But at eight o'clock that morning in Houston I was suddenly aware that my loss, of the finest and closest friend I had ever known, was a much greater loss to our country and to the principles which he had served so courageously.

I finished dressing, went to the convention hall, and waded through my speech. The audience was aware of what had happened and was tolerant of my poor presentation. Several people expressed their dismay over the murder, and most seemed to understand that condolences were best left unsaid for the moment.

It never occurred to me to change the immediate plans that Medgar and I had made to present testimony in Washington that day. I knew that he would have been upset if such important business was interrupted for any reason. I flew to Washington that afternoon. I appeared before the House Judiciary Committee at ten o'clock the next morning and reported on Mississippi as I saw it, including what I could remember of Medgar's testimony. The committee had asked us to paint an accurate picture—one that usually sounded far-fetched to people who had not been there. That day, however, those present seemed to accept everything I said, and, several years later, Congressmen Brademas and Lindsay told me that they still remembered my testimony.

When I got back to Clarksdale, I realized that I had left my car in Jackson. I usually left my car at airports and picked it up on my return, but this trip had been so hectic that I had forgotten where I left it. I had a friend drive me to Jackson, and, before I left, I promised Noelle that from then on I would have someone take me and pick me up at airports.

As soon as I returned to Jackson, I went to see Myrlie, Medgar's wife, and she told me exactly what had happened. Her doctor had her under sedation, but she insisted she wanted to relate the entire story to me. She had been in bed and heard the car drive up. Over the years, she had learned to identify by sound precisely whose car came into the driveway at night. When she was unable to determine whose car it was, she expected trouble, and she relaxed when she heard the little engine quirk that identified the car as Medgar's.

Then she heard the car door slam shut and immediately the thundering roar of a high-powered gun. Myrlie leaped from her bed and ran to the kitchen door. Medgar was facedown on the concrete driveway and crawling toward the house. She ran into the yard, followed by the children. He was almost to the steps when she got to him, and there he went limp. A wide, dark smear of blood traced where he had pulled his body over the pavement, and the blood was flowing profusely from his back and seeping from under his body. As Myrlie bent over him, the children were crying and screaming, "Get up, Daddy, get up." But he couldn't get up and was pronounced dead on arrival at University Hospital.

I learned later that several of the neighbors had heard the shot and had called an ambulance. One neighbor, Houston Wells, ran into his yard and hid behind a clump of bushes for a moment, fired a pistol into the air to scare off the sniper, and then ran to Medgar's body. The police later found a rifle with a telescopic sight nearby and decided it was the murder weapon. A week or so later Byron De La Beckwith, a fertilizer salesman from Greenwood, was arrested and charged with the murder. Despite vigorous and unrelenting prosecution by the state's attorney, William L. Waller, the following February, a mistrial was declared in the case, and Beckwith went free.

Response from Jackson officialdom after the murder was prompt. Everyone said they detested the violent act, but there was little evidence of real sympathy. Governor Ross Barnett's statement said: "Apparently it was a dastardly act, and, as governor of the state of Mississippi, I shall cooperate in every way to apprehend the guilty party. Too many such incidents are happening through the country, including the race riot last night in Cambridge, Maryland." Barnett later appeared at Beckwith's trial and shook hands with him.

The day after Medgar's death, over two hundred people were arrested in a series of marches. The day of the funeral, police refused to grant permission for us to march from the service to the funeral home, but we planned to march anyway. Jackson authorities seemed apprehensive in the face of such an enormous gathering of Negroes on the heels of the brutal death of a person they respected more than any man, black or white, in the state of Mississippi.

The service was at the Masonic Temple, and Dr. T. R. M. Howard gave the eulogy. He had returned to Mississippi for the funeral and told how he had recruited Medgar into the civil rights movement through the Regional Council of Negro Leadership. Roy Wilkins, national director of the NAACP, spoke, and the service ended with the song "This May Be the Last Time." It is a sad hymn, and we began to cry. The words rang so true for us all.

The crowd was seething with sorrow as we left the temple, and the police saw that we intended to march with or without permission. A city official quickly granted the permit but said that the crowd was to disperse when it reached the funeral home or there would be trouble. We began the march down Lynch Street, three-thousand strong, singing and crying, to the funeral home on Farish Street. Just as it had been in Belzoni on the day of George Lee's funeral, there was not a white face in sight as we walked.

This changed at the funeral home when a brigade of police with nightsticks met us. They had been told to break up the crowd immediately, and they began to shout rudely, telling us to go home. You could feel the anger rising among the marchers. "To hell with that." We turned left on Farish Street and met a line of highway patrolmen blocking the street. We marched into them. They started beating people and trying to push them back, and the crowd retaliated by throwing rocks and bricks and bottles.

A full-scale battle was developing, and, as it worsened, John Doar from the Justice Department moved into the middle of the street and raised his hands above his head. He stood there for a moment and then shouted, "This is John Doar. Everybody here ought to know me. I am your friend. This is not the way to settle an argument. I want *you* people over here, and I want *you* people to assemble over there." It was amazing. Like the Lord had spoken. Everybody did what he said. The fighting stopped, and both sides drifted away.

It was ironic that Medgar's funeral almost exploded into violence. I believe a main reason that he was able to lead the movement with unflinching courage and dedication to justice was his early exposure to violence and death. He once told me about an experience when he was only fourteen years old at his home in Decatur, Mississippi. A close friend of his father had been lynched for allegedly insulting a white woman, and young Medgar and his brother, Charles, had seen them bring in the body. He had heard his father say that his friend had done nothing—not even spoken to the woman. Yet he was dead and nothing could be done. Medgar told me that for him it was the turning point—from then on he felt a deep bitterness toward a system that allowed this. During his ten years in the civil rights movement he saw case after case of raw brutality against Negroes, and he abhorred the violence. His funeral should not have been an occasion for further violence.

Chapter 11

Clarksdale Garbage

The July following Medgar's death, the Clarksdale NAACP chapter tried to meet with Mayor Kincade to discuss our grievances. In keeping with the pattern across the state, he ignored us after we wrote and requested a conference. Then we sent him a telegram, and he ignored that, too.

As a last resort, a large group of us went to city hall and sat in front of his office. He continued to ignore us for a while but finally walked out and asked what we wanted. We had our business stated in a petition, but I told him most of our demands before giving it to him. We asked for the rights that white citizens of the city enjoyed. We reminded him that the median annual income for Negroes in the county was less than a thousand dollars. We talked about the deplorable public school system and said that it would probably remain that way as long as segregation prevailed. And we advised him that, of sixty-nine thousand Negroes who had tried to register during the past four years, only four thousand had succeeded. Mayor Kincade accepted our petition and said that he would be in touch.

At the end of the week, there was no answer, so a committee went back to his office. Mayor Kincade told the committee that there was nothing in the petition that he was able to grant and added that conditions were not as bad as we claimed. He refused to set up a biracial committee or to even discuss any of our problems. Our only resort was a mass demonstration protesting unjust conditions. A few days later we converged on city hall from four directions, carrying picket signs. Since we were coming from all directions, the police had a tough time positioning themselves. They ran to one side to stop a group and then rushed over to stop another group, but we all kept coming. I was one of the first to be arrested, and, as I sat in the police car, I could hear the police radio dispatcher. She was located in city hall, and she was yelling over the radio in a high twangy voice, "Look at the niggers coming. There are niggers coming from everywhere."

Eighty-six of us were arrested the first day, and from then on there were sympathy demonstrations outside the jail. Most of the leaders were locked up, but local supporters held their own with songs and prayers. Soon they were also arrested, and finally two hundred men, women, and children were incarcerated. There were so many of us that we filled the city and county jails. We made no attempt to post bond and were prepared to stay in jail and force authorities to sentence us to road work details to dramatize the situation.

Most of the arrests were made on Friday, with trials the following Tuesday. Sixty men and forty women were sentenced to thirty days in jail and fined one hundred dollars for parading without a permit. None of us appealed, and the city's only recourse was to send us to the road gangs. We were assigned to work crews to clear rubbish, dump garbage, and dig ditches for a new sewer line. The women were made to clean city buildings or cut grass. We worked daily from eight to five and then returned to jail. This continued for eleven days, and the most upsetting thing for me was how my mother took it. One morning she looked out the door of the house where she had raised me, and there I was picking up garbage. She had always encouraged my civil rights activities, but that was almost too much for her.

After serving eight days of my sentence, I bonded myself out and went to New York to raise funds to free the rest of the demonstrators. The NAACP officials, with some assistance from SCLC and CORE, readily put up the money—about forty-thousand dollars.

While the jail-in might have pricked a few consciences in the white community, it did not have a healthy effect on the local civil rights movement. Most people were afraid of jails and police. When a white man is beating you, it is possible to run, but that is not possible when you are locked up in a cell. In spite of this, the movement's enthusiasm and voter registration work soon picked up. And the strategy had worked. Publicity had been our purpose, and the paper ran frontpage pictures of everything, including the work details.

Right before the jail-in, when I had gone to city hall for the parade permit, Chief Ben Collins had refused. I told him we would march anyway, and he said, "Tell you what, Aaron, before you march, how about letting me take out some life insurance on you?" "Man, you're crazy," I told him.

"You know you owe me fifteen thousand dollars, don't you? Somebody's gonna kill your ass," he said, "so why don't you let me be in a position to get my money when they knock you off?"

"Man," I told him, "ain't nobody gonna bother me unless it's you."

Sure enough, a day or two before the march, Ben sent a life insurance salesman over to try and talk me into letting Collins take out a policy on my life. I told him he was crazy, so he went to Jess Brown, my lawyer, and tried to talk him into it. When I think about Ben's proposition, I recall an affidavit filed with the Justice Department. A Clarksdale Negro named Charlie Black stated that Ben Collins offered him ten dollars to kill me.

About this time, the local NAACP was becoming increasingly concerned for my safety and the welfare of Rebecca and Noelle. While I was in jail after the demonstration, they hired an armed guard service to protect my home, but this was too expensive to keep up for long. I still was operating under the principle that either something happened or it didn't, and elaborate precautions were not worth the problems they created. But I agreed it would be sensible to get some protection, and I spoke to Sheriff Ross about it. I asked him if it was within his scope of duty to have some of his men keep an eye on my house at night. He said that local law enforcement agencies weren't prepared to take this on and suggested that perhaps the federal government would now do something. We both had known for years that this was something that they could not legally do. Ross did advise me that if he were in my position he would take steps to get protection for myself and my family.

While I was still in jail, the local NAACP branch set up a system of ten or twelve rotating guards, each of whom took one night in turn. Several nights after this started, Ben Collins came along and saw two of the men changing the guard. They were standing in the side yard by the garage talking, and, when they saw Ben, one of them pitched his pistol into his own car, which was parked in my driveway. Ben came into the yard, questioned the men, reached into the car, and took the pistol. It was reported in the

Press Register that the police had seized a pistol from an armed guard at my home, alerting white hoodlums that my home was being guarded. Even if a newcomer came to town some night and asked, "Where does that son-of-a-bitch Aaron Henry live?" he would be told, but also warned that there was an armed guard at the house.

But the novelty of the guard system wore off, and soon only Reverend Willie Goodlow came to the house every night. He came after dark and sat in the living room all night with a loaded shotgun. He was a great morale booster for Noelle and Rebecca. Noelle and I no longer agreed about "reasonable precautions." I knew that no guard would have been effective if a brigade of ruffians descended upon the house intent upon destroying it and my family, but an awake and alert guard was still important. In the past when the house was bombed, by the time I could get dressed and run outside, the culprits were gone.

Another Clarksdale Negro youth was shot to death by police in September 1963. The killing climaxed an argument over whether Ernest Jells had tried to steal a banana. Jells had gone in the Fair Deal Grocery Store, owned and operated by Mr. Abraham. One of Abraham's sons accused Jells of trying to steal a banana, and Jells fled from the store. Abraham ran after him and fired a pistol at the boy as he was running down the street. Several policemen were parked nearby, saw a white man chasing a Negro and shooting at him and took up the chase with no knowledge of the circumstances. They chased him into an alley, and the boy started clambering over garbage cans trying to get onto the roof of a building and get away. Jells was hanging onto the edge of the building trying to pull himself up, and the policeman fired bullets into him until his perforated body fell to the ground. No report was ever made on the number of slugs in this boy.

The reaction in the Negro community was bitter. The police said that Jells had thrown a gun onto the roof of the building and was climbing up there in order to get a better vantage point for firing at them. They even produced a rifle that Jells had supposedly thrown onto the roof, but none of the boy's friends or family knew anything about his having a gun of any kind. No charges were ever brought against the police.

Chapter 12

The Freedom Election

The most ambitious and perhaps most worthwhile COFO effort of 1963 was the mock participation of an interracial slate of candidates in the state gubernatorial election in November. The two leading regular candidates were trying their best to outdo each other in racist statements. It also came at a time when Senators James O. Eastland and John Stennis were in Washington telling Congress that the only reason Mississippi Negroes did not vote was that we were too slothful and unconcerned to register.

Allard K. Lowenstein came down in July 1963 to offer his help to COFO and our voter registration efforts. My friendship with Al went all the way back to 1949 when I was a delegate from Xavier to the United States National Student Association Congress. He later became president of that group and was respected by students on many campuses throughout the country. The plan that emerged was that we would attempt to show the nation that we would indeed vote if allowed to do so. It would be the first big test of our concentrated program of voter education and registration. We hoped to show how meaningless Mississippi lily-white campaigns were and to show that each major candidate promised to do more than the next to deny us political rights.

James P. Coleman had been eliminated in the Democratic primary for governor, mainly because of his support for John Kennedy, so the November race was between Democrat Paul B. Johnson, Jr., and Republican Rubel Phillips. The crucial issues were clouded by a thick haze of racial prejudice. Johnson's main campaign issue was that he "stood in the doorway at Ole Miss" when James Meredith was trying to enroll. His supporters said proudly, "Paul stood tall at Ole Miss," adding, with reference to his stand against legalized whiskey, "Paul will stand tall against alcohol." Johnson also said that a strong and united Democratic party would make it easier to keep a sharp eye on Negro activities.

Rubel Phillips maintained that Johnson had been willing to "sit down and play cowboys and niggers with the university." He said that with a Republican governor and two strong parties, the state could keep two sharp eyes on the Negroes. He was saying that, with his election and the election of Republican Barry Goldwater to the presidency in 1964, the Negro problem would be solved. So these were our top contenders for governor. They both referred to Mississippi's being the greatest state in the union, but neither was openly concerned about the economic issues—our gravest problem. Thirty-two percent of the people earned less than three-thousand dollars a year, twenty-six percent earned less than two-thousand dollars annually, and, in the Delta, fifty-one percent of the people—black and white—earned less than two-thousand dollars a year. This was real poverty. The candidates made superficial allusions to bringing more industry to the state, but the campaign standard was seeing who could yell "Nigger" the loudest.

We could do nothing "official" to combat these forces, so COFO decided to have an "unofficial" election of our own. I would be the candidate for governor, and Edwin King, a white Methodist minister from black Tougaloo College in Jackson, would run for lieutenant governor. Ed King was a Mississippian from Vicksburg. Bob Moses would manage the campaign, and we would stress the important issues that Phillips and Johnson were ignoring, as well as show the potential strength of our vote.

Among our many problems, the lack of a good political speechwriter was the greatest. We also needed national publicity and coverage that would reflect the significance of our effort. We needed people who knew about political organizing—we had had little experience in this field. Once again, we turned to the outside for help. Joe Lieberman, editor of the *Yale Daily News,* was in Mississippi at the time doing a series of reports on the activities and programs of SNCC. He became interested in our plans and assured us that he would spread the word at Yale about the type of help we needed. He thought our needs would have strong appeal to students majoring in journalism and political science.

Within a few weeks the students came—from Yale, Harvard, Dartmouth, and Fordham—forty strong, and their interest in the campaign was as keen as our own. They knew how to write campaign literature and how to organize meetings and rallies. They were able to get the news media to almost every mass meeting that we held in the state. Our main instrument for spreading the word was a little newspaper, "The Free Press," and Bill Minor and R. L. T. Smith helped us get it printed.

I toured the state making speeches and waving my hands and yelling, and I guess some of the Negroes thought they had their very own Bilbo or Barnett. I spoke in Holly Springs, Oxford, Greenville, Clarksdale, Jackson, Gulfport, and Hattiesburg. We had good campaign tours in Clarksdale and Greenville, because whites left us alone and did not try to break up the rally. In Greenville, they even let us use the Washington County Courthouse and—most amazing—the police even arrested several whites for harassing participants.

Gulfport, Vicksburg, and Hattiesburg were another story. In Hattiesburg, the police barged into the civil rights headquarters the day of the rally and closed it down as a fire hazard. We had to go to a church. When a white girl tried to join the rally, the police arrested her and put her in a patrol car. She was screaming and kicking and biting, but they wouldn't let her come in. And the rally had barely started when we heard seven or eight police cars circling the church with their sirens growling. Then came four or five fire trucks with their whistles screaming and their bells clanging. It was impossible to speak above the roar of the official harassment. In my speech I shouted to the audience that we were glad that the fire department was outside but that the fire within us could not be extinguished with water. Lawrence Guyot, then director for SNCC in the Hattiesburg area, spoke right after me. While he was speaking, some firemen came charging into the church yelling that they were looking for a fire. Guyot yelled for the crowd to let the firemen through. A couple of dozen firemen soon stood in the front of the group, in full regalia, some snickering and some actually looking around for a fire, but all looking like damn fools. There was a moment of silence, and the firemen were looking to their captain, Moore, to tell them what to do. Then Guyot told Captain Moore, "We're going to have a meeting here tonight, and we don't give a damn what you do." Captain Moore did not reply but turned and led his men out of the church.

We had the same sort of official harassment in Vicksburg. The police and firemen surrounded the building making all the noise they could muster, but they had gotten the word from Hattiesburg that it was best not to go into the building and be laughed at by a bunch of progressive Negroes. In Gulfport we held the rally at the Back Bay Mission, which was staffed by and served both races. It was just between a Negro and a white neighborhood and had never had any problems over its integrated ministry. But during the rally, a large number of whites converged on the building, and we heard sirens wailing. The noise increased, and finally rocks and bottles started crashing through the windows. The police were there in full force. They stood and watched the whites throwing whatever they could at the windows. Every window in the mission was broken.

We were aware that we were trying to be politicians on this trip, so in a statement to the press we made the most charitable remarks that we could contrive about our reception in Gulfport. We said that we were sorry that some hoodlums had broken the windows and marred what would otherwise have been a pleasant visit. The next morning outside of the mission several white ladies came up to me and said, "Those weren't hoods that threw those bricks. It was us."

We covered as many communities and rural areas as possible and dipped into places as yet untouched by any civil rights activity. The campaign reminded us of how much remained to be done, as we saw thousands of new faces wrinkle with fear at the mention of total desegregation of the schools. We went to places where Negroes tried to escape even being asked to come to the rally. We added all of these places to our list of areas to reach in the future.

But there were some counties that we did not go to at all because of plain fear and good sense—like Issaquena, Amite, and Neshoba, where we were afraid we would be shot. Any Negro we might approach in these sections would have feared for his life, and the collusion between the lawless elements and law enforcement officers would have made our effort foolhardy.

We ended the campaign with a jubilant, backslapping fish fry at a country church in the backwoods near Lexington. We felt we had done well and were relieved that we had made it through with no deaths or serious injuries. Our public relations were remarkably successful, and, even as far out in the country as we were, a big passel of reporters, photographers, and television people were on hand for the event and enjoyed it as much as anybody.

We got as much attention during the race as either of the major candidates. No newsmen in the state had any doubt about what Johnson and Phillips were going to do and say, and they were delighted to have a little diversion. For the first time in over a century there was a real campaign, unofficial as it was, dealing with the real problems facing the state. We provided a chance to air these problems in the press, and no doubt white Mississippians learned a few things as well.

Our campaign was colorful in more ways than one, because of the antics of fire departments and law enforcement agencies blowing sirens and ringing bells. It was certainly more unpredictable than the campaigns of twin-like candidates trotting around the state leading hillbilly bands and yelling "NIGGER."

To tabulate the results of our efforts, we set up ballot boxes in churches, businesses, and homes. Ballots had all names of candidates for governor and lieutenant governor, which gave our voters a choice of three slates. Voting took place over a whole weekend from Friday until Monday. Many church congregations voted at Sunday services, and records were kept to keep people from voting more than once. In some places, such as Greenwood, there was trouble from the authorities when five voters were arrested and charged with disturbing the peace.

When the "freedom votes" were counted, it was found that more than eighty-thousand people had participated in an election which they knew they could not win. Quite a turnout for a people who Senator Eastland said were too lazy to even register. Those eighty-thousand votes for freedom quashed whatever hopes he and other segregationists might have had for continuing to sell our laziness as the sorry excuse for lack of Negro voter registration.

We knew that there were also a few write-in votes all over the state for Ed King and me, but we could never find out the exact count. Under Mississippi statutes, write-in votes invalidate a ballot unless the official candidates happen to die before the election. To my knowledge, Clarksdale was the only community to tabulate the number of write-in votes, and the election officials announced that write-in votes received by Henry and King had reached about six hundred, and then there were no more reports.

The election had shown the country that Mississippi Negroes would vote if given the chance. It was established that the sacrifices of the people and the labor of the civil rights movement were not in vain, and this evidence was to spur groups on to even more industrious activity. And perhaps most important, white college students from the North had seen what a significant role they could play in the Mississippi struggle. Al Lowenstein, with his wide contacts at Yale, Stanford, and other colleges, had played a major role in bringing these students down. Within a week after the freedom election, plans were being made for a massive influx of college volunteers for Freedom Summer, 1964.

And there were other encouraging signs. Paul Johnson defeated Rubel Phillips using old issues, but, in his inaugural address, Johnson hinted at a change in the state's official line on race. He may have been frightened by the strong expression of would-be Negro voters and had a legitimate reason to say, "I want my people to know that Paul Johnson is fully aware of the forces, the conflicts, that fashion our environment. Hate or prejudice or ignorance will not lead Mississippi while I sit in the governor's chair." He spoke of industrial development: "I would point out to you that the Mississippi economy is not divisible by political party or faction, or even by race, color, or creed." Never before had a Mississippi governor uttered such bold words—a fine reward for our freedom election.

Chapter 13

The Mississippi Freedom
Democratic Party

During the early days of 1964, awareness of our situation was slowly growing outside the state. While we were still reeling from the January murder of Louis Allen in Amite County and a statewide resurgence of Klan activity, college students who had come down and worked on the "freedom vote" the previous fall were spreading the word of our dilemma. [Allen, a witness to the murder three years earlier of Herbert Lee by a state legislator, was himself gunned down outside his home.] In particular, young people at Stanford and Yale were urging classmates and professors to come to Mississippi in the summer and donate their political and organizational abilities to help us acquire basic rights.

Early in January a Supreme Court decision ordered the registrar of Hattiesburg, in Forrest County, to stop discriminating against Negro voter applicants. The decision came fifteen years after the first affidavit on voting discrimination had been filed with the Justice Department. Our voting rights movement steadily gained momentum from the day that order reached Hattiesburg until we made our display the following August at the Democratic National Convention. There in Atlantic City we would gain the attention of a national audience.

After the Forrest County decision, we scheduled a Freedom Day in Hattiesburg to discuss the best way to implement the decision. COFO workers from all over the state convened on January 22 to encourage local Negroes to take advantage of the order and to prod the Justice Department into enforcing it. I spoke to a group and said that we planned to remain in Hattiesburg until the Justice Department took the county registrar by the hand and made him follow the order. Leaders of all the civil rights groups in COFO and representatives of national church groups were present at the gathering, and it was clear to local Negroes that they were backed by the best the movement could offer.

During the meeting, we also discussed general plans for the coming year and agreed that we should shoot for a massive voter registration program the following summer. Through our mock gubernatorial campaign the previous fall, some of the finest students and professors in the country had become active supporters, and we felt we could expect that to continue and increase. Interest inside the state was at a new peak, and the perfect touch was to aim toward the Democratic National Convention. There could never be a better time to launch a full- scale effort, and we began to think about a "challenge" to the right of the regular all-white Mississippi Democrats to represent the state at the party's national convention. It seemed to us that the Mississippi Democratic Party, which controlled the state government and maintained control by perpetuating the disfranchisement of a large segment of the population was, in simple fact, constitutionally illegal. It seemed poor business on the part of the national Democratic Party to continue to tolerate a state party which openly and often malevolently condemned the party's national candidates. We were in a good position to make a strong political protest.

Our nucleus of commitment and ready-to-be-tapped energy lay in the eighty-thousand people, some registered and some not, who had participated in the mock governor's election in the fall of 1963. Until that time many Negroes had been reticent about becoming involved in any sort of civil rights activity, and the mock election had served to ease those fears. There had been few reprisals, because most hostile whites considered it a game we were playing and never took it seriously. They preferred our seemingly harmless games to our filling the streets and jails.

In normal state party politics, potential voters are invited into an established party within the political subdivisions, but we could not invite these people into the Mississippi Democratic Party, because we could not get in there ourselves. Of course, the same held true for the Republican Party. The only answer was to create our own party, organize it in accordance with the laws of the state, and eventually ask for a charter.

The Mississippi Freedom Democratic Party (MFDP) was born from these broad ideas, and the midwife was the Mississippi Freedom Summer, dependent on the full cooperation of all civil rights groups and every volunteer we could recruit. We knew we had to have help from the outside. Bob Moses would direct the Freedom Summer project, and Dave Dennis, a CORE field representative, would be his assistant.

Originally, the Freedom Summer project had several goals, the most important of which was to register as many Negroes as possible. Freedom schools were planned that would offer remedial instruction in basic courses, including political science. We planned to set up community centers that would provide job training and general health and hygiene education. The culmination of the summer program was to be a challenge of the right of the regular Mississippi delegation to be seated at the Democratic National Convention in August of 1964.

Bob Moses was the real architect of the program. We all contributed ideas, but whenever he felt strongly about a particular suggestion, we would heed his advice, and usually it proved to be solid. Al Lowenstein's participation was also vital to the early planning.

By the end of February, we had a pretty definite outline for the summer program and the goals we hoped to accomplish. An important first step was to recruit college students from all over the country to come to the state and spend the summer living and working with Negroes and teaching the necessities for better living and fundamental political involvement. We had established contacts at many northern and midwestern colleges and universities, and we set about getting in touch with them. Bob Moses, Dave Dennis, Hunter Morey (a young white SNCC worker), and I took the responsibility for recruiting college students, and we spoke at schools all over the country. We knew the necessity of outside help, and, in this drive, it was more important than ever. We simply did not have enough capable Negroes and sympathetic whites in the state to organize and implement our plans.

Recruiting college students was not difficult. We appealed to their idealism. Mississippi had so violently distorted the national dream that these students wanted to help get the state on the right track. We told them of the illiteracy of Mississippi Negroes and of the lack of state programs to correct this. We explained that Mississippi provided no community programs for teaching home economics or better living to adults who were no longer in school. And we said that hundreds of thousands of us were being denied the right to vote. We asked them to come help us, and the response was gratifying.

A typical example of a recruiting tour was at Queens College in New York. Some students we knew had arranged an assembly where we could speak. Bob Moses and I went, and many of the students brought their parents with them to hear our appeal. Everyone was offering assistance of some sort. At the reception following our talk, a sharp-faced, intense young man approached me with his parents. The boy explained to his parents that I was the person who had convinced him that he should spend the following summer in Mississippi. The boy was named Andrew Goodman. The next time I heard of him he was being reported "missing" near Philadelphia, Mississippi. Later in the summer, Goodman and two other civil rights workers were found buried beneath an earthen dam in Neshoba County.

That news alone was a good reason why I never got out of the civil rights movement and why I never wanted to leave the state. I have encouraged too many people like Goodman to sacrifice everything to help us, and there are thousands who have suffered severe physical and economic reprisals because they listened to civil rights leaders. I have been far more fortunate than most in these respects, and the least I can do is remain active in efforts to secure civil rights and civil liberties. I have such respect for Medgar Evers and Andrew Goodman and all of those who gave their lives. The only way I can do justice to them and others who made sacrifices is to remain in the movement and fight for what they believed in. I have thought long and carefully, and this is all I can do.

Along with recruiting students, we began a simultaneous campaign to get Democratic councils in other states to pledge their support to the unseating of the regular Mississippi delegation to the national convention. As early as February 23, 1964, the California Democratic Council unanimously adopted a resolution supporting the seating of the Freedom Democratic Party at the national convention. In Massachusetts, several of our summer workers returned and appealed to prominent Democrats for their support. The Massachusetts convention turned the question over to a special committee. Representatives from all active civil rights groups presented arguments before the committee, and a healthy debate centered around the ethics and judgment of taking such a step. But after a few days the committee reported favorably, and the Massachusetts convention opted to support the seating of the MFDP at Atlantic City.

Most of us planning Freedom Summer were a little vague on the legal technicalities involved in the organization and functioning of the FDP. We simply knew we were right and that it was unconstitutional to deprive our people of the vote. Our problem was solved when Bob Moses spoke at an Americans for Democratic Action conference in Washington to explain what we hoped to accomplish at the national convention. There he met Joseph Rauh, chairman of the District of Columbia Democratic Party and a talented lawyer and political advisor. Rauh was extremely sympathetic towards our efforts and volunteered to be the counsel for the MFDP seating challenge. We gratefully accepted. Rauh outlined a procedure for us to follow in order to give the challenge the best possible chance for success. The plan called for us to attempt participation in the precinct, county, and state conventions of the regular Mississippi Democratic party. When this failed, as we knew it would, we were to hold our own precinct, county, and state conventions. Throughout, we were to follow closely the technical procedures of the regular Democrats, and we were to pay close attention to all state laws governing political parties.

By this time, interest on our behalf was stirring all over the country, and, with Rauh's office located in Washington, it became clear that we needed to open an office there as well. We didn't have the funds necessary to do this, but Ella Baker, who was on the advisory committee of SNCC and known to all of the major civil rights groups, volunteered to do the job. The Washington office opened on April 23, 1964, and a steady stream of letters flowed to prominent Democrats all over the country urging them to persuade their delegations to support us in Atlantic City.

While progress was being made on the national level to develop support for MFDP, support at our new party's first rally back at home was a disappointment for me. It was held April 26 at the Masonic Temple in Jackson and only two hundred people were there. We had been in the national press a good bit, and we realized that we had not had time to get the word around in Mississippi. The volunteers had not yet begun arriving in the state to tell the people what we were trying to do and to teach them how they could help.

In the meantime we had been able to attract the attention of the National Council of Churches (NCC), an organization with a seemingly unlimited supply of funds. The council had decided to provide money for orientation sessions for the summer volunteers before they came into Mississippi. This training period was designed to weed out undesirables and to instruct those who would come concerning just what they should expect and how they should react. Money was one of the essentials for the successful implementation of our plans, and this was beginning to trickle in from individuals and organizations all over the country. The Voter Education Project of the Southern Regional Council in Atlanta had withdrawn their support in 1963, but their grants of around fifty-thousand dollars had certainly made our job easier in facing early problems in black voting in Mississippi.

The filibuster against the 1964 Civil Rights Act by southern congressmen was in progress during that spring, and I went to Washington to join members of the National Council of Churches in a plea for the passage of the bill. The council set up daily vigils of small groups at the Capitol, and I took part in one of the large demonstrations known as the NCC Pilgrimage. We congregated and prayed and then went to lobby members of Congress. I testified before the House Judiciary Committee in support of the bill and explained that firsthand experience with the injustices in the Deep South would make any sincere American vote wholeheartedly in favor of the bill's passage.

As soon as I returned home we began a campaign to write letters in support of the bill. Across the state at every NAACP meeting, the people were not allowed to leave until they had written either a postcard or a short letter saying why they wanted the bill made into law. Ten thousand letters were written and sent from Mississippi.

That spring I also joined with Dr. Everett Parker, director of communications for the United Church of Christ, and Reverend R. L. T. Smith in a request to the Federal Communications Commission to deny license renewal to a Jackson television station, WLBT. The station had refused to sell me time for a political advertisement in my run for governor and had refused time to Reverend Smith when he ran for Congress. The station manager had told me that "niggers couldn't buy time."

By May 1964, four MFDP candidates had qualified to run in the Democratic congressional primary, including Fannie Lou Hamer, who later was one of the top drawing cards at the MFDP challenge in Atlantic City. The four knew from the beginning that they had no chance of winning, but the purpose again was to show the country how many Negroes in Mississippi would vote if given the chance. Rallies in support of the MFDP candidates were held across the state, and thousands of Negroes signed up for the freedom registration. All four candidates lost in the official primary election, since a very small percentage of Negroes had actually been able to vote. Nonetheless, the great body of disenfranchised Negroes—the people whom MFDP was designed to represent—was being aroused. Steadily the body was gaining strength.

I was in Washington at the national NAACP convention when word came that the three civil rights workers were missing in Neshoba County. My young friend from Queens, Andrew Goodman, and two of his friends, Mickey Schwerner and James Chaney, had disappeared mysteriously and local authorities were saying they had no knowledge of their whereabouts. When we heard the news, Charles Evers, appointed NAACP field secretary following his brother Medgar's murder, and I were on the telephone almost all night trying to find out when and where they had last been seen. But when we had exhausted our sources, not one person, black or white, had any concrete information.

When the first session of the NAACP convention opened on Monday morning, I went to the chairman and told him we needed the help of all members to pressure the government to find those young men. He allowed Charles Evers to speak to the convention, and Charles told the delegates of our futile telephone efforts the night before and that we had received no cooperation from the Justice Department when we had asked them to call all the jails in the Neshoba vicinity to try to learn if the boys were being held. He related that we had telephoned the FBI in Meridian and had been told that the trio had not been missing twenty-four hours and that there was no evidence they had they had been kidnapped across a state line. They said bluntly that the FBI could be of no help and that we would have to rely upon state authorities.

When Evers finished speaking, the convention delegates were ready to storm the Justice Department. We immediately scheduled a march to the Justice Department and arranged a conference with Attorney General Robert Kennedy. The convention was recessed while most of the delegates picketed the Justice Department and contacted influential people for their help. The entire convention was quickly mobilized into a team of people demanding that something be done by the government to locate the three missing boys.

Several of us, including Evers and Roy Wilkins, met with Robert Kennedy and presented our request for assistance. He was sympathetic but explained that he necessarily had to remain in an advisory capacity for the time being. At one point, while we were picketing his office, he came out and said "I agree with you," put on a picket sign and got in the damned line and marched with us. Bobby Kennedy stayed in touch with me through most of the hard times. He would call me up and start the conversation with "Hey Big Daddy South."

It was decided that Allen Dulles would be sent to Mississippi with me to expedite the search for the missing workers, and we were grateful for at least that much. Kennedy wanted Evers and me to brief Dulles on the general situation in Mississippi and what to expect in this particular case, but John Doar pointed out that Dulles's effectiveness would be seriously compromised if the state found out that he had been briefed by Evers and me in Washington. So we flew home to confer with Dulles on Mississippi soil.

We discussed the apparent abduction, the way things were going all over the state, and the possible scenario for the future. Dulles listened more than he talked, and we explained that we often failed to get effective FBI assistance with our problems. He appeared to be sympathetic with our problems and said he would do what he could to find the missing workers. Evers and I left Dulles in Mississippi and flew back to Washington for the remainder of the NAACP convention. Six weeks later, with full federal assistance, the bodies of the three boys were discovered.

But even with the brutal murders of the three workers at the beginning of the summer, students flocked into the state from all over the country. They were screened and processed at the orientation center at Oxford, Ohio, and then they came into the state and worked and lived in Negro communities. There is no way to estimate the services that they rendered. Naturally I am biased, but my impression of the students who came to Mississippi during that summer is that they were the finest in America. Many of them were idealists and talked about the American dream and the dignity of the common man, but they were dedicated to these ideas and proved it by their coming. I am certain that they were the greatest assets to ever come our way, and without them our road ahead would have been far more treacherous and uncertain. I am sure there were a few thrillseekers among the volunteers, but most of them were decent young people with a genuine interest in trying to fill the cultural and educational and political void that had resulted from decades of our second-class citizenship. I visited many of the freedom schools during the summer, and it was clear to me that the summer workers, black and white, were extending their efforts into areas where Negroes had never even heard the term "civil rights." Courage and dedication were necessary for this, and it is ironic that the qualities with which the summer workers were so heavily endowed are the very qualities that many white southerners cherish as their own—except when it comes to racial questions.

The accomplishments of the summer volunteers were great, and the levels of political and academic education of Mississippi Negroes were significantly raised. Most important, Negroes all over the state came to realize their personal obligation to improve themselves and become useful citizens.

Another aspect of that summer's accomplishments had to do with the deeply imbedded bitterness and hatred of whites in the minds of many Mississippi Negroes. It began to subside as they saw these white college students sacrificing everything in order to help them. With the murder of the three workers and the constant intimidation of Negroes who tried to be active in the movement, many colored people had simply given up trying to forgive the white man for his sins. But the fact that whites from the rest of the country—the same color and looking a lot like the ones already here— continued to work with us and live in our houses, even when they were bombed and shot into, gave Mississippi Negroes a new image of the white man. This beginning of understanding was invaluable and one of the factors that restrained ideas of bloody retaliation that still lurked in the minds of many Negroes. The summer volunteers gave civil rights leaders an argument for our continued profession of love as the solution to our problems.

In early June, the leaders of the MFDP set about trying to penetrate the regular Mississippi Democratic Party, in accordance with the directions from Joseph Rauh. Simultaneously, we began to organize county MFDP units around the state and to register people on our own freedom registration forms. The plan was to organize along both lines and have dual assurance in making our case for acceptance by the Democratic National Convention in Atlantic City.

The MFDP unit leaders from all over the state met at the Masonic Temple in Jackson to decide how many delegates each precinct, county, and district would be allowed to send to the state convention. We were not organized in every political subdivision, so it was impossible for us to plan a convention to meet the exact specification of the regular Democratic Party rules. But our rules paralleled those of the regular Democrats as closely as possible.

At this meeting, we also planned the other half of our strategy—how to penetrate the regular party structure on the precinct level. The regular precinct meetings were scheduled by law to be held at 10 a.m., June 26, at the place in the precinct where ballots were regularly cast. In many areas, Negroes were not permitted to attend these meetings at all, while, in some areas, they could attend, but their participation was limited by their own ignorance and the maneuvering of the whites. Our plan called for as many Negroes as possible to try and gain admission to the precinct meetings and to participate as fully as the whites would allow.

Our experience in Clarksdale was probably typical of the attempts all over the state to participate in the regular Democratic precinct meetings. On the specified day, about twenty of us went to the south Clarksdale precinct at about twenty-five minutes before ten o'clock. There were five white people there when we arrived and by ten o'clock only about seven— giving us a numerical edge of thirteen. This, of course, caused some consternation on the part of these whites, who had become accustomed to years of political inactivity on our part and apathy on the part of whites. The chair of the meeting conferred with several of the whites and announced that the meeting would be delayed because Leon Porter, the secretary, was not present and that we would start as soon as Porter could be located. We knew this was a stall, because Leon was a former city judge whom we all knew, and we had just seen him in the building. During the delay, whites from the south Clarksdale precinct began straggling in, many of them asking each other why they had been called. A white acquaintance of mine came in the drugstore a few days later and said to me, "I'm sure glad y'all went down there to the voting place. They never have let us get involved before, but when y'all showed up, they called us and let us have something to say at last."

When the meeting finally started, the whites far outnumbered the blacks. I was nominated by the blacks to be delegate to the county convention, and the whites nominated Vincent Brocato. He beat me by forty votes to twenty, which shows how many whites had been called into the meeting.

In other communities, where Negroes were not even allowed inside the door, various ruses were used. Sometimes, the meeting place was changed at the last minute without public notice. In other communities, signs appeared on the buildings where the meetings were usually held saying "No Meeting Today," while the meeting was actually going on inside. And, of course, there was always the threat of intimidation hanging over the head of any Negro with an idea of participating in a precinct meeting.

In some parts of the state, FDP members tried to get into the county conventions after they had been defeated at the precinct level. But this did no more than dramatize our deprivation, and in Coahoma County we decided not to waste our time trying to crash the county convention. Under the law, we had no right to be there unless we had gained a seat through the precinct election.

Across the state our efforts to participate in precinct meetings were frustrated. Since we had been stopped at that level—the basic step toward the national convention—we had exhausted all possibilities for participation in the state's regular Democratic Party. While some Negroes were able to vote as Democrats in the primaries, none of us had been able to participate in the party machinery as convention delegates or as officials on the county district or state level, or even as influential voters in basic elections. No Negroes participated in the state convention. There was nothing left for us to do but continue to develop the Mississippi Freedom Democratic Party. Quite simply, the MFDP went to Atlantic City because we were not allowed in the regular Democratic Party in Mississippi. Typically, the state's regular delegation insisted that we had contrived the entire charges against them.

Following the precinct meetings of June 16, we began to set up parallel structures towards our own convention. From the start, the undertone of our efforts was our intended support for the Democratic national nominees, while the regular Democrats in Mississippi had no such intention. When we got our papers in order and went to the secretary of state, Hebert Ladner, to register as a party, he refused and told us there was already a political party in the state which called itself "Democratic." We declined his offer to register as a third party and explained that, although the regular party bore the name "Democratic," it had failed to support the national party's presidential candidate in 1960. We pointed out that even the party leaders themselves claimed to have no affiliation with the national party. And we told Mr. Ladner that we were the ones who represented the philosophy of the Democratic Party. But he was firm in his resolution not to register us as anything but a third party.

During all of this we were anticipating the passage of the civil rights bill. Our plan was to begin testing the new law as soon as it was passed by Congress. The bill became law July 2, 1964, a date I am not likely to forget, because it was also the date of my birthday and that of Medgar Evers. On that very day we got enough money together to pay bonds if it became necessary, and we began our attempts four days later to implement the public accommodations section of the bill. We tested public facilities in Clarksdale, Jackson, Vicksburg, Biloxi, Gulfport, Natchez, and Laurel, and in most cases we were successful. In all of the cities, local people tested the restaurants and theaters. But we had out-of-town people test the motels and hotels, since some places had legitimate policies against renting rooms to local customers. Within a month, we had tested all of the public facilities in Clarksdale, and all had either integrated or had suits pending against them.

We spent July canvassing the state and signing up members for the MFDP, and at the end of the campaign we had nearly one hundred thousand people registered. Still, our greatest problem was the reluctance of so many Negroes, particularly in rural areas, to have their names placed on the rolls.

The roots of fear went back to 1955 when we were trying to get signatures on petitions protesting segregated schools. The people who had signed the desegregation petitions remembered that their names and addresses had appeared in the local newspapers, and many had suffered severe and often brutal intimidation. Many remained hesitant to sign anything to do with civil rights. Their fear was even greater than in 1955, because nine years earlier they had been more naive. So we had to convince prospective signers over and over that their names on voter registration lists would not be made public and that, in fact, nobody would ever know about it except those in sympathy.

Once we got momentum started for the freedom registration, Martin Luther King, Jr., agreed to come to Mississippi and help build enthusiasm for the challenge. He was the very best person because of his tremendous appeal to the masses and because almost all Negroes considered him the most dynamic and powerful civil rights leader of all. King came the third week of July and went from town to town making speeches urging the black community to participate. At the end of the trip, Dr. King and I appeared together on a Jackson television station discussing the challenge and giving it our full support.

That same day we had a rally at the Masonic Temple that drew about two thousand people—a happy surprise after the two hundred that had shown up several months earlier. All the civil rights forces in the state had worked together to plan this rally, each trying to outdo the other in attracting people to come. King made a rousing speech on unity and said that the MFDP was one of the important tools that could fashion the freedom that we would all enjoy one day. He called the MFDP a true grassroots movement—the kind of revolutionary movement essential to the gaining of our rights.

Along with the immense bolstering of the spirits of people who had come from all over the state at jeopardy to their very beings, came the public pledge of all the civil rights groups to help defray the expenses of going to Atlantic City. More than a thousand dollars in contributions was collected that night. I felt that MFDP was headed for success.

During July, we redoubled our efforts to get Democratic convention delegations from across the country to commit themselves to our cause. We went on more speaking tours, and summer volunteers began returning home to talk to prominent Democrats in their states to persuade them to endorse our effort. This was valuable and speaks well for the calibre of young people who came to us that summer. Officials in their states would listen to first-hand accounts of what they had seen and learned in Mississippi. Through this effort, ten delegations endorsed our challenge to the seating of the regular Democratic delegation from Mississippi. They were California, Colorado, District of Columbia, Massachusetts, Michigan, Minnesota, New York, Oregon, Washington, and Wisconsin.

Towards the end of July, a newspaper reporter called to tell me that Senator Paul Douglas had proposed that the Democratic National Convention seat both the MFDP delegation and the regular delegation and allow the two groups to split Mississippi's votes. When influential people like Douglas, who are sympathetic to your cause, make a suggestion, it must be weighed carefully. We could not afford to alienate people like Senator Douglas. However, we considered his suggestion totally unacceptable. The issue was simple in our unpolitic minds. The regular Democrats boasted about their disloyalty to the national party, while we promised to campaign vigorously for all of the national candidates. Therefore, it seemed that we should have the full voice to support candidates and not be weakened by the racist-minded delegation representing so-called Mississippi Democrats. We felt that the regulars should not be allowed any seats in the convention—that we had a rightful claim to all sixty-seven seats. Excluded from the consideration of seating us was the parade of injustices we had witnessed in trying to participate in the regular Democratic organization. We had taken affidavits from people who had been turned down in their attempts to participate, and, by following the legal advice of Joseph Rauh, we had multiple and solid grounds for making the challenge. For all of these reasons, including the simple principle that we were right and they were wrong, we could not accept Senator Douglas's proposal with an easy conscience.

As it turned out, we would have been wise to accept the Douglas proposal and work toward gaining one-half of the convention seats, since it was far more than what was finally offered to us. But I believed then that we had to fight for the full seating, and it would have been a severe blow to MFDP morale to accept such an early compromise. We had spoken so much about the principles involved in the challenge that it would have bordered on

Mississippi Freedom Democratic Party 175

hypocrisy for us suddenly to become calculating and practical and political. We were so naive. We didn't realize that the great liberals of our times, such as Douglas, Hubert Humphrey, and Lyndon Johnson, talked more about principles than they lived by them. We were to learn that this was one reason why they got elected to office. The essence of our challenge was a moral appeal decorated with an array of legalities that were being handled by people other than the rank and file of the movement. So, it was only after the convention that we would see that we should have worked for the Douglas proposal. But even to this day most of us believe that we would have succeeded in our attempt for full seating had it not been for the last-minute maneuvering by President Johnson to keep our seating question off the convention floor, where almost certainly we would have been successful.

The MFDP convention was held August 6, at the Masonic Temple in Jackson, and it was organized along the lines of most political conventions, including music and colorful hoopla. Delegates had been elected in many counties, and, in places where it was too dangerous to hold a local convention, the delegates were seated just prior to the state convention. Ella Baker, legndary organizer for the NAACP and SCLC and advisor to SNCC, was the keynote speaker, and she got us off to a good start. Her words rang out: "Until the killing of black mothers' sons becomes as important to the rest of the country as the killing of white mothers' sons, we who believe in freedom cannot rest." She continued, "MFDP will not end at the convention. This is only the beginning. You are waging a war against the closed society of Mississippi." Before long, people were marching around the auditorium chanting "Freedom" and clapping and singing.

Joseph Rauh was there and explained our legal position as it then stood. He advised us that we had a poor legal case, mainly because the Democratic Party is not governed by external laws in its own organization. It sets its own rules on procedures and policies, and it must function in accord with various national laws governing all political parties. Rauh explained to us that nothing we were asking was impossible—the Democratic Party could accept us as the legitimate Democratic delegation from Mississippi if the convention pleased. Or they could turn us away. Or they could break all precedent and offer us votes at large. The convention could vote to do anything that it pleased, and precedent and existing rules were of no mandatory consideration. Rauh made it clear that we had done all that was possible to show the national Democrats our sincerity and genuine problems and that it was in the hands of the convention delegates—or those people who controlled what transpired at the convention.

This general explanation let us know that at least our judges would not be the Mississippi Democrats to whom we were accustomed. Our destiny would be decided by national Democrats in Atlantic City. Then Rauh began talking about various political angles that gave our challenge a strong chance of success—provided that Lyndon Johnson maintained a benevolent neutrality. This brought wild cheers from the crowd, because the mention of President Johnson's name stirred thoughts of total commitment to our cause. Rauh said that as long as Johnson did not actively oppose us, the MFDP should be able to unseat the regular delegation. He explained that the president could not afford to openly support us, because that would amount to flagrant alienation of a previously accepted segment of the Democratic Party. It would be a personal alienation if the president did it himself, but it would be an impersonal matter if the convention as a whole decided upon it. Most of the delegates were elated over this, and the general feeling was that Johnson, in view of his liberal stance in civil rights matters, would do nothing to prevent our seating. And even trying to figure it politically, we saw that the Mississippi regulars were openly opposed to Johnson, while we were willing to campaign all over the country for him. This seemed like an additional reason for him to help us. Enthusiasm was at a new high by the end of Rauh's convention speech.

In an informal talk with us after the meeting, however, Rauh gave disheartening news. He said it would be extremely difficult to get President Johnson to go along with us, and he predicted further that chances were strong that Johnson would work against our being seated. This seemed incredible, but, as Rauh talked, it began to make sense. He told us that if Johnson didn't stop the MFDP from being seated, he could possibly lose five southern states, including his native Texas, in the November election. There was reason to think that the delegations of these five states would get up and stomp out of the convention if the MFDP was seated, a frightening prospect to a man like Johnson, who would like to take every state in the union.

So, our high hopes were soon deflated, but we were determined to make the best effort possible. If the White House was against us, and if President Johnson sent down the word, we had little chance. We could only hope that he would remain quiet. As this more discouraging news spread throughout the convention that night, animosity toward Johnson began to develop. We just couldn't believe that Johnson would work against us, but we also were convinced that Rauh would not tell us anything that he did not believe.

Other business at the state convention included the selection of an executive committee and the organization of the official delegation. Travel plans were made, and sixty-four Mississippians were selected to go. They would represent almost one hundred thousand Mississippi Negroes who had never before had any representation in their government.

The executive committee sent a letter to the secretary of the national Democratic Party, certifying the MFDP delegation, and this was the last step in fulfilling the various formalities. Next stop—Atlantic City. The executive committee also sent a letter to the national chairman, John Bailey, informing him that we were coming to the national convention and asking that we be seated as the legitimate delegates from Mississippi. We sent him newspaper clippings in which our prominent regular state Democrats renounced any affiliation with the national party. We tried to convince him that the MFDP was the true voice. Bailey's reply was simple and noncommittal. He said that he had received our letter and that he gathered we planned to come to Atlantic City. He closed by saying that our position would be decided at the convention by the delegates.

Up to this point, Mississippi officialdom had confined itself to laughing at us and denouncing the national Democratic Party. But then on August 12, Attorney General Joe Patterson got Judge Stokes Robertson to issue an injunction ordering all MFDP officials not to leave the state and go to Atlantic City. The injunction also prohibited the leaders from engaging in any further MFDP activity, all of which amounted to one of the most ridiculous stunts they ever tried. We didn't even consider obeying the order, and we knew that if they carried it out, they couldn't incarcerate us until we got back from the convention. This last-minute display of arrogant manipulation of judicial power on the part of the state's leading Democrats was a good example of what we faced in Mississippi. We were glad that this would be fresh in the minds of the people at Atlantic City.

The little knowledge we had of state politics had been acquired by watching men like Robertson and Patterson, and we had enough Mississippi blood in us to stir up an even bigger legal mess at the last minute. As soon as we learned of the injunction, we immediately filed suit in federal court asking that sixteen Mississippi segregation laws be invalidated. Actually we had a legitimate case, and this was something we would have gotten around to anyway, but it caused lots of last-minute confusion for the white power structure, just as we were leaving for Atlantic City. As it turned out, the confusion was just beginning.

Chapter 14

Atlantic City—Heartbreak And All

Several of us went to Atlantic City one day before the arrival of our entire delegation, hoping to raise funds to offset the huge expense involved in bringing sixty-four people to the Democratic National Convention. Fannie Lou Hamer, Annie Devine, Victoria Gray, and I appeared on a program arranged by parents of students who had worked that summer in Mississippi. We discussed the hard work that had gone into the challenge and tried to make clear our precise goals at the convention. We explained why we felt entitled to the sixty-four seats normally occupied by the regular Mississippi Democrats. Proceeds from that meeting helped towards our costs.

The buses from Mississippi started rolling in on a hot Saturday morning, and everyone was directed to the Gem Motel. Ella Baker had made the arrangements and had done the best she could with limited funds. The Gem Motel provided the worst accommodations imaginable, and it was several miles from the convention hall. We had to sleep five and six to a room, and there were never enough beds to go around. People were sleeping under the beds and in chairs, and no room was considered filled until there was no lying room left. Although this was uncomfortable, the main problem was that we were so cut off from activities at the convention. We felt isolated, and most of us were lost in Atlantic City. Few had been there before, and none had spent enough time to become acquainted with the town.

Joseph Rauh was probably our biggest help and easily the best friend we could have had—other than Lyndon Johnson, if he had made that choice. Rauh was on the credentials committee and knew what was going on. He had heard the arguments of the regular Mississippi delegation and knew the best position for us to take. His legal staff, along with many volunteers, worked to give us the best advice on keeping the challenge on the right track, and he even took charge of seeing us around Atlantic City and making sure we were at the right place at the right time.

Charles Diggs was the other person who took a keen interest in our well-being. He was the Michigan congressman who had been at my home the night of the 1963 firebombing. He was on the credentials committee but told us from the beginning that we would not get all that we asked for and advised us to think about alternatives to our hope of unseating the entire regular Mississippi delegation. He explained that our position would not be endorsed ultimately by the convention and that we should face the political facts of life.

While the Mississippi delegates were still arriving, we met on the veranda of the Gem Motel for a pep rally. We were enthusiastic, and it seemed clear that everyone wanted to push for full seating. The attitude was, "We have come here to be seated, and we will be seated. If not, we will pack up and go home." No one seemed willing to accept a compromise. We had learned bitterly at home that compromise was usually to our disadvantage.

Our first hearing before the credentials committee came on Saturday afternoon in the grand ballroom of the convention hall. With the direction of Rauh, about fifteen witnesses were prepared to testify about being deprived of their right to vote or to participate in political activities. Fannie Lou Hamer was one of the first. In surely one of the most colorful and most uninhibited presentations ever made in the convention hall, Mrs. Hamer told her story to the committee. She had been a tenant on a plantation in Sunflower County, Senator James O. Eastland's home county. She had been put off the plantation after she went to town and registered to vote. Her landlord cited her voting activities as the reason for her expulsion and had been very frank about it. She was arrested for other civil rights activities and had been beaten while in jail. Her rendition of her experiences created new tension among the committee members. It was clear that many of them had never seen a woman like Mrs. Hamer nor heard a firsthand account of Mississippi goings-on.

Mrs. Rita Schwerner was another extremely effective witness. Her husband, Michael, had been one of the three civil rights workers murdered near Philadelphia. She described the work that she and her husband had done prior to his death and emphasized that his death could be made meaningful through giving Mississippi Negroes the rights that they deserved.

Others testifying before the committee included Ed King, the chaplain from Tougaloo, and national civil rights leaders Martin Luther King, James Farmer, and Roy Wilkins. The main purpose of their testimony was to show the credentials committee why we should be seated as the delegation from Mississippi. Rauh tried to show that Negroes in the state had been abused physically and psychologically in their attempts to register and to vote and participate in the functioning of the Democratic party. He wanted to show that our exclusion was the result of the efforts of Mississippi Democrats who were not in sympathy with the principles of the national Democratic Party, while our delegation gave them full support.

A central point in Rauh's argument was that there was no "legal" question involved. He emphasized that the Democratic Party was not governed internally by statutory laws, but that it functioned in the same way as a private club. It could accept as members whom it pleased, and it could reject persons on the same grounds. The true and legitimate Mississippi delegation could be decided entirely by the convention with no external factors involved.

As some credentials committee members persisted in saying that we had no "legal standing," Rauh continually presented the rebuttal—that it was unrealistic for our delegation to be expected to express and present ourselves through channels provided by Mississippi law. We had tried to register the MFDP and had carefully followed the law, but, when everything else had failed, we had set up our own party. In short, the state of Mississippi had refused to allow us to comply with its own laws.

Moreover, we were ready to pledge our full support to the national candidates—no matter who they might be—in contrast to the regular Mississippi delegation, which was uncommitted. The state convention of the regular party had recessed until after the national convention before deciding on their support for the national candidates. If "legal" questions were to be raised, it seemed to us that the regular delegation was on poor footing and that we were in an excellent position.

We tried to convince the credentials committee of the abuse and intimidation our delegation had suffered. We supported the national party, and other state delegations seemed sympathetic to the plight of southern Negroes. We saw no reason why we would not have the entire delegation seated. The future looked brighter than we had ever expected.

After our people had testified before the credentials committee, Mississippi state senator E. K. Collins, the spokesman for the regular delegation, took the floor and denied that we had any difficulty voting in Mississippi. He said that Negroes "are absolutely free to participate in state Democratic affairs, including the selection of national convention delegates." I don't believe that Senator Collins convinced anyone—he didn't even believe it himself. It was simply outrageous.

The press was attentive to us from the moment of our arrival. Some of the newsmen had followed our activities in Mississippi and were men that we knew and had come to like, having been glad when they were on the scene during demonstrations and protests. But most of the newspeople had never before seen sixty-four Mississippi Negroes in a group and were keenly interested in us and what we were trying to accomplish. They appeared very sympathetic, and the press was siding with us, on purpose or otherwise, just as they had during dangerous racial turmoil back in Mississippi. Also, since the political conclusion of this Democratic convention—as far as newsmen were concerned— was settled far in advance, most of them were glad of a little diversion.

Foremost for the press was the question of what compromise we would be willing to accept. They seemed to think we had come asking for far more than we had expected to win and were hoping to reach a satisfactory compromise. Repeatedly they asked about this, and just as often we told them that we had no intention of accepting any compromise. Following the credentials committee hearing that Saturday, the press told us that they had heard that the Freedom delegation would be recognized as "honored guests of the convention," and that the regular Mississippi delegation would be seated. We told them we would not accept the offer—that we could sit in the balcony in Mississippi and that we certainly hadn't come all the way to Atlantic City to accept a "back-of- the-bus" deal. Actually, the MFDP Executive Committee had discussed the possibility and probability of a compromise before we even left Mississippi, but in the heady atmosphere of the convention, we continued to insist that we be seated as the official delegation or be ignored entirely.

Right after the credentials committee hearings ended, we began our intensive lobbying sessions with state delegations. Never have I been through such a harrowing experience. It was practically a twenty-four-hour-a-day job, and even then it seemed there was never enough time. I have never slept so little. We tried to convince the other state delegations to support our challenge to unseat the regular delegation. Most of our delegates participated in this caucusing, and I personally met with twenty state delegations. In many cases, a student from a particular state who had worked in Mississippi Freedom Summer would present one of us to the delegation from his home state. In his introduction, the student would relate what he had seen during his stay in Mississippi. Usually we would meet informally with the delegations in their motels and explain our challenge and why we must be seated. We were always open for questions during these sessions, but there were very few, and in every case we were received enthusiastically. By the time our lobbying was over, it seemed evident that the rank and file among the delegates were with us all the way. But these were delegates who felt no blind loyalty to the party—delegates who were deciding things on a basis of right and wrong, irrespective of party lines. However, the leaders of the delegations, who usually sat quietly and listened to us, were generally with the party line, right or wrong, and they were the important figures. This is what we didn't understand at that point—it isn't how many people you have with you, it is *Who* you have with you.

At noon that same Saturday, a quiet demonstration got under way on the boardwalk in front of the convention hall. Everything centered around large charcoal portraits of the three civil rights workers slain near Philadelphia, Mississippi, the previous June. One of our purposes was to provide the public with a constant reminder of the brutality often faced by our people when they demanded the right to vote. Our demonstrators were joined by people from all over the country who wanted to see the Freedom Democratic Party seated. Mostly under the leadership of SNCC, the vigil of around one hundred people went on twenty four hours, day and night, for the entire time the convention was in session.

The credentials committee met on Sunday to consider our case. David Lawrence presided over the meeting, and Ed King and I represented the MFDP. We had no voice in the meeting but were allowed to be present to see how our case was handled. As it turned out, there was little need for our presence, since our position was so ably presented and defended by Joseph Rauh, Congresswoman Edith Green of Oregon, and others. Invariably the question arose as to whether our position was strictly moral rather than legal, and, no matter what Rauh said, the question of our "legality" persisted. It was clear during the meeting that when committee members referred to our actions as "illegal," they really simply meant that it had never been done before. If we made our point that legalities had nothing to do with our position, the members of the credentials committee never understood—or chose not to.

The solution that the press had tipped to us was proposed at the meeting, and it apparently had the backing of President Johnson—that we be seated as honored guests of the convention. The president would make a glowing reference to us in his acceptance speech. This would be a satisfactory acknowledgment of the MFDP and also show a unified front in the effort to beat Republican Barry Goldwater. The proposal would actually have our delegation seated in the gallery of the convention hall—back to where we had sat for two centuries in Mississippi. We had risked everything to go to Atlantic City for this?

The only meaningful compromise offered that afternoon was Edith Green's proposal that every delegate—regular or otherwise—be required to take a loyalty oath to support the national candidates. Those who took it would be seated,and those who refused would not. If all concerned—regular and FDP—took the oath, then each delegate would have one-half vote. Most of us in the FDP felt that this was the one compromise we could accept if compromising became necessary. But the party leaders—Lyndon Johnson and Hubert Humphrey—could not accept this proposal. It possibly would jeopardize the loyalty of the other southern delegations, and the risk was not worth it.

Our friends on the credentials committee said that unless the committee provided the MFDP a right to vote, the matter would be taken to the convention floor, where it surely would be settled in our favor. They were refusing to accept anything short of our eligibility to vote in the convention, but others felt differently, and the meeting ended in a deadlock. Chairman David Lawrence appointed a subcommittee to consider the question further and report back to the full committee.

Then began the pressure from all sides. Sunday night a meeting was arranged with Hubert Humphrey, and we got our first dose of real national politics. Martin Luther King, Jr., Bob Moses, Ed King, Roy Wilkins, and I were invited. Rauh accompanied us, and we met at the Pageant Motel with Humphrey and several White House aides. In a cordial atmosphere, Humphrey told us that he had been a strong supporter of Negro rights for a long time, that he personally supported our position, and that he didn't want segregationists representing the Democratic Party in Mississippi. However, he only wished that our position were "legal" so that he could give us his full and unqualified public support in our attempt to be seated. Then he said he was going to make some proposals to us, and, if we went along, he would look to us in the future to rebuild a new Democratic Party in Mississippi. Most of us knew then what he was leading up to.

Humphrey told us that there was no "legal" way that we could be seated by the convention and made the same offer the credentials committee had made—that we be considered "honored guests." One hell of a lot of good that was going to do. We knew that Humphrey was acting as the spokesman for President Johnson, and we had every reason to believe that if he didn't settle this intraparty squabble he would not be offered the vice presidency. As for the president, he knew that the MFDP could not muster enough votes to carry Mississippi, and, if we were seated, it could not gain him any states. It could only anger other southern states and harm his chances of taking them. Johnson knew that Mississippi or Alabama alone could not lead a walkout from the convention that would take other southern states with them, but he also realized that certain states, such as Georgia, were prepared to pack up and leave if he allowed the Freedom delegation to be seated in the place of the regular Democrats from Mississippi. He also had reason to believe that his home state of Texas would possibly do the same and cause him a tremendous amount of embarrassment.

The president's position, as we learned through Humphrey, was that our case must be settled in the credentials committee—not out in the open on the convention floor, where a harmonious party facade might be publicly ruptured. The pressure was on us, and it was even hinted that if we did not comply with the presidential wishes, there might be a different vice presidential nominee who could possibly be far less sympathetic to our cause than Hubert Humphrey was. In retrospect, it seems that everything possible was done to pressure us into the "honored guests" position—with the exception of a direct request from the President himself.

Had we been more politically sophisticated, perhaps we could have seen that, on the national level, the party comes before issues, no matter how important they might be. We felt issues were most important and that the party should conform. We were confronted with two choices. We could fight to have the issue taken to the convention floor if we failed in the credentials committee or we could go home. Quite clearly, our group would first fight for the seating, and, if this failed, we would go home before accepting the compromise. Generally, most of the members of our delegation were indignant over the offer.

From the first voting sessions in the credentials committee, it was clear that we would not receive their support. The next step was to try to round up eleven members of the committee who were willing to sign a minority report calling for the seating of the MFDP delegation. With this minority report, the issue would be placed on the convention floor. Once it was on the floor, we would have to have eight delegations back our requests for a roll call vote on our seating as the regular delegation. At the time, it was all bewildering for most of us, and, without the technical guidance from Joe Rauh and his associates, we probably would have been completely overwhelmed.

Following our meeting with Humphrey, Dr. King called a press conference and said that, if the credentials committee approved the compromise proposed by the White House, the natural reaction of Negro voters on election day would be to go fishing. He suggested that the Democratic Party should have no reason to expect the support of Negro voters if the MFDP was not seated as the regular delegation from Mississippi. In response to this, I announced that I intended to support the Democratic candidates, regardless of who they were and whether or not we were given the seats. I had made this pledge to support party candidates before I left Mississippi, and I intended to keep my word. This was not the first time that Dr. King and I disagreed, and it would not be the last.

The first session of the convention was Monday night, and David Lawrence announced that the credentials committee had not resolved the dispute over the seating of the Mississippi delegation. This led to broad speculation that the committee might continue to postpone a decision until the convention was over. That was the most noncommittal way for the issue to be settled, and we were learning quickly that politicians on that high a level don't like to be committed to anything that hasn't got several convenient exits. Most of us were irritated that the committee might possibly evade the issue entirely. It seemed outrageous that they could lack the integrity to face the matter squarely, come to a decision, and provide reasons for that decision. But we were also beginning to realize that most anything could happen.

Then, several members of the delegation were asked to meet with Hubert Humphrey on Tuesday afternoon at three o'clock at the Pageant Motel. We didn't hear about the meeting until that day. The first thing I did was to try to reach Rauh to discuss what was going on. I kept trying to reach him by phone until the last minute. I couldn't find him and later learned from Rauh that he had been trying to get in touch with me at the same time. I went into the almost impromptu meeting with Humphrey without Rauh's advice.

Dr. King, Bob Moses, Roy Wilkins, Ed King, and Bayard Rustin went to the meeting, and, to our surprise when we walked into the room, there sat one of the oldest friends of the civil rights movement—labor leader Walter Reuther. Humphrey was there, of course, and the room was filled with people who had always had a sincere interest in the welfare of blacks. But our welfare was not foremost in the minds of Humphrey and Reuther on that particular afternoon. President Johnson had sent Reuther to Atlantic City from the bargaining table where he was working towards a settlement on a union-management dispute in the automobile industry. It wasn't often that

Johnson considered something so important that he would call away a top participant in a labor dispute to settle a political squabble. Johnson knew that we respected and trusted Reuther, and thought that the combination of him and Humphrey should be strong enough to persuade us to accept a compromise.

But that day, Reuther used poor strategy. He chose the one line of reasoning that we found intolerable. He first reminded us that he had been a friend of the movement for years. Then he put his figures on the table: "When the NAACP needed forty thousand dollars to get buses for the Washington march, I got the money for you, Roy. Martin, when you needed six thousand dollars for the Montgomery boycott, I got it for you, didn't I?" Certainly he had done these things, and we were grateful to him. But he was talking mainly to King and Wilkins and telling them that favors done for them in the past now called for repayment. It might have been effective with them alone, but he was asking King and Andy Young to persuade Moses and me to go along with the compromise. Reuther's approach was almost ridiculous. King could not claim to represent the feelings of Mississippi Negroes who had never felt the results of Reuther's good will—they didn't owe him anything. After Reuther's performance, there was little chance that King would be able to get the FDP delegation to go along with the second proposed compromise from the White House.

This compromise called for two "at large" votes for us, and it specified that Ed King and I would be the two delegates seated. We asked them why they had settled on two votes. Why not four? Humphrey and Reuther said that could be adjusted. Then we objected strenuously to their specifying the two delegates by name, but they said that would have to stand as presented. Their refusal to try to work with us on this matter clearly indicated that President Johnson had assured Reuther of getting what he wanted in the labor contract negotiation if he settled the convention dispute. And it was still very clear that the president had told Humphrey that his nomination as vice president rested on his ability to resolve the controversy. None of us ever doubted that the two men were personally sympathetic with our cause, but we knew they were acting on direct orders of the president of the United States. Acting on those orders placed them in the role of playing national power politics with a bunch of country bumpkins from Mississippi. They thought we were matching them in a power game, but we didn't even know what the game was. In short, the sincerity and moral concern and integrity that these two men had shown in earlier times was not present on that Tuesday afternoon in the Pageant Motel.

If they had only said we could have two votes and left it at that. Maybe then, we could have taken the two votes and divided them among all sixty-four delegates, giving each delegate one-thirty-second of a vote, and all of us would have been admitted to the convention. But we were through with the business of whites, whoever they were, picking our representatives for us. The people in our delegation had come to Atlantic City at a tremendous sacrifice. By simply being there, we were violating a Mississippi court injunction, and all of us were subject to being jailed upon returning home. No leader worth his salt, under these circumstances, would have accepted the compromise proposed by the White House. And just as bad as the assignment of two certain delegates to represent us was that our two votes would come under a designation of "at large." The compromise gave our delegation no recognition as Mississippians. Our two votes would not even be under the Mississippi banner, and they would not be cast from the state of the people we were representing. The proposal was paternalistic in every sense. Ed King kept asking for Humphrey to admit to this, but to no avail. We finally told Reuther and Humphrey that we would not accept the compromise and betray our people.

While we were meeting with Humphrey and Reuther, we were completely unaware of a conspiracy under way at the convention hall. A credentials committee meeting had been scheduled for six o'clock Tuesday evening, but, without our knowledge, the time had been changed to four o'clock, the time when Moses, Wilkins, King, and I were conferring with Humphrey and Reuther. Rauh had found out about the change and had tried to get in touch with me, but he had no way of knowing that I was off at the Pageant Motel. I had no way of knowing that the committee was meeting two hours early. So, while Humphrey and Reuther were trying to persuade us to accept the compromise, that same compromise was being accepted by the credentials committee without us there to express our objections. Rauh was telling the committee that he could not accept the two-votes-at-large compromise without talking to me, as chair of the delegation. Humphrey knew what was going on. He knew where Rauh was and he knew where I was, and he was certain that he had us in a position where we could not get together. And he was exactly right. We weren't exactly held captive at the Pageant Motel, but Humphrey and Reuther could keep the conversation going until the credentials committee agreed to the compromise without us there to put a monkey wrench in the works.

The high-power strategy failed. Humphrey and Reuther seemed to think we would be more susceptible to compromise if they could get us away from Rauh. Instead, we just refused to do anything without consulting Rauh, and, more importantly, we knew our delegation had to make the decision.

Towards the end of our meeting in the motel, the telephone started ringing. The phone was in another room but close by enough for us to hear the man talking on our end. He turned our way and said, "Robert Kastenmeier has accepted the compromise. Joe Rauh has accepted the compromise," and so on. It was obviously an effort to stampede us into accepting the White House proposal. Later we learned that at the point of the phone calls, no one had accepted the compromise.

I am convinced that Tuesday afternoon was filled with maneuvering and manipulation calculated to keep us away from Rauh and to force our acceptance. I discussed this with Rauh, and he agreed, but he later told a press conference that he believed that no fast deals took place at the convention. Rauh, too, was firmly entrenched in the Democratic Party establishment, and what he might say to the press may not have been what he actually believed.

We were not the only ones who didn't know about the early meeting of the credentials committee. Not all committee members were able to get there, and it seemed that those who were notified were not particularly sympathetic towards our goals at the convention. When Rauh learned about the meeting and couldn't get in touch with me, he notified several other members of the MFDP delegation of what was happening. It seemed that the extremely favorable public reaction to our appearance the previous Saturday had pressured the president into making the tangible offer of the two votes at large. The president wanted as little public demonstration from us as possible, since that could jeopardize the committee approval of his compromise.

Congressman Corman of California, a member of the committee, presented the compromise proposal. The plan also called for notification to all state conventions that in 1968 they must send integrated delegations to the national convention. Some members agreed with the compromise proposal, but most of those who would have balked at such a drastic compromise of our goals were not there. Things were moving quickly at this point—considerably faster than our people could think or act, especially with their leadership shut up in a motel with Hubert Humphrey and Walter Reuther. The credentials committee accepted Corman's proposal and appointed Ed King and me to represent the MFDP at the convention with two votes at large.

I was genuinely sorry that Johnson had not offered us a more favorable compromise, because it is difficult to refuse to cooperate with the president of the United States. Our delegation discussed the business of the two seats at large and the fact that they meant nothing. The two votes were not from Mississippi; they were two votes in addition to the total votes of the convention and could have little bearing on the courses taken by the convention. If we had even been offered two of the official Mississippi votes, possibly we could have persuaded our delegates to accept. Or even if they had offered us no votes and then refused to give votes to the regular Mississippi delegation, maybe we would have found that acceptable. But we couldn't accept a compromise that didn't at least place us on an equal footing with the all-white regular delegation from our state.

While we were meeting with Humphrey and Reuther, our delegation back at the church was also becoming extremely bitter about what they were hearing. They were being told that their leaders had accepted the compromise. They felt that we were selling them out as well as the people back in Mississippi that we were supposed to be representing. The feeling against the president was particularly bitter, and the delegates were saying that if he had stayed out of it, we would have won the seats.

They remembered a meeting in Jackson prior to Atlantic City, where Rauh had assured us that our chances were good as long as President Johnson didn't become involved. He had become involved, to our detriment, and this translated into his being against our delegation and therefore against the things we were seeking for the black people of Mississippi. Most of the delegates felt we should be offered Congresswoman Green's proposal that both delegations take a loyalty oath and that the vote be divided among those who signed it. None of the delegates cared about being "honored guests"; they felt that the two at-large votes were unacceptable; and, above all, they would not have the president make "glowing references" to us in his acceptance speech.

When we got back to the church after the meeting with Humphrey and Reuther, we found most of the delegates furious over the rumors. By then, we had gotten word of the proposal that the credentials committee had accepted, and there wasn't a cool head in the delegation. There was a general demand to vote that very minute and reject the compromise, but I felt strongly that we should wait until we cooled down a bit. Bob Moses and Ed King argued about this, and I felt that we should wait and let the delegation hear the opinions of Dr. King, Roy Wilkins, Bayard Rustin, James Farmer, people who had been working for our goals since the beginning. They had helped gain the support that we did have, and it didn't seem ethical or sensible to cross them off our list at the very moment when their judgment was most needed. Moses would listen to none of this. He had always been one of the coolest people working in Mississippi—no matter what danger he faced, he remained collected and reasonable. But he seemed a different person that day. I had never imagined that he could be so irreconcilably opposed to postponing a decision until calmer heads might prevail. I realized that he felt we had been double-crossed—just a repeat of Mississippi treatment—but I believe what upset him the most was that our delegation had been persuaded that their leaders, including Moses himself, had been in on the double-crossing.

Emotions were pitched high, and radio and television reports were convincing the delegation further that President Johnson and the credentials committee had sold them out. Moses knew that the delegation would reject the proposal if an immediate vote was taken. We voted, and about seventy percent of the delegation voted against the compromise.

While this frenzied meeting was going on, some of us were aware that there was still a chance that we could be seated. After the credentials committee accepted the compromise, we had several hours to round up eleven members of the committee who would be willing to sign a minority report calling for the seating of our delegation. Then we could get the issue to the convention floor. Seventeen or eighteen committee members had at one time committed themselves to signing such a minority report if it became necessary. But those people who had been so keen on our being seated, no matter what, were not to be found that afternoon. Obviously, they had gotten word from the convention managers that the president didn't want the issue aired publicly any more—that he didn't wanted us seated in place of the regular Mississippi delegation. The credentials committee had been called early—without notice. Humphrey and Reuther were in charge of keeping the MFDP leaders out of commission for several hours. Everything was moving smoothly for the powers behind the Democratic National Convention, and it appeared that even the people we considered our strongest allies had been set against us.

We were able to find nine members willing to sign a minority report, but it was impossible to find the two more necessary to get the report to the floor. It was confusing, because several members had contacted us who might have signed but had been told that we had accepted the compromise. When the deadline for the filing of the report had passed, we were still looking high and low for our "friends." I will always resent the underhanded manner in which the White House handled the entire affair, and calling it "just politics" does not excuse the people involved. For example, Charles Diggs, a longtime friend of mine who had been willing to sign the report, was not to be found. He had turned out to be a party man. When I saw him several hours later, I didn't ask him where he had been, because I didn't want to embarrass him, and he didn't offer any explanation or apology. Perhaps this shows that the very best kind of people can become so much a part of the machine that they can only think in terms of the party's welfare. Then it becomes impossible for them to support anything which might cause difficulty within the party.

The convention met at eight-thirty Tuesday night and immediately approved the compromise proposed by the credentials committee. A voice vote was taken, which kept any of our "friends" from having to go on record with their underhanded cooperation with President Johnson. Moreover, I do not believe that a majority of the convention really voted for the proposal, because the southern voters were as much against it as the liberals who were still holding out for our best interests. The nays were much louder than the ayes, the way I heard it, but this doesn't matter with a chairman who hears what he wants to hear. Senator John Pastore was the chairman, and he had probably been in on much of the planning that went into settling the dispute. Anyway, our hopes of being seated were quashed.

Our delegation members were rallying in front of the convention hall, and, shortly after the credentials committee proposal was accepted, I spoke to the group and tried to explain that it was time to approach the situation positively—that we couldn't just get mad and sing songs. I tried to convince them that we should be thankful that we had come as far as we had and that this was not the time to stop. I said that the national spotlight was on us and that we ought to keep it there as long as possible. Other civil rights groups, far more radical, were threatening to break up the convention with acts of civil disobedience. We needed to keep the publicity with us and our goals, particularly since the newsmen gravitated towards us wherever we went.

After I spoke to the group, we tried to get into the convention hall, but the guards stopped us. No reason was given. Each delegate had full credentials for admission that had been supplied by Senator Wayne Morse, who had been advising us and speaking at our street rallies. As we stood there asking the guards why we couldn't be admitted, we noticed that people were getting in at other entrances. We decided to split up into groups of five and approach different gates, and, if others got in, we would, too. After we stationed our groups at different entrances, the guards continued to refuse us admittance. People were beginning to pile up at the ends of our lines, and finally word came from somewhere that we were to be admitted. I learned later that this little mess was the result of a poor decision on the part of the guards, who had decided that we were going to storm the convention.

From the beginning of the convention, neither the MFDP nor the regular delegation had been allowed to occupy the seats in the Mississippi section of the convention floor. Our delegation had made no attempt to occupy them—we had allowed them to stand empty as a symbol to us of the vacancy of Mississippi politics. But on Tuesday, the convention decided that members of the regular delegation would be seated if they signed the loyalty oath and that none of us would be seated. It seemed that a protest was in order. We decided to show our dissatisfaction by claiming the seats under the Mississippi banner, which we thought would be the best way to maintain the attention of the national press. When we got onto the floor, the seats were still vacant, so we claimed them. No one had told us we could not sit there, and we had a greater right to them than anyone else in Atlantic City. I cannot speak for the other members of our delegation, but if the sergeant at arms had asked me to vacate my seat, I would have done so immediately. But he did not, and I sat there through the remaining part of the session.

Our delegation met at ten o'clock Wednesday morning at the Union Temple Baptist Church to discuss whether we should reconsider our rejection of the compromise. My main interest was still in having the delegation at least listen to Dr. King, Bayard Rustin, Roy Wilkins, and James Farmer. I knew there wasn't much chance of the delegation rescinding the rejection of the compromise, but we owed these men the common courtesy of listening to what they had to say. But many of the delegates were not interested in what I was saying, and this was the first time I saw a blind belligerence that later would come to typify for me the attitude of many SNCC leaders. At the time, I thought it was mainly a reaction to unfair treatment, but it blossomed into much more than that. Many of the delegates were voicing loudly the idea that white people everywhere were against them. I told them that I hoped they would be as tough on white people when they got back to Mississippi. The opposition to hearing Dr. King and the other leaders amounted to an outright kick in the face as far as I could tell, and I wouldn't have blamed King for completely losing interest in what we were doing. It was clear to me that we were not in a position to get on the bad side of anybody who was basically sympathetic with our goals. If we alienated these civil rights leaders who had helped us get this far, we would go back to Mississippi and have no one left to turn to for advice in national dealings in the future.

There were other reasons to reconsider our rejection of the compromise. Humphrey had suggested that we could possibly get a commitment for more civil rights legislation—maybe even a promise of administrative support for voting rights. But when I told that to the delegation, many of them still refused to budge an inch. Finally, after many exchanges, the delegation agreed to hear the national civil rights leaders and to reconsider the compromise proposal. The meeting was Wednesday afternoon, and Dr. King, James Farmer, Bayard Rustin, Senator Morse, and Bob Spike and Jack Pratt of the

196 *Atlantic City*

National Council of Churches, among others, came before us. All of them told the delegates that they had won a victory in the offer of the compromise and that we should accept. King told the group that it was the greatest decision that they would ever make and eventually would be felt around the world. The delegates expressed little reaction to all of this, and I suspected that they were not very impressed.

Then the opposition to the compromise gave their side. Bob Moses, Jim Forman, and other spokesmen from SNCC said that the delegation had been sold out. Rita Schwerner, wife of the murdered civil rights worker, supported the SNCC argument that the delegates should reject the compromise. The SNCC cadre was vehement in the rhetoric that later became typical of the Mississippi Freedom Democratic Party—that the political and economic systems of this country were no good and that the systems had to be replaced before any progress could be made and before an acceptable society could be attained. The national parties were no good and should be wiped away. But they never said what would replace the existing systems.

Most of the delegation felt that afternoon that the American system not only had betrayed us in Mississippi but was now doing the same thing at the convention in Atlantic City. Frustration was the main feeling, over having done all that was possible under the existing institutions and still getting nowhere. After the delegation reluctantly listened to the pleas of Dr. King and others, a vote was taken on the compromise offered by the credentials committee, and seventy percent opposed it—the same as the vote that been taken the day before.

For me, the SNCC ideas were frightening, because they were about something as foreign to the American system as white supremacy was. There we were, trying to do something about segregation and white supremacy, and some of us were proposing something that seemed incongruous with the American way of doing things.

Longtime SNCC workers were angrier than most of the other MFDP delegates, and the attitudes presented that day by the SNCC leaders represented the first concrete evidence of the ideological conflict between the more moderate NAACP leaders and the radical SNCC cadre. SNCC executive director Jim Forman asked the delegation why Ed King and I had been arbitrarily named as the delegates at large in the compromise. Forman told the group that if anyone was named it should have been Fannie Lou Hamer, the person who best represented the illiterate field Negroes of Mississippi. This was the beginning of the division that would come to characterize two distinct factions in the Mississippi freedom movement. It was a painful time.

In my estimation, the only workable answer to the overall problem of race goes back to the ethic of love, which means forgiveness. It erases the hostilities of the past and calls on man to embrace his brother, although his brother has wronged him. Those who are in positions of leadership must insist on this if they expect a smooth transition through the times of adjustment which we face. We should make certain that we are never guilty of the wrongs attributable to the white supremacists.

But when it comes to politics, love often isn't the best formula. My idea of the MFDP in the beginning was that it would be a real political party—a party of inclusion for labor organizations and liberal whites, as well as for much of the black population. I had hoped that we could supplant the old-guard Democratic Party in Mississippi. I had also hoped that the MFDP would be able to maintain their political activities and their civil rights work separately. I felt that each individual could continue civil rights activity under the banner of SNCC or the NAACP—or whatever group they chose—and at the same time have an interest in a unified MFDP. This didn't work.

In retrospect, I think we did the best we could at the Atlantic City convention, and I lost no personal respect for the people who had tried to help us. They gave us what President Johnson would allow. We did all we could do and learned a great deal about the way things work up in the world of high-level politics—heartbreak and all.

Chapter 15

From Freedom to Politics

Aaron Henry's oral history ends in 1964. In this chapter he relates some of his feelings about the deep changes in the Mississippi freedom movement and indicates his determination to build a representative Democratic Party, beginning with the seating of the Loyalist delegation at the 1968 convention in Chicago.

Following the August 1964 challenge in Atlantic City, the organizations were in disarray. Disappointment, disillusionment, and disenchantment were the order of the day. Leaders and others who had been the backbone of the movement searched for reasons and pointed fingers in various directions. Aaron Henry passionately expressed his own doubts, questions, and attempts at answers in his musings when he was back in Mississippi in the fall of 1964. He began to see the complications resulting from differences in generations, conflicts in organizational approaches, and distinctions among classes. In the heat of the movement, from 1960 until 1964, the difficulties had not been so apparent.

The problem of broadening ideological differences between the NAACP and SNCC had been brewing even before Atlantic City. It was natural that followers of one group would develop strong feelings about followers of the other. During the summer of 1964, the SNCC youngsters openly criticized the NAACP for our judicial approach to many problems. The NAACP's attempts to work things out through the courts took a long time, and SNCC people felt it was ridiculous to wait so long. I still don't know exactly what they would have done instead. The difficulty was very much like the problems that arise in a home between children and parents. A boy of eighteen often thinks his father is the biggest fool in the world. By the time the boy is twenty-five, he realizes that either he was the fool or his father had learned lots in the meantime.

Basically, it involved two different approaches. The NAACP believed in thorough and basic gains—all within the framework of the law—while SNCC believed in snatching as much as possible at any time. For this reason, SNCC spokesmen felt that the NAACP was too much a part of the existing power structure—too willing to accommodate, too willing to compromise with the white forces, and not in a big enough hurry to gain the rights that we knew were ours and were determined to have. The NAACP said that SNCC was a group of young upstarts not even dry behind the ears who didn't know what they were doing.

My personal upbringing and my instincts made it natural for me to lean toward the NAACP way of thinking, possibly because, after we left the plantation, I was reared in a relatively middle-class home. I felt that the NAACP way of achieving goals was within the American framework and that the ends achieved were much more substantial than would be gained by a more radical approach. In most ways the goals of both groups were the same—justice for blacks in the South and the opportunity to exercise our rights as American citizens.

There is no question that SNCC's radicalism did some good for black people in Mississippi. SNCC workers were able to gain close ties with many of the state's most impoverished. Along with devoting energy to giving immediate aid to people, SNCC also attempted political indoctrination. It was quite appealing to a poverty-stricken field Negro to be told that he might be a senator some day. The SNCC workers motivated a large number of illiterate Mississippi Negroes to become conscious of what was going on around them politically and economically and to assert themselves to improve their lives.

But sometimes, I felt that SNCC wanted to see the Negro in political and economic supremacy in the South—a situation which would be precisely equal to the system of white supremacy. In small meetings and personal conversations with SNCC advocates, I sometimes got this feeling, and often their philosophy zoomed off into that nebulous paradise that they declined to define. Once we got beyond the basic achievement of rights, I was left far behind. Whenever I asked what they would put in place of basic American institutions, they never seemed to have the answer.

But while I agreed with much of the criticism directed toward SNCC, I knew that the suggestion that it was communist-inspired and directed had no foundation. People who say this are confusing a new radicalism with an old one. I have been called a communist myself and have been investigated by state groups and the FBI—to no avail. I feel certain that I have never met a communist. The word has been so misused, and I am thankful that the things that segregationists identify as communistic are actually far removed from the ideology. If the rights we seek are communistic, then I am afraid we would all be communists. But we are fortunate in that our own Constitution grants us those rights—at least on paper.

At the Atlantic City convention, I got the first crystal-clear idea that SNCC was distancing itself from our political goals, and I began to see that the MFDP was organized pretty strongly along those lines as well. White Mississippians needed to take a close look at this. Perhaps one good effect of the SNCC philosophy was that it caused many moderate whites to join forces with more moderate civil rights groups. Whites came to see that they were going to have to deal with someone, and they realized that the voices of the NAACP and others were preferable to those of SNCC radicals. The best way to squash radical ideology was to grant blacks the basic rights of American citizenship. As basic rights were gained, the SNCC revolutionary fervor would subside.

SNCC spokesmen believed that Mrs. Hamer was the symbol of the Mississippi black sharecropper, and this was probably true, but they also said this was why she was the most qualified to speak for the black masses in the state. Was their reasoning that, once Mrs. Hamer became formally educated or trained in the workings of representative government, she would no longer be qualified to speak for the masses or to truly represent them? They were saying that the downtrodden masses must be represented in a democratic government by their own kind of people and they must be represented now! If this was impossible under the existing system, then the system was wrong and must be abolished and reconstructed along different political lines. In a way, this is not unlike the idea of the old Populist parties, when members believed that "the people"—citizens who were at the bottom of every social and economic scale—should have as major a voice in running the government as the educated. This theory rules out the value of education, and, if one sustains the theory, it practically insists upon a status quo of ignorance.

The radical attitude that developed during the national convention insisted that the abolition of middle-class institutions must take place before decent rights for the masses could be achieved. SNCC spokesmen, particularly Bob Moses, reasoned that as long as the upper and middle class held the wealth of the country, the poor people would never get their share. If full political participation could be gained for the masses on the bottom, they eventually could wrench this wealth through political means, and then the wealth could be distributed equally. This thinking did not emerge from the cotton fields of Mississippi. These were theories brought into the state by various highly educated people who came here and lived and worked with the people for a short period of time. It was a new breed of radical thinking, and it is likely that some of the philosophers and political scientists who came here viewed Mississippi as a perfect testing ground for their ideas—almost a test-tube situation, where they had half a million subjects to work with. Of course, the philosophies were not presented to the masses in ideological terms—the masses were simply offered the possibility of gaining the comforts of the middle class, which is the same old cycle.

Compared to the total number of Mississippi blacks, those in the middle class were few. However, middle-class blacks have had an influence far disproportionate to their number. Thousands of Negroes who labored on the Delta plantations and lived in poverty in the towns and cities looked up to those few of their race who had somehow been able to overcome the disadvantages. I didn't believe that Mississippi Negroes wanted to destroy the middle class but rather to join it and be like them, to share the comforts offered by that status. It meant having a position of respect, a good paid-for car, a decent house, running water, and the means to give something better to their children. Combining the black middle class and those who respected them, you covered the vast majority of blacks in this state. Blacks who would have sided with SNCC, if ever there was a division between the two philosophies, were the ones who had been helped by SNCC and felt some personal obligation. Or, in other cases, it might be a reaction to the

American system as manifested in Mississippi. In no case would it be near a majority of Mississippi Negro citizens.

The question for me lurking in the later SNCC philosophy was what would replace middle-class institutions once they were destroyed. They had no program outlined. One situation just fell into another, and they seemed to create lofty principles and ideals to support whatever position they took. But when they took step one, they weren't sure where they would be in step three and hadn't the slightest notion where step six might leave them. In the NAACP we tried to plan everything as carefully as possible. A simple comparison between SNCC and the NAACP might be made on the way we went to jail. When someone in the NAACP was jailed, he knew that he would immediately be released on bond, because he had been certain before he was incarcerated that enough money was on hand. But in SNCC they purposefully got thrown in jail and then started worrying about where bond money would come from.

By August of 1964, the SNCC forces had already given the MFDP an entirely different coloration from what was originally intended. I listened long and hard to the philosophies that emerged in connection with Atlantic City—I had to, because in the early days of COFO, in spite of my NAACP background, I welcomed and embraced everyone. But the MFDP was rapidly becoming an active civil rights organization in itself, cutting off the possibility of the party becoming a coalition which could combine forces with other liberal groups and win elections. Before long the rigid SNCC philosophy became so pervasive within the MFDP that the two organizations were virtually indistinguishable.

Naturally, this drove away many potential allies in the white and black communities who might otherwise have been interested in the MFDP. The MFDP lost a good opportunity to become the nucleus of a new Democratic Party in Mississippi.

Whatever disillusionment Henry may have felt in connection with Atlantic City, his belief in and loyalty to the national democratic Party did not waver. He was convinced that the election of Republican Barry Goldwater to the presidency in the November 1964 election would be a disaster, and, at Hubert Humphrey's request, he and

Fannie Lou Hamer campaigned vigorously all over the country for the Johnson-Humphrey Democratic ticket. Also, for some who had been to Atlantic City, there remained the promise of better things at the 1968 Democratic convention in Chicago. The national Democratic Party had set up a special Equal Rights Committee to write rules that would insure the selection of future state delegations without regard to race. It was chaired by former Pennsylvania governor David Lawrence, and, after his death, by New Jersey governor Richard Hughes. For the next four years, Henry worked tirelessly to form a coalition that would choose a truly representative delegation for seating at the Chicago convention.

By 1968 we had amassed a greater mixture of people in Democratic Party politics in Mississippi—the AFL-CIO, NAACP, Young Democrats, the black Prince Hall Masons, MFDP, and the black Mississippi Teachers Association—all these units working together, yet no one had to reject their own position. Unite on some things and do your own thing on the side. We also had a vote equity distribution in this cross section of the population to present to the national credentials committee of the Democratic Party. We made a tactical decision that it was better to go to Chicago as the Democratic Party of Mississippi. It was the press who tagged us "Loyalists"—meaning that we were loyal to the national Democratic Party. And the MFDP was as much a part of that unit as any of the other groups. MFDP was like a gadfly to the Loyalists. It pushes you, whizzes by, says "move," but it had no separate party structure or meetings. MFDP was just accepted as a unit within the party. Our constituents included Fannie Lou Hamer, Reverend Harry Bowie, Unita Blackwell, and Bob Clark.

The recognition of our Loyalist Party at the 1968 convention meant more politically than civil rights wise. The Hughes committee document gave substance to the philosophy that there is no such thing as legal fruit from an illegal tree—that is, the whole party has to be right for any part of it to be right. George McGovern extended that further so that the national party did not rely upon the governor of the state to implement the rules and regulation of the party. It depends upon the party executives from each state—the chair and the democratic committeemen and committeewomen to make sure the rules of reform are carried out. We had tremendous assistance from the Democratic National Committee in drafting our documents of procedure. The DNC is the unit that operates the party during the four years between conventions. It has four commissions, and we had at least one person on every commission, mainly because Senator Fred Harris understood what novices we were—that we needed support and opportunity to learn what the party was about. Mississippi was the only state in the nation that had somebody on every commission within the DNC.

I was reminded again in Chicago of the disparity of justice. I knew it in 1963 when the white kids came and started going to jail and being hit, hell, we had FBI agents coming out of our ears. The conclusion had to be that the system doesn't respond unless a white American is being victimized. Same thing at the Democratic National Convention in Chicago. Forget the march from Selma, the Meredith March, and many more—you never heard a cry and uproar over that violence, but you sure heard it in Chicago because it was white kids out there in the park getting their heads beat. I recall an action of mine at that convention that I regret to some degree. A white fellow came down to our Mississippi section and said, "Do you mean to just sit here and let those kids up in the park get whipped?" We'd been fighting to get into the convention since 1964, and I said, "What's that got to do with us?" "Mississippi ought to lead a walkout," he said. "Man, you are crazy as hell. It's our first time here after a long battle. Do you think we're going to walk out now? And look—black kids have been getting their heads beat all these years and you white folks ain't said nothing. If anybody needs to lead a walkout, you white folks are up, because I am staying right here. We're the Mississippi delegation, I'm the chairman, and get out!" That was cruel, but it was a very subjective and emotional reaction, and I'm sorry I responded to him so harshly. If I could find that fellow again, I would apologize to him, even though most whites are still not sensitive to black victimization.

So Chicago was a victory in many ways. We were proud that our work in the 1964 challenge laid the foundation for the 1968 challenge to the old-guard Georgia Democratic delegation. We got to vote to seat Julian Bond and his group in Chicago—the only southerners to do it. At the same time, Chicago was sad, because the Vietnam war and the demonstrations and arrests became the reality, and the fights over the presidential candidates we supported divided us. The unity of our purpose and goal for justice and equality for black people was fragmented.

Chapter 16

Who He Was

Oral history excerpts in this chapter are intended to give further insight into the life of Aaron Henry. Some of the people interviewed knew him before 1968 and talk about their work or contact with him during that period. Others elucidate his activities in the years following 1968 until his death in 1997.

It is important to note that before the 1964 Atlantic City convention, Henry's leadership was accepted almost without question by organizations and individuals alike in Mississippi. His feelings of alienation from SNCC and MFDP are apparent in his own words in previous chapters, and there is no question that some people in both groups felt betrayed by his actions at the 1964 convention. Because of his role in accepting the compromise offered there, his commitment to changing "movement" politics into coalition politics, and his part in the Head Start and other battles over federal programs for the state, he was called "defector" and "Uncle Tom." Critics have also said that his work as an elected official in the state legislature was minimal, and some have questioned his holding on so long as chair of the state NAACP.

The anecdotal material in the interviews sheds light on some of the controversies. It has been compiled from more than twenty-five interviews that I conducted between January 1997 and January 1999. I hope that these stories will show not only what Aaron Henry did but also who he was.

Not Lucky—Blessed

Rebecca Henry lives in Clarksdale, Mississippi. She is the only child of Aaron Henry and Noelle Michael Henry. She runs a gift shop called Noelle's Flowers and More.

My mama worked in the Methodist Church during the summer, and her job was to travel around and get vacation Bible schools started. When she came to Clarksdale, in the late forties, she stayed with my grandmother, Mattie Henry. Mattie asked her for a picture, and the next thing Mama knew, Daddy was writing her from wherever he was stationed, telling her when they were getting married. So everybody met Mama before Daddy did—he had never laid eyes on her. He wrote her that he would finish the service, finish school, and then they would marry.

Noelle Michael was born and reared in Jackson. She had seven sisters and two brothers. She was actually named Christmas, because she was born on December 25. Children teased her, and in third grade, she changed to "Noelle" when a teacher told her it was French for Christmas. She graduated from Jackson State, and I believe she was one of the teachers at the Smith Robertson school in Jackson. It's a museum now, and there's a picture of some of the teachers on a bulletin board just as you come in. She's the prettiest woman in the picture—Noelle Michael.

My mother didn't have a lot of friends in Clarksdale, because people were often jealous and envious and didn't like to see folks get ahead. They tried to stay in folks' business. Now there were some people who were really good to her and would look out for her, which was important with her diabetes and congestive heart failure. And with being by herself a lot someone would come over and stay with her. Then when I lived in Jackson, she would come down to see me and her four sisters who were living there at the time. When I was working in West Point, she would come to visit, but for the most part she would be by herself.

Mama read a good bit, and she was a strong believer in God. She taught school in Coahoma County eleven years until she was fired because of Daddy's civil rights activities. Since he worked for himself at the drugstore, they couldn't touch him, so they fired her. Then when the antipoverty programs started, she worked in several of those until she retired. After that and before her health got bad, she was the top volunteer at the hospital in Clarksdale—the auxiliary where they had the gift shop and would serve coffee and distribute the mail to patients. She got awards several years for having the most volunteer hours. And she could really raise funds—she could charm folks out of their money for the church building fund or for Rust College, a United Methodist school and my alma mater.

Now, I didn't discuss much with Mama or Daddy my feelings about him not being there for me. I would ask why do you have to be gone so much, and he would tell me, "I'm doing this for you and all the other children." Quite a conversation-stopper. And that's all well and good, but when you want your daddy to do something, you want him to be doing it for you alone. Still, I was proud of him. I remember when he was first elected state NAACP president. I couldn't sing and he couldn't sing, but Vera Pigee, NAACP youth advisor, and Wilma Jones, president of the youth council, and I, the treasurer, were at a church in some town every Sunday God sent, teaching them to sing "We Shall Overcome." So I was proud of him, but I did miss out on so much.

Daddy was a believer. He went to Xavier, a Catholic university, and was active in the United Haven Methodist Church, and we always had the Bible in the house. You know that was one of the only books that a lot of people had. I don't know if he actually studied the Bible, because for the most part he was not around. He makes references to God and Christ, but with us, and even with his brothers and sisters, when he was grown, his relationships and his religion were civil rights and politics.

I resented that when I was little and still do—big time—always getting somebody else to take us places, and, at my high school graduation, we had marched in and everybody was sitting down and my daddy was not there. He finally did get there, but for the things that other kids' daddies did with them, he wasn't around. We had one family vacation in 1961. I was ten years old. And that was the first. We went to St. Louis to see my daddy's sisters, Aunt Thelma and Aunt Ethel Mae, and even then all these people came around to see him. We went to Chicago, Illinois, and to Grand Rapids to see more relatives, but he would call friends, and they'd come and get him, so we still didn't do things together.

My mother didn't seem to resent him being away all the time. You would have to know my mother to understand. She was the most cooperative person I have ever known. Because had it been me or most other women, we would have been long gone. But he told my mama that when he was in the service and saw black people being treated so bad he had promised the Lord that if

He let him live to come home, he would spend his days working for his people. So he told her that, and she told me, "Well, that was a promise that he made to God." And I would say, "Yeah, but he's done enough now. The Lord will let him slide on by." I needed a daddy and my mama needed a husband.

If it hadn't been for her, he would not have been able to do all that he did. She was there, she was the one that answered the phone threats when they said "we're going to kill you" and "we're going to throw a bomb and your man won't be coming home." She was the one that lost her job because of his activities. She was the one that had to sacrifice. She was the one that stayed there and had to go through all that and still remain good-natured. Because I was an absolute wreck. I didn't answer the telephone for years—I was just that nervous. Her husband was never there to do things that she needed him to do. Well, she loved him a lot, and people don't understand what her contribution was. Daddy wasn't lucky in having Mama—he was blessed.

I didn't understand a lot of things until after she died. She would talk to me, but I just didn't realize all that she was going through. You've got a husband, but you have to get used to somebody else doing for you, because he's got places to go and things to do. When I really got upset with Daddy—but he never knew it—was when Mama was in a coma before she died. She stayed there for eight weeks down in Jackson. And Daddy had an NAACP board meeting in the Bahamas, and he told me to come to Jackson and stay with her while he was gone. I know that was his life, but just the idea of my mama laying there in a coma, us not knowing when her last days would be, and he goes to the Bahamas for a meeting. Now, really.

I was thirteen when things started heating up during 1964 Freedom Summer. Mama would send me to Jackson to stay with my aunts and grandmama, because she said Daddy would be going to jail and didn't want me to be in jail, too. When I was at home, there were always students there. I didn't know who was who, but I would think, "Oh, my God, another one." And we had to be careful about where we went, what we did, what we said, because we didn't want anybody to shoot us. It's a wonder I'm not a basket case. And there were always so many other things that kids were doing that I couldn't because of his visibility and position.

Daddy was a forgiving man—he forgave when he didn't need to and held on to what he didn't need to hold on to. Some people did some heartbreaking things to him, and he'd just forgive them when everyone else was pitching a fit—"why did you bother with him or her?" And he would say, "You keep the peace for the cause." Whatever they did to him—he put it behind him and drove on as helpful and doing just as much as he could as ever. I'd be ready to tell them where to go. I know you are supposed to forgive, but it seemed like people that treated him the worst are the ones he treated the best. And it wasn't just a political thing, because even when I would go on about how somebody had done me wrong, he would jump all over me. That's one thing I didn't take after him. My mama told me I was going to hell because I don't forgive. I hold things in. I'm getting better as I mature, but there was a time—no matter who you are—if you did something to me, I was going to get you. People would do him so bad—he'd just go right on and then they'd call him and he'd still call them back. He always got the big picture—not holding grudges—not petty—and he tried to teach me that. He was also very sensitive, in spite of his ability to go on, and sometimes he came off as arrogant—but it was a shield. I know when he lost that election for the legislature a few years ago—it did something to him way down deep. He lost by such a few votes, and we heard that the person who ran against him was paid by the white community to run. And although he never would say it, I saw the decline. He's a Cancer—born in July—and, like that crab who has a hard shell, it's hard to get through, but you are hurting inside and don't show it much.

That Wrongs Be Made Right

Charles Young, lifelong friend of Aaron Henry and NAACP activist, lives in Meridian, Mississippi, and is a member of the state legislature.

My father, my grandfather, and his brothers were active in black economics. They started an organization called the Holbrook Benevolent Association to help black people have access to hospital facilities and, in some cases, an opportunity for a decent burial. They built one of the major buildings in Meridian to house these activities.

Because of this interest in medical facilities, pharmacy products, health care, my father had established contact with Aaron Henry even before I met him. In 1954, I went to the Fourth Street Drug Store selling hair care products. I had heard Daddy talk about the drugstore and the pharmacist there, and of course they knew each other through the NAACP. My father and my uncle were pioneers of the NAACP here in Meridian as far back as 1931. Another NAACP connection was through C. R. Darden, our state president in the early years, because he was from Meridian.

Aaron and I hit it off immediately. Like him, I was brought up believing that we needed to be free, and my parents and my grandparents were sticklers for standing up for what you believed in. After Aaron got elected president of the Clarksdale NAACP and began getting involved in state activities in the fifties, he would call and say we needed to be here or there and we needed to do this or that. Then when Aaron welcomed Bob Moses and the young SNCC workers and CORE and SCLC in the early sixties, he would call more than ever and tell us what we needed to do. He knew there were certain black people like my family that were independent enough to not bow to white pressure. He was one of the ones that promoted and organized COFO here in Meridian, because he always felt that there was a place and a need for the different organizations. I remember one day when Aaron called to tell me that a young white volunteer named Andrew Goodman was coming our way. Goodman went straight to the COFO office. I never did see him when he got here. He got together with James Chaney and Mickey Schwerner, and they went to Philadelphia, Mississippi. When they didn't get back by the prescribed time, Sue Brown, who was working in the COFO office, called me. When our contacts couldn't find out anything, we were so worried and later called the FBI, who said that they could not do anything until after seventy-two hours had passed. We told them that within seventy-two hours, they'd be dead. And they were, and it was the saddest thing for our Meridian movement and for Aaron, who knew Andrew Goodman's parents.

From 1964 on our major thrust was in politics. We had been working with the Freedom Democratic Party, but things were pretty confused after Atlantic City, and we began working with a group called the Mississippi Democratic Conference, which included Claude Ramsey from the AFL-CIO and Tom Knight and Charles Evers and several others. We were trying to open the doors in the local Democratic Party structure. Aaron loved the party dearly, and he was not organizing for blacks alone. He was equally concerned about everybody. He wanted Native Americans to be involved and worked with a Choctaw named Beasley Denson, and Phillip Martin, a tribal chief in Philadelphia, Mississippi.

Aaron knew that the political arena could change the conditions of human beings. He reminded us often that one stroke of the pen of the Supreme Court and we could be back where we were in the nineteen sixties. You can see some of that taking place today. Aaron's activities in political organizing led us to the convention in Chicago, led us to the convention in Miami, led us to the convention in New York.

At the Miami convention in 1972, I came up with the idea of having a vice-chair of the convention. Aaron was very supportive of that concept and went to Hubert Humphrey and George McGovern to sell it. They agreed to buy the concept if we would help find a person that would represent all of us. So Fannie Lou Hamer and I worked diligently, and I finally called my sister in California, and she suggested a young lady by the name of Yvonne Burke. I called Yvonne and she said she would love to do it. I told her not to tarry, to catch a plane and get to Miami right away. She caught the plane, was introduced from the platform of the Democratic National Convention, and was elected vice-chair.

Now, it was my responsibility to be in charge of some activities at those conventions, including the number of people that could be involved on the convention floor. Aaron's philosophy was that the more people that could be exposed to the convention floor, the better off we would be and the more support we would get back home. At both the New York and Miami conventions, we operated what we called the "underground railroad," which was our way of getting all of our people who weren't delegates or alternates onto the convention floor for a while. So you can see the kind of activities that Aaron did within the party.

Aaron and I both got elected to the state legislature in 1979. Those were some struggling years, and probably not the time of his greatest contribution. He sometimes didn't go to committee meetings, and he was more interested in making sure legislators knew the historical context or background on some of the bills or issues they were discussing—still interested that wrongs be made right. He was active on the Ways and Means Committee, and he was always pushing measures that boosted educational opportunities, but he just wasn't nearly as aggressive as he had been. For most of his life, he kept a schedule that would kill a horse, but his health began declining, and you could tell he was feeling weaker and weaker. I went to see him in the hospital, and it almost felt like he was ready to go. At the funeral, I refused to view him, because I have an image of Aaron in my heart that I want to keep. I just appreciate God letting me live during the era when I could work with a person like Aaron Henry.

Staying the Course

Robert Smith, a native Mississippian, graduated from Tougaloo College, completed his medical training out of state, and returned home in 1962. He was a key figure in the establishment of the Medical Committee for Human Rights. He lives in Jackson.

I was a student at Tougaloo College in 1953 when I first met Aaron. He and a handful of other black leaders like Dr. Emmett Stringer, Dr. A. H. McCoy, and Reverend R. L. T. Smith would come out, invited by Dr. Ernst Borinski, who used to conduct social science forums. He was white, and our college president, Sam Warren, was a white Quaker. Tougaloo was United Church of Christ; it was known for its liberal policies, and it always kept a close connection with the Quakers.

Aaron also came to learn and to be educated himself and to take a breath of fresh air. Tougaloo at that point was one of the few places in the state where these kinds of social science forums would take place. They weren't only about race. They were about international affairs, domestic affairs, education, the whole gamut of human endeavor.

When I attended Tougaloo College, it was the only school open to blacks in the state that promoted itself as having a formal pre-health program. Alcorn, a state supported college, had previously trained physicians, but funds were cut, and state schools no longer trained black physicians. After the 1954 *Brown* decision, the mid and late 1950s brought the Emmett Till murder and other acts of violence as well as the white Citizens' Council and passage of segregation laws in Mississippi. People who supported civil rights and the NAACP had their loans recalled, and doctors lost segregated hospital privileges. Many hospitals in the state were even more racist and would not admit black patients or physicians. The black patients and physicians were relegated to substandard facilities, and many of the physicians left the state. Obviously the national office of the NAACP recognized the problems we were experiencing in Mississippi because we were one of the few states that had a field secretary. Aaron was instrumental in bringing Medgar Evers to that position.

When I came back to Mississippi in 1962, I started attending mass meetings and got involved with Aaron and the movement. As one of the few trained black physicians, I became known as the physician to the movement, treating students and faculty, local blacks and liberal whites as well as volunteers from outside the state. There were so many significant health and social problems—poverty, hypertension, diabetes mellitus, high maternal and infant mortality, heart disease, and degenerative joint disease to name a few. Understandably, many of the blacks didn't trust their local white physicians.

Meanwhile, there were beatings and jailings by highway patrolmen, police—horror stories you wouldn't believe. We didn't have FBI investigations and reports and media coverage like we had later with Freedom Summer. As the movement began to grow, particularly in 1963, black physicians were still moving out of the state. A group of us, including Dr. James Anderson and Dr. A. Benjamin Britton, Jr., started organizing locally what became the southern Medical Committee for Human Rights. Aaron Henry was there for us, with any resources he could find and always carrying the NAACP banner and pointing out the need for care for civil rights workers. Improving medical services was where he and I worked most closely. We investigated and documented many cases where workers were being beaten. Most local physicians, black and white, were afraid to treat civil rights workers or to get involved in anything that would endanger their work or families. The Medical Committee for Human Rights brought in physicians from the outside to serve the SNCC and CORE kids and NAACP people throughout Freedom Summer.

Then the neighborhood health center movement came into being, which grew out of the civil rights movement, and Aaron played a vital part in that movement. That's one of his most significant contributions, as far as I'm concerned. You see, when the antipoverty program was founded in 1965, there was actually no provision for health services. Neighborhood health centers were left out. The only provisions for health care at that time came in the Head Start programs, and that came out of the deplorable conditions that the movement workers found among the children with whom they worked. So it was a blessing that people like Aaron and Medgar Evers and Amzie Moore welcomed Bob Moses and the young people, embraced their direct confrontational tactics, and resisted the old traditional NAACP approaches. They knew it was going to take something more dramatic to break Mississippi.

The suit against WLBT, the Jackson TV station, also brought major changes, and Aaron was a significant player. It goes back to 1963 when Aaron was running for governor in the freedom vote, and he and Reverend Smith went down to purchase time on the TV station. The station manager told them, "We don't sell niggers air time." And Aaron went back and reported this to some visiting lawyers and churchmen who insisted on going back to hear this for themselves. But it was not only that. All you had to do was listen to the evening news—if it said anything about black people at all, it was nigra this and nigra that, or that nigra Martin King—all the lingo of segregation. Anyway, WLBT's license was set aside. Thus, the suit filed by Aaron and Reverend Smith changed the airways of America. Reverend Ed King, Aaron's running mate for Lt. Governor and Chaplain of Tougaloo College, also participated in the TV suit, as did Dr. Dan Beittel, the President of Tougaloo. Dr. Beittel made arrangements with Everett Parker of the Communications Office of the United Church of Christ to develop the legal challenge to remove the license of the TV station. All over the country we saw stations bringing on black anchor persons and increasing black participation on television in programming, employment, and even as owners. These stations were fearful that they would also be sued and lose their licenses like WLBT.

Aaron's being elected chairman of the station's board was not without its problems. At that point, most whites and some blacks thought Aaron was not of the stature to sit on the board with them. It was people like me who pointed out that he was the man who had filed the suit in the first place. We also had to convince Aaron that it was not sinful to have some capitalistic ownership in the television station. It took a lot of doing, and I spent hours trying to "corrupt" him on that deal. He needed some corruption! He spent a childhood pinching pennies. For years we had struggled to raise money to send him to New York or Washington or wherever he had to go. He was used to living on a shoestring.

I think Aaron's leadership of the Mississippi Freedom Democratic Party and later in the Democratic Party and American politics, in general, is important. Blacks in the Democratic party were tokens all over this country, not only in Mississippi. Some people said Aaron sold out at the 1964 convention when MFDP was given only two seats in the delegation. I had friends on both sides, and looking back now, I know that SNCC and others could not have gotten us to Atlantic City by themselves. In his own style, Aaron did what had to be done to open the Democratic Party all over the country. He was the stabilizing influence in terms of activism and reality-based change. Aaron had no public relations agent. His name is not a household word. History cannot be revised. It will show the changes Aaron wove in the basic fiber of American society.

Despite character assassinations and threats on his family, despite lack of protection from the law, despite the Citizens' Council, Aaron had led the only remnants of activism that had existed in the state since the fifties. He was loyal to the NAACP in their dedication to education, voter registration and litigation. He and a few others, sometimes without the support of the organizations' leadership, moved to the front lines. Aaron Henry put his life on the line and was not afraid of dying. No, he was not afraid of dying, even after his best friend, Medgar Evers, was murdered, and even with the knowledge that his name was also on a hit list. (No question about it! I've seen the list. It is around.) If Mississippi had not become so much of a national focus, they would have picked off the people on the hit list one by one, with the sanction of the law and powers that be. Aaron knew this!

When the sixties came he moved along with the demands of the freedom movement. Later he fought for equal education, voting rights, health and housing services, child care, TV access, and basic social services, dealing with a racist society and willing to stay in his Mississippi for the battle. Doggedly hanging on, courageous, forgiving, able to work with people across many lines, he was not afraid to proceed as he saw new ways open. He stayed the course and laid the framework for significant change in Mississippi.

Aaron never forgot his past. He never got a blown-up sense of his own importance. He believed that right could, should and would triumph. He believed in the traditional institutional church and had his own deep abiding faith. He never gave up in spite of the horror and deaths. Aaron could have left, but he didn't. I have known many of the great people of the civil rights era, and I have heard that people such as Martin Luther King, Jr. only come along once in a century. I am not trying to compare greatness, but Aaron's work with the NAACP, his work with other activist organizations, his diplomacy, and his contributions to change and improving the quality of life of people is on par with anyone I was exposed to in the movement. The important thing is his making a difference in the lives of others! I feel that Aaron, maybe because of his long span of time or because he was a native leader here in Mississippi, exuded something that I am still looking for in a replacement. He believed with all his heart that change would come, even in the belly of the beast—his beloved Mississippi.

A True Believer

Ivanhoe Donaldson was a SNCC organizer in Mississippi in the 1960s. He is now a businessman in Washington, D. C.

I first met Doc Henry when I brought some supplies down from Michigan State around Christmas 1962. I knew that he was head of the state NAACP and that he was a pharmacist, and he turned out to be this wonderful human being—alive, full of energy, zest, combative, lots of courage, and guts. Doc was an impressive man by my twenty-one year old standard.

In 1964, when I went to the Atlantic City Convention as an organizer for the Mississippi Freedom Democratic Party delegation, at twenty-three, I believed our cause was righteous. We had done everything correctly to get our delegation seated. We crossed all the t's and dotted all the i's. We were going to be seated. I was a true believer. We had a lot of friends on the Credentials Committee, and what startled us was that we weren't defeated by our enemies, we got defeated by our friends. There are all these stories about who did what and what Lyndon Johnson was doing behind the scenes, but we didn't know all of that. We felt that if we could have gotten the issue of the seating of the MFDP to the convention floor, for a vote by all the delegates, we would have won. I still feel that today. The Committee short-circuited the democratic process—the very concept the MFDP was fighting for. Of course, it did lead to a restructuring of the Democratic Party rules under McGovern years later.

I never lost any respect for Doc, even after Atlantic City. There were obviously some deep divisions within the Mississippi community as well as the civil rights organizations. SNCC was particularly bitter about the compromises—trying to figure out what we should do next and what kind of direction that Doc was moving in. But I realized that Doc was always "locally driven." He had to live within the realities of his environment in Clarksdale and the state and do what he thought would be most effective. I don't think Doc ever lost any respect from anybody. We, the SNCC family, were disappointed that Doc supported the proposed compromise and probably angry at the time, but when all was said and done Doc was a committed partner in the freedom struggle. He was a hero in the civil rights movement, but Doc never had the intensity of affection that we felt for Fannie Lou Hamer. We looked at her as a SNCC person—after all she was one of our field secretaries, and we saw her as being really grass roots. Mrs. Hamer was a shining example of what SNCC was trying to organize: people who worked the land and then evolved into leadership roles in the community. But I never thought our advocating for Mrs. Hamer was based on class. Doc was just Doc, and disagreements and discussions were all in the family. Doc was already a leader, and SNCC often pooh-poohed existing leaders no matter how we loved them, even our own. I remember us thinking that to be chairman of SNCC was the worst thing and that the chairman's only purpose was so the outside world would have someone to talk to. Within SNCC, the chairman was just a co-equal; people didn't have to pay any attention to the chair.

After 1964, there was the expansion of white middle class people into our political world and the move to be seated at the '68 Democratic Convention as an interracial delegation became one of their major priorities, and Doc believed in that coalition. By that point in time, SNCC was no longer a viable political entity anyway. We felt that the 1964 convention experience required us to re-examine politics, in general, about where people were going. Look at the meaning of being told in Atlantic City that we would be given two seats-at-large and then told who was going to sit in them. Forget the whole concept of whether there should be any compromise here at all. We recognized that the compromise would take electoral politics in a direction that would not be grassroots-based. It would, in fact, be middle class driven. That is eventually, of course, what happened in Mississippi. The issue wasn't that there was anything wrong with the middle class, but if you are trying to build a grassroots organization you have got to give them the hooks to manipulate their own institutions. It is important for people to represent themselves as opposed to being spoken for and on behalf of by people who are more articulate, smarter, and already able to manipulate the political arena.

A Moment Of Grace

Patricia Derian was an activist in Jackson during the 1960s and was instrumental in the reshaping of the Democratic Party in Mississippi.

After Atlantic City, the Democratic Party, humiliated by its failure to respond to the Freedom Democrats, needed to show that though it had stumbled badly, it was intent on reform. To that end the National Committee passed a firm resolution requiring inclusion and ordering state parties to affirm their intent to conform. Our state party gave no assurance and in 1968 set out to select delegates as they always had.

A small biracial group of Democrats, in agreement with the national party, met several times. Somewhere in the early stages Charles Evers introduced me to the group. That's when Aaron and I, who had met several times, got to know each other. The group decided to participate in the existing party process from precinct to state convention. At the end it was obvious that the state party was not in compliance with national requirements. After we saw the results, our group then chose to act as the Democratic

Who He Was 219

Party of the State of Mississippi (it became known, familiarly, as the Loyalist party) and elect a delegation the right way.

Our group met endlessly. We had to decide how we would meet the national mandate. Everybody was keen on having the delegation half black and half white. There was some tension when I added that it should also be half male and half female. Most of the men found this disconcerting . . . in the way that they might have reacted if I'd dropped a bomb in the room. But, if you're going to be fair you can't add women the way the Regulars did . . . most of those women were not only all white, but widows or wives of big donors or other male delegates.

Aaron and I had quite a few, somewhat heated discussions about it, and at first he just couldn't understand why I wanted to complicate things. However, the way Aaron approached discord was to smooth things over. His position was that it was not the person you had to fight, it is the idea you're trying to get into action. He was as philosophically oriented as anyone I ever knew.

He knew how life ought to be. His high standards were interspersed with sweet maudlin poems, songs and quotations from Tennyson to Irish blessings which underlined his vision of life as it should be. We "climbed Jacob's ladder" a thousand times. So there we were dealing with a philosopher always in search of a just democracy—the idea of the country. That's what made him so brave . . . a rock hard commitment to freedom and justice.

Aaron finally got the message about the women. It was like turning on a light bulb—total identification: what pertained to discrimination against black people pertained to women as well. In any case, women were half the delegation when we went to the convention.

Rules were decided, the national party was notified, and the entire delegate selection process was repeated from precinct through state convention. Delegates, co-chairmen, and national committee members were elected. Aaron and Hodding Carter (now my husband) were co-chairs of the delegation; Charles Evers and I, the national committee members. The Regulars tried to get the seats. They sued us in Federal court and lost. Off we went to make our case to the party, where the judge said it should be made. And after a dramatic presentation before the credentials committee, the challenging "Loyalists" won the Mississippi seats. A wonderful moment that still satisfies these 31 years later. We were in Chicago!

At some point between the credentials decision (which had astounded an outraged, discredited, and used-to-be/would-have-been Mississippi delegation) and the start of the convention, Aaron, Hodding, Oscar Carr, Charles, and I were invited to meet with Hubert Humphrey and Orville Freeman. Doug Wynn, from the Delta, who was working for Hubert, was also there, anxious and trying to keep us all in a group.

Our little knot of victorious pols had been standing by the hotel elevators on a floor of private meeting rooms, waiting for someone to show us the meeting place. Rarely, some exceptionally remote person would appear to say we'd have to wait. We had been delighted to receive the invitation. Hubert was a longtime and strong supporter of integration efforts in Mississippi. After 30 or 40 minutes our delight began to fade. Charles Evers and I, neither of us patient waiters, were commenting on the topic of discourtesy and threatening in annoyed and stern tones to leave. Wynn's anxiety rose and nearly everyone looked uneasy as we staged a dialogue of things that were polite and right and things which weren't.

We waited about an hour and Charles and I had summoned the elevator several times. Just as it arrived again, we were invited in. After a seated wait at a very big round table, Hubert and Freeman entered, shook hands, and briskly took their eats. Hubert made a nice speech, victory, wonderful, etc. and then raised the issue. They wanted us to give up a certain number of our seats to some of the Regulars! We were shocked and adamant. (I still wonder what on earth the party was thinking . . . Those guys weren't going to vote for the Democratic candidates . . . They simply felt that the seats had always been theirs and belonged to them.) Charles had been silent throughout. It was as though he had moved out to some other place.

Hubert said something and asked Charles Evers, "Don't you think so, Chuck?" Charles did not look up. Everybody knew that he was talking to Charles but Charles didn't say anything because "Chuck" is not his name. A small shadow crossed Hubert's face...something is wrong. So, he turned to Aaron who did respond and then turned back to Charles, "Well, what do you think, Charlie?" He made his way through a few more names, and by the time he got to the fourth, Charles was really mad and puffed up. Wynn was practically wringing his hands. Aaron tried to keep the conversation going in his best statesman-like manner, but the tension mounted.

Then, in the middle of all this, in walked a waiter with a great big tray. It was around lunchtime, everyone was hungry, and the table brightened. The waiter set two places, put plates with club sandwiches and potato chips down—one in front of Hubert and one in front of Freeman. Both men were oblivious, and Hubert continued to talk. The two men began to eat. Southern tension ensued and the group closed up. In a room full of southerners, forget the color line, nothing could be more discourteous.

Aaron looked around in a panic and realized we were about to get up and leave. He then reached over, while talking spiritedly to Hubert, (he was sitting right next to him), and took a section of sandwich and began to eat it. Hubert looked as though he'd been pole axed. Aaron continued to chat, leaning in at Hubert, nibbling away. Ah, it was just a wonderful moment. All of the southerners relaxed, even smiled faintly—trying to stay polite. Aaron had saved the day.

Hubert and Freeman seemed finally to realize that a faux pas had taken place and it wasn't committed by Aaron. Aaron ate about half the sandwich in the most natural kind of way—a moment of grace, indeed! He finished up, we rose, said our warm farewells and went home with all the seats we'd come with.

Chicago Insurgents

Curtis Wilkie is a journalist and author. He lives in New Orleans and writes for the Boston Globe.

I was with the Clarksdale *Press Register* from 1963 until 1969. At first, I was the youngest reporter and would be assigned to the night meetings and the civil rights rallies. I was over at Aaron's house in the spring of 1963 to interview Congressman Charles Diggs right before they firebombed the house. Medgar Evers was there, too, and we sat around and drank beer. So I had known Aaron almost right from the start. He was a very good source.

He would call me up and tell me about harassment or arrests or meetings or who was coming to town. I remember sitting at a rally in one of the churches in 1964. I had heard of Jim Forman, the articulate, intellectual director of SNCC, but I had never met him. I'm sitting on the front row, the only white guy in the church. There is a guy sitting next to me, and he looked like a field hand. He had a big club and he's shaking the club and cheering the speakers on and he's poking me with his elbow and winking— just great theater. Aaron was the emcee of the program and says, "Now our guest speaker, Jim Forman." The guy sitting next to me gets up. You could have knocked me over. I was expecting this erudite, pompous guy. He gave this great fire-and-brimstone speech.

So Aaron and I were in almost daily contact, and I think he respected me as a journalist because I treated him honorably. If he told me something off the record, I wouldn't use it. Once in early 1964, Aaron called to tell me that Al Lowenstein and Steve Bingham, a political radical from New York, were over at his house. They were arrested by police when they came out for violating curfew. Back in those days in Clarksdale there was a midnight curfew that was only applied to blacks or white civil rights workers. The rest of us could go as we pleased. I was still going to the city jail every morning to look at the police blotter, and I said, "Anything interesting going on?" I had never seen the name Al Lowenstein before, and the police sergeant said, "Yeah, we had an interesting case last night. We arrested two New York Jews over at Aaron's house. We gave 'em their phone calls, and do you know who that son of a bitch Lowenstein called? He calls Franklin Delano Roosevelt, Jr. So we said, 'Holy God! We have to let these guys go.'" Back in those days, FDR to a certain extent was some people's saint, in Mississippi, and they let them go.

Later Aaron and I became friends and then political allies. As a journalist I couldn't get very deeply involved, but I was interested in following the changing face of Mississippi politics and certainly pulled for anybody who represented any kind of progressivism in the Democratic Party. Probably after 1965, Clarksdale was at least sixty percent black, and the county had a probably even heavier black percentage. I was involved with the paper, almost editorially, to encourage some black representation on the school board, city council, other public entities. For me that sort of dovetailed into what there was of the antiwar movement in Mississippi. I was very much opposed to the war by 1966, so we liberals (all twelve of us) were united in support of civil rights and antiwar activities. I know that I was encouraging Aaron subrosa to get out the black vote and coalesce behind some good candidates. Then about that time, the War on Poverty guidelines brought integrated meetings and, God forbid, integrated staffs. Aaron was a central figure in all of that, particularly in the Community Action Program agency, Coahoma Opportunities, that virtually got all the Office of Economic Opportunity money in Coahoma County.

I was not personally involved in the politics surrounding Atlantic City, but my sense is that Aaron bought into that compromise, feeling it was at least a leap forward, if not a great one. The more radical people involved felt it was a betrayal on Aaron's part, an unprincipled decision, and that he should have never agreed to be seated. I think Aaron was deeply hurt by their reaction—people he had chosen to work with at peril to himself and his family now calling him a sellout. Some factions even depicted him as a kind of "Uncle Tom"—it was just a terrible, nasty falling-out. The more radical groups seemed to have forgotten his welcoming reach a few years before. Stokely Carmichael, Ivanhoe Donaldson, and many more stayed at his house.

Aaron was always very inclusive, of whites, of people in the movement. I mean he craved acceptance. And he wanted to accept people. I'm sure that is one of the reasons he bought into the Atlantic City compromise. It was just out of character for Aaron to reject any kind of hand that was extended to him if he thought it was a step forward.

After 1964, SNCC people were leaving, and the seeds of wanting to have a coalition party, a Democratic coalition, had been sown. MFDP couldn't pull it off, because many Mississippi people after Atlantic City thought that it was too radical. Some white liberals thought that the message from the 1964 challenge was a chance to reform the regular Mississippi Democratic Party. The moderates, centrists, whatever, and we few on the left were hopelessly outnumbered and always trying to figure out how to assure better political leaders and black representation—anything that would revolutionize the state Democratic Party. Many of us that were involved were looking for any way to wrest the party away from Jim Eastland and the courthouse crowd that had kept the state backwards for all of those years. At that time you really didn't have a Republican Party in the state. There was just the Democratic Party, which had always been divided between the more moderate people and the yahoos. And 1964 was the starting point for it all, with the critical mass coming with the passage of the Voting Rights Act in 1965, followed by a true working relationship between some whites and some blacks in the state. It all came together in 1968 with our seating at the Chicago convention.

We had to go all the way from the precinct level right up through the state meeting to get a delegation. In the meantime, Governor John Bell Williams chose an all-white delegation with two token black exceptions. So, given the pledge from the national party leaders in Atlantic City to not seat segregated delegations, the regulars were in an untenable position. Our group was called the Loyalists, but I always called us the Insurgent Democrats, rather than Loyalists.

The regulars never even got as far as Chicago. Some of their representatives showed up at a Credentials Committee hearing prior to the convention, but our people were already there and the fix was in. They told the governor's delegation that they would not be seated. It was the first time that an entire delegation had ever been rejected.

We elected our Loyalist delegation at a state convention in Jackson in the Masonic hall about two or three weeks before we went to Chicago. It was heavily attended. I remember Mondale was there representing Humphrey, and McCarthy and Kennedy both sent representatives. Everybody got together Saturday, and we had a big party at a hotel right near the capitol, and suddenly a group half black and half white were all eating together in the dining room, just blowing all sorts of minds. Jackson had never seen anything quite like this. Things were legally integrated, but we had several hundred whites and blacks partying together. And then the meeting was Sunday, and, to ensure that we would have a racially balanced delegation, Aaron and others put together a slate of twenty-two whites and twenty-two blacks. It represented everybody from more traditional leaders to Guyot and the old SNCC people to Aaron and Charles. Then whites like Hodding Carter and Patt Derian were included—trying to balance all the various factions.

We also tried to balance it in terms of presidential preference. I was identified as a McCarthy guy, and Aaron is the one who asked me if I would be willing to be a delegate. I remember thinking that would be really dumb as a reporter to become openly involved in something like this, but I told him immediately, absolutely, I'd be delighted to do it. I was flattered to be asked and knew it would be exciting.

At that Jackson meeting, there was a movement by some black leaders to upset this carefully crafted delegation and to have elections from the floor. It would have ensured an almost all-black delegation, which would be self-defeating, and there was a huge fight on the floor. Harry Bowie from McComb got up and made a beautiful speech. He was an identified MFDP person, and he made an extraordinary appeal for everybody to agree upon this group that had been carefully thought out and to not be divisive and defeat our purpose. He prevailed. Then there were various challenges to Charles Evers as national committeeman, and they had a big fight over that. Charles had a rock band that suddenly started playing, and they were drowning out the speech of whoever his opponent was. It was a very rowdy afternoon. There was participatory democracy at its best—and worst!

So we all took the overnight train to Chicago. Most of the blacks didn't have any money, and some of the younger whites like myself needed help. I barely had the proverbial pot to take a leak in back in those days and went up there with about fifty dollars. A northern foundation probably paid for our hotel rooms, and I think our tickets were provided by some of the more wealthy whites in the group—the Carr brothers, Hodding Carter, and Wes Watkins. I have never to this day, in all the things that I have attended or covered, experienced anything like that 1968 Chicago convention. It was incredible and the most exciting weekend of my life.

There was so much confrontation, challenge, and change. The Georgia delegation faced their own challenge by insurgents like Julian Bond and Taylor Branch. There were the antiwar demonstrations and many arrests. My activist role was yelling and screaming on the convention floor. We rowdies would have done anything to keep Humphrey off the ballot, because of the war. It didn't have anything to do with race. Humphrey's credentials on race were impeccable, although there were people who felt he was party to the sellout in Atlantic City. I got in a fight with somebody from Ohio who was a Humphrey delegate. I mean it was boiling on the floor. People were shoving and cursing. It wasn't pleasant. I remember two or three of us went over and joined the Wisconsin delegation. They were raising more hell than anybody. We were hollering at Mayor Daley and all of the Humphrey people. Then we went downtown and all got teargassed by the police, demonstrating in front of Humphrey's hotel.

In our own delegation, everybody laid aside their animosities for about a day or two. Then it began to deteriorate in our caucuses and factions, some based on our presidential candidate choices, but also based on some old battles and rivalries held over from Atlantic City and the Head Start controversy. Ed King, Guyot, and MFDP people were mostly McCarthy people. Aaron was deeply committed to Humphrey, and some of the whites were for McGovern because he had inherited what was left of the Kennedy campaign. People were sarcastic and often scornful of Aaron, although he tried his best to be a peacemaker. I didn't participate in the tribal warfare in our caucus. I was a McCarthy guy and that was it.

If you were not a Humphrey supporter, when you left Chicago you left with a literal heartache. I left there swearing I would never vote for Humphrey. In the end I did, but I held my nose. I remember I didn't lose a night's sleep over Nixon's election. I was so bitter against Humphrey and the establishment that controlled the convention.

So, in a way, the only victory in 1968 was that our delegation was seated, and it then led the way to essentially the blacks taking over the Democratic Party in Mississippi and driving the old-guard whites out of the party. Aaron became state chairman, and then in the seventies more whites came back in and we basically had an integrated party.

I heard people express all sorts of angry feelings about Aaron over the years. I don't think I ever heard Aaron speak evil of anybody. He would certainly deplore their conduct, but he never deplored them personally. Now, the essence of Aaron is in this story. It has been told to me more than once. Ross Barnett, ex-governor of Mississippi, staunch segregationist, in his dotage was going up to Washington one day. Ross sometimes didn't know where he was, and Aaron happened to run into him at National Airport. It was clear Ross was disoriented, and Aaron went up to him—again your classic Aaron—forgive everything. "Governor, this is Aaron Henry. Can I help you?" Barnett is going to the Mayflower Hotel and doesn't know how to get there. So Aaron got him in a taxi and went with him and took him to the registration desk. The people at the registration desk were sneering at the blundering old fool (Ross is about eighty-five at the time) and Aaron was patiently explaining that this is a very famous Mississippian—"He was the governor of our state and you should make every kind of accommodation to make him comfortable here." The clerk finally looked over his glasses and said, "And I suppose you are the head of the Mississippi NAACP."

When to Deal

L. C. Dorsey was born on a cotton plantation in Washington County, Mississippi, joined the movement in 1964, worked in Head Start, received a D.S.W. in social work, and has remained active in prison and health reform work. She lives in Jackson.

I had heard about Aaron Henry, long before I met him, through Amzie Moore, an NAACP community activist, who, under the cover of being in a spiritual quartet, went around the countryside and spoke at churches about the NAACP. I was twelve years old and living on a plantation between Drew and Ruleville in Sunflower County, and the four men, including Amzie, came to my church, Pilgrim Rest. It was in the early fifties and there would always really be some singing, but Amzie talked to us about the issues being addressed by the NAACP, and he told us about Aaron Henry working up in Clarksdale. During those times, there was still a day in the month of February when all the schools celebrated black history, and, by the fifties, we began to hear about local black people who were making contributions to history. Aaron Henry—he was always called Dr. Aaron Henry—and a black physician in Ruleville were two of the local people that were discussed.

That made an impression, but I also came from a home where my father and mother wanted us to understand that all the black people in the country didn't chop and pick cotton and weren't desperately poor. Daddy always got the *Chicago Defender*, the *Pittsburgh Courier*, and sometimes he would buy *Jet* magazine. Mama could read and write, and, on the weekends, Mama would read the paper to us so we would know that black people in the rest of the country had different lifestyles and enjoyed freedoms denied to us—they had decent houses, jobs where they collected a paycheck every week, and didn't live in fear of the Ku Klux Klan.

But mostly we didn't even realize that we lacked dreams of a different life. Like Aaron in his childhood, you just knew that this was your life and everyone else's. You went to school, you had food, you had shelter, you had your parents who loved you. There were a few youth groups like the 4-H Club and Tri-Hi-Y, and little organizations like the Knights and Daughters of Tabor who had chapters almost everywhere and Saturday afternoon meetings. There were the churches with their socials and picnics, and the Baptist Training Union.

Now, my mother was a Methodist (AME) from Alabama, and she never warmed to the Baptist Church. But the Methodist Church was not welcome on most plantations in the Delta, because Methodists required that their ministers be educated and often backed the progressive activities that were going on. Our Baptist preachers were picked, set up, and controlled by the plantation owners. They couldn't talk about anything to do with freedom or registering to vote or challenging the status quo.

Then in the sixties, through the freedom movement, we began to see leaders like Aaron Henry at mass meetings around the state. Owen Brooks from the Delta Ministry actually introduced me to Aaron in 1965. I was glad to finally meet him face-to-face (but understand that in my early contact with Aaron, he was at a leadership level and I was never a leader—I was always a follower). I would see him at mass meetings or at the big rallies, and we all were in marches and demonstrations, including the Meredith March in 1966, but our leaders were three or four miles up the road and we were in the back.

I was very active in the NAACP, and Aaron was state president, and, in the late seventies when I moved from the Delta to Jackson, I got to know him better. Aaron didn't just hold meetings. He believed in action, and that's what people miss about him. He understood the danger that was involved in action, but he also understood that there was strength in numbers to support a person being terrorized and tyrannized in some small backwoods community. It also made white folks understand that if a hundred and fifty or two hundred people came to town for a meeting around an issue and marched through town to show their strength and solidarity with the person, the issue wasn't over. We spent time all around the state wherever there was trouble. For instance, when a boy was killed in Belzoni, Aaron had the NAACP state conference meet there to visit the family and to let the black folks know we were supportive of whatever road they would take. We would march on the police station, the school board—wherever the problem lay. And that's why you see all these old folks who feel so loyal to the NAACP. They may not be happy with how the national NAACP, the state NAACP, or their local chapter are doing things now, but they remember how it was. They remember what it stood for. And they keep holding on because they understand like Aaron did that life is a constant battle for justice, and addressing issues head-on will come back round.

Often, in the seventies, Aaron and I would be riding in the same car and get chances to talk. I worked with him around prison issues. I can't say that I introduced him to the problems in the prisons, but I certainly helped make him aware of what was happening inside them. As a result of my interest, he named me chairperson of the Prison Affairs Committee for the NAACP state conference. I reported directly to him for a number of years until I finally left and went back to school.

Aaron understood the prison issue because he knew that issues change their faces. He knew that the worst threat growing up in Coahoma County as a young black male was being lynched by the Ku Klux Klan. Then we saw where the biggest danger for young black males became the Mississippi criminal justice system. That system would get them not one by one, but in droves, hordes. I mean the prison is filled to bursting with young black men, and the laws are still being written to keep them there. Aaron was a visionary, and, more than most, he understood that there was money involved in incarcerating these young people. The hordes of young black men being jailed for drug-related crimes—robbery, burglary, carrying, or dealing—we saw it happening and understood the two factors at work. It was easy to track. First, the education system was failing young people miserably—keep us ignorant and we stay in our place. Second was an actual campaign, developed allegedly by the KKK, to control young black men. Aaron helped circulate the material on this, showing the moving of lynching to a more sophisticated level. They took off the sheets and moved into banking and politics and three-piece suits, and they actually instructed teachers in public schools to expel black students. Then we began to see it happening—expel kids from school and track them from there to the juvenile justice system to county jails and on to prison and some to death row. And before some of us figured it out—that as you send more people away, you had to build more prisons—Aaron saw the economics and the money behind it. But more important he understood they were doing it to keep the black men out of the community. Whites weren't fearful of black women. It was black men who had to be controlled. Aaron knew this from his own experience in Clarksdale when they had curfews for blacks in the thirties. He knew the double standard when it came to the issue of sexual relations for black men who even looked at a white woman, and he knew the numbers of black men who had been lynched for real and perceived violations of the strict sexual segregation between black males and white females.

By the time he was in the legislature in the eighties, we were really into this explosion of young people in prison, but we couldn't work up enough steam to make it an issue. And during the last decade of his life, his health failing, there was virtually no interest in what was happening in the prisons. Politicians were still more concerned about what was happening with crime than what was happening with black people's lives.

But Aaron was always responsive to the tides of change and what was happening and needed in the state. When you talk about his complexity, I think it was because he was concerned about the human condition. Aaron saw life as a human condition, and he'd experienced that condition. He had been in prison. He had been chronically ill. He had been hungry. He'd been poor. He'd been denied adequate education. He'd been discriminated against in this state by white people who were in power. And he'd been harassed by police who were also charged with protecting him, his house had been shot into. He had lived all of this.

It's important to know that Aaron, unlike most of us, knew the history of his people. He knew the contributions they had made, and he had read many books that they had written. So he understood life from an intellectual experience as well as from having practical knowledge. He would talk about the killing of Bigger Thomas in Richard Wright's *Native Son*. He had the intellectual background, the grasp of history, his own knowledge, and a lot of guts. Even knowing what they do to the Bigger Thomases of this world, he stepped out into a leadership position in Mississippi.

In spite of his education, Aaron never became pretentious. I grew up with this whole business of being in your place. You certainly knew what your place was with white folks, but you also knew what your place was with important black folks. I sometimes had this great sense of my own unworthiness and where I should be in the whole spectrum of things. So I was always a little bit nervous and tongue-tied and I guess fearful of being rejected by people who were important. Aaron was never that way. I don't care how he felt, he always had a smile. He was glad to see you and ready to stop and listen to whatever you had to say regardless of how insignificant it may have been. I remember coming from the Delta when he was in St. Dominic's Hospital in Jackson. I persuaded the nurse to let me see him—that I had come a long way. When I walked in the room you would have thought that Queen Elizabeth had arrived. He made me feel ten feet tall. He lifted me. I've had the experience of reaching some profound point of view and telling it to some men, and they don't listen. Or they listen with a kind of "Oh, I wish you'd hurry and get through with this mess." Aaron was never like that.

I recall a time, for instance, when both of us worked with Charles Tisdale and were on the board of the *Jackson Advocate*. We were discussing an interview, and, at that time, I was thinking that I was a pretty good writer and I wanted to do the story. Charles Tisdale, Aaron, and I were sitting at the table, and Tisdale said something like, "Naw, we're going to get a professional writer to do this." And he said it without a thought to how his words and tone impacted me. And I *was* crushed. Aaron was sensitive enough to pick up on it and to try to take away some of the hurt by saying, "Well, you may get a person who has more credentials, but you won't get anybody who is more professional than L. C." And, of course, he was directing this to me. He never felt the need to destroy people in public—never needed to step on your ego to boost himself.

Yes, Aaron certainly believed that women could make equal contributions, and I never experienced any sexism with him at all. He valued my opinion on issues when he talked to me, and I've never been in a situation where he asked a woman to get him a cup of coffee. We didn't even know these feminist questions, and people don't understand that freedom was the thing that was important. All of a sudden, in the sixties freedom fight, it looked like we might have a chance, but we mainly wondered if we could sleep at night without fear of being dragged out of our house and killed, or whether they would set the house afire and burn us all up in it. Also, I had six kids and had the horrible experience of having to listen to those kids cry themselves to sleep because we had no food and no money. So that was what freedom meant to me—never having to go through that fear and pain again. Maybe the women's issues will be more important to my granddaughter. But as for Aaron, he seemed not to care about class, sex, gender, or race, and as much as he knew about white people, he never really hated them.

If you happen to talk about the downside of Aaron, I know that some people considered him a compromiser over the Mississippi Freedom Democratic Party in the 1964 Democratic convention and in building the Loyalist Democrats. Some of the SNCC people especially felt he gave in too easily to seating just two members rather than the whole MFDP delegation, but sometimes a compromise is a good thing. An activist has to know when and where to deal, because if you miss that point of when to deal, when to negotiate, you have lost the whole thing. Aaron knew when to deal, and that's different from being a compromiser, which can have a bad connotation. Negotiating from a power place after you have marched or demonstrated lets people know your strength. People perceive power differently based on their own experiences. For instance, Aaron's perspective was to take those two seats as a beginning—the first wedge in reforming the Democratic Party in Mississippi. Some people from the outside, advising the delegation, had never been denied the opportunity to vote, had never lived in near-slavery conditions, had never been abused or violated by law enforcement or the criminal justice system and police force. They could not understand why you would even consider accepting just two seats.

Looking at Aaron from just a purely intellectual point of view or from the perspective of history, I think he played an absolutely necessary role. Aaron understood that we needed dialogue between the racist white folks and the good white folks—and between the good white folks and black people— that we all had to live on this planet together. Aaron was serving at a time in Mississippi history where you had the white Citizens' Council over here prepared to do whatever they could to stop integration, you had the Sovereignty Commission over here prepared to do their evil, and you had the Ku Klux Klan just waiting to do violence. And you had powerful white people who controlled the money, the police force, and everything else ready to finance all these other agencies to keep us from ever attaining any measure of freedom. And then you had the more radical black young people saying we want it all now, with their fervor and the high pitch of Freedom Summer and history pushing them to say, "Let's take it now." All over the country, you had folks prepared to say, "If I can't have it you won't either—we'll burn it down first." Martin Luther King's nonviolent movement got more support when white people were faced with the spectacle of thousands of seemingly enraged people following Stokely Carmichael and black power—"burn, baby, burn." The alternative was the nonviolent approach with black people singing and praying—people who said, "if you hit me on one cheek I'll turn the other, and why don't we sit down and talk." So that may have been Aaron's role in Mississippi history—he saw things as a continuum of action within the circumstances that you faced at the time.

"Bring Some Clean Drawers"

Winson Hudson, born in 1916, has lived all of her life in the Harmony community in Leake County, Mississippi. She and her sister Dovie helped lead the fight to desegregate their schools in 1964. She has served as president of the local NAACP since 1962.

What inspired me to first love Aaron Henry so was back in the sixties when I was looking at my black-and-white television and saw six black men over in the Delta working on a garbage truck. They had been arrested for civil rights work and Aaron Henry was the leader, and I said to myself, now that's a man I want to work with. We were trying to get the NAACP organized and to save the Harmony school in our community. Medgar Evers was helping us, and we had to have fifty members to get a charter and had a hard time because everyone was afraid of the NAACP—even to say the name. But we scraped up fifty-one members, and we warned the whites that if they tried to move or close our school, we were going to their schools. They told us, "Well, you and your children and your children's children will never live to see it." That was during Ross Barnett's time, and someone from his campaign even came to see us and told us that our "children's blood would be spilled in the streets like water before integration came." But we had the NAACP Legal Defense Fund behind us, and their lawyers and Medgar were encouraging us to integrate and go to the "best school." So, we started going to meetings in Jackson and all over the place, and that's when I met Aaron Henry. Aaron and Medgar were real close, and they both knew about death. I was thinking at Aaron's funeral that he was going to see his friend Medgar at last.

Aaron and I went all over the state and demonstrated and protested together, and I got to know him very well. He had more sense than any governor we ever had. And we trusted him both as a person and as a leader. You couldn't buy him. Aaron would call us about a meeting and say, "Y'all come on, bring some clean drawers because you might have to spend the night." And I followed him all over this country, working with the Mississippi Freedom Democratic Party and went to two national Democratic conventions with him—one in Miami, Florida, and one in Kansas City, Missouri. I was right with Aaron and Charles Young and all that crowd when we sent the Mississippi white delegates home.

We followed him everywhere, to everything that was all-white. Once we protested to break up that all-white Mississippi Health Coordinating Committee. There were about thirty or forty of us waiting at their meeting place, and when they arrived, we started singing and sang everything 'til we ran out of songs. It was in July, and we sang "I'm dreaming of a White Christmas." They couldn't have the meeting because we were there singing. Then they tried to move to another place and we followed them. Finally they put me on the health care commission, and I served there I don't know how many years.

So Aaron had us ready to demonstrate any time. First he would talk to them, and when they wouldn't do, then he would do. If negotiation didn't work, then he'd call and we'd get together, and he would keep our spirits up and always tell really funny jokes. Aaron didn't care too much about money, fine clothes, and stuff. When I first met him, his shoes were run over and his pants were wore out behind, and he was just going like he wasn't paying nobody to give him anything. Aaron didn't care whether you praised or down-graded him—he just worked for the people.

Once Aaron had us to come up to Clarksdale to a state conference in the late sixties. Times were still rough then. We got up there, and some blacks were walking in to eat at this Holiday Inn on the main highway. When we drove up, we were told to leave somebody with our truck because some klansmen were just going by with their guns out. I guess it was the first time that blacks had gone to the motel in a group. We weren't staying there—we stayed in people's homes, but we were testing public accommo-dations in the restaurant, and attorney Joe Rauh and NAACP national office leader Gloster Current were with us. We just had a bowl of soup, and they were slamming it down in front of us. We were eating and scared to death that those Klan people would come in there and sit right by us. Last time I was up there, they had a big sign welcoming the NAACP.

Now at that Clarksdale meeting, we were sharing our community prob-lems, and I raised my hand and told about us trying to get telephones into our Harmony community—all through the civil rights movement from 1964 on. We tried everything. We had young people, white and black, that had representatives all over this country, and they still couldn't get tele-phones in here. The companies would come all around us with telephone wires but never into the community—just like they did with roads. We had to go all the way into Carthage to use the phone. And so Joe Rauh and Gloster Current said they knew some people who knew the president of Bell Telephone Company and that we would be hearing from them when they got back home. And the next week, I had a letter from New York—said they had contacted the president of South Central Bell in Jackson and that he would be getting in touch with us. That president wrote me a letter and said he did-n't know that we weren't able to get telephones, that we would stay in touch and we would get telephones. Within three months we got phones here and in other little black communities around here, and our telephones would be just ringing and ringing. And people didn't know how they got them, and that white telephone guy in Jackson, we stayed in touch and any little phone problem—he'd straighten it right out. So we were willing to take a chance on our lives with those klansmen and things, because we were depending on

Aaron and the civil rights people because they were so smart and knew how to get things done.

Now when Head Start came into Mississippi, you know, there was a kind of a conflict between the CDGM [Child Development Group of Mississippi] and MAP [Mississippi Action for Progress] and all these groups that wanted to run the program. And Aaron called around, me included, and told us what to do, who to meet, where the meetings were being held and what to say, and before the white folks knew anything, we had control of the Head Start, because we had good ties with Hubert Humphrey and Sargent Shriver and the people at the top. Now a lot of people said that Aaron was up in Washington compromising too much, but, at the same time, if we ever went to Washington, you'd find old Stennis and Eastland treating us like white folks for the first time. They were afraid of Aaron. Aaron did a lot of compromising to keep us eating bread, and that was important, because if they had closed down Head Start, a lot of us wouldn't be here now—would've had to leave Mississippi. My family had this farm and knew how to survive, but there's a lot of people that was on the white folks' place, and, with no money coming in from jobs like Head Start, they had no place to go. And it was especially hard when those civil rights workers came from the outside. Now they did a whole lot of good, but they left.

Aaron didn't make any racket, he didn't bother you, he didn't dominate, didn't care about praise. He was never the type to push women back, respected us in places of leadership—all of us in the struggle together. Sometimes we used to get mad at him when he let people run all over him—just let people do anything. So Aaron and I just stayed together working in the NAACP and the Democratic Party—they were two things that we loved the best. Some people think we got money out of it, but there's no money in it—just fighting for our rights.

"Tell Him Aaron Henry's Here"

B. T. Jones is President/CEO of MINACT, Inc., a Jackson-based management and training company.

I first heard of Aaron Henry through my family in Holly Springs, Mississippi. I was discharged from the military in 1966, returned to Memphis in hopes of going to college, and went to visit my family. They kept talking about this man—what a hero he was—that he would stand up to any white man—stand up and be counted. At first, I didn't have a clue about him. In fact, when they first mentioned his name, I thought they were talking about the baseball player Henry Aaron.

About four or five years later, I was working at the Job Corps center in Kentucky and living in Evansville, Indiana. Dr. Henry was on the board of directors of an organization called Joint Action and Community Service (JACS). They had a support contract for returning Job Corps students to the community and helping them get settled. My center director said to me, "We got Dr. Aaron Henry from JACS coming up here. Would you take him to dinner tonight?" I proudly said "yes."

Then in 1977, I came to Mississippi to start the first Job Corps center in this state, in Crystal Springs, about twenty-five miles south of Jackson. Aaron contacted me and asked if I would come to the state conference of the NAACP in November to explain to the conferees what the Job Corps was going to be like in Mississippi. While I was there, I said, "Aaron, come January, we're going to be celebrating Dr. Martin Luther King's birthday at the center with our staff and students. And I'd love to have you come down there and speak." He pulled out his big brown book, wrote it down, and said, "I'll be there." Well, Hubert Humphrey died a few days before the celebration, and I knew that Dr. Henry had been extremely close to the Humphreys. So, I had assumed that I would get a call from Dr. Henry saying that he was not coming to the Job Corps center to speak to the students, that he was going to join the Humphreys for the funeral. And I did get a call from him, but, surprisingly, he asked when we were going to pick him up. And I said, "Doc, where are you?" "Well, I'm in Clarksdale," he said, "but I'm going to be in Jackson tomorrow. What time am I speaking?" I told him, "Well, now, I can have someone pick you up in time for the talk, but Doc, I want you to understand that I know that you were a very close personal friend with Senator Humphrey." And Aaron said, "I appreciate that but I gave you my word that I would be down there to speak to the kids.

And while I'm there I'm going to have a few words to say about Martin and a few words to say about Hubert."

Aaron came down to the center, spoke to the staff and students as he had promised and then got on a plane that same day and went to Minnesota and joined the Humphrey family. And I thought, "A man of his word." That was the impression that he left on me.

A year later I had this dream about starting my own company, and one of the persons I wanted to involve in it was Dr. Henry. So I asked him to join me in this business venture, and he was on the MINACT board until his death. No matter how many important people he knew, he never forgot the little people in our state or in this country.

And it wasn't the easiest thing for him to get around. He had a license, but drove rarely. Aaron had a tendency to just fall asleep. Sometimes even at a major event, he'd drop his head. At a board meeting, he'd fall asleep but know everything everybody said—he would not miss a beat. I think someone told him he ought not to drive because of this tendency—at least not long distances—and he usually got people to drive him around.

I saw a lot more of him when he served in the legislature and started living in Jackson. We began to travel together on MINACT or Job Corps business to speak to staff and students. It amazed me that every community we went to, somebody there knew him.

I watched him the twenty years I knew him and was struck that he had done so much for so many people. I know what he did for MINACT and for me and my family. I mean he cut through a whole lot of horse manure and got to the decision makers very early, and they were all very interested in giving us an audience. We would never have had that opportunity had not it been for Dr. Henry's reputation, credibility, integrity, character—all of those things that he had built up over time.

And I'm talking national level here. See, by then, contacts he had from the civil rights movement had evolved into significant positions in Washington. For example, MINACT got the contract to operate a Job Corps center in St. Louis, Missouri—in 1979, I believe, and Aaron had already committed to come the day we decided to have an open house. Now it just happened that Ray Marshall, who was then the secretary of labor, was going to be in St. Louis the same day, and somehow the two of them met up, and

Ray Marshall came to our open house and he's talking to everyone about his experience with Dr. Henry. I hadn't realized that Marshall had been in Mississippi—maybe at Ole Miss—and had written a good portion of a book at Aaron's kitchen table in Clarksdale.

So, right away, MINACT had instant credibility—not because of what we had done, but because Aaron Henry was a part of the company. And that's what I mean about cutting through a whole lot of layers. He gave us that credibility, and then it was left up to the rest of us to make sure we always got things right for Doc. Aaron's main quality was his stick-to-itness. Once he decided to do something, he never got off track. It goes with his July zodiac sign of Cancer—the crab—he grabbed with those claws and wouldn't let go.

He used his influence to improve the lives of black people and ultimately for white people, too, by helping us get those federal programs for our state. We went to Washington once, and I will never forget this. We had been working on a contract to operate a Job Corps center in Grand Rapids, Michigan. We decided we'd go walk the halls of Congress, and Aaron said, "Well, I'm going to go by and see Don Regal, Sandy Levin, and Carl Levin [representatives from Michigan who worked in Aaron's campaign in the 1963 freedom vote]. I want them to know we are now in Michigan." We would go in these doors, without an appointment, and he'd say to a receptionist, "Tell him Aaron Henry is here," and then the senator or congressman would come out! I mean it was incredible. So that's what I mean about the genuine respect that he gained from people he had worked with over time.

"Get More Kids"

Frank Melton is president and chief executive officer of the Jackson, Mississippi, television station WLBT, the NBC affiliate.

I was living in Texas in the 1980s, and my company was trying to buy WLBT, the television station in Jackson. Dr. Henry was chairman of the board and one of the owners at that time, and we wanted to keep him in the transactions. A small group of us bought the station in February 1984, and I began spending a majority of my time in Jackson, as president of the television station.

Now, Dr. Henry and others had filed suit against the station in 1963 when they refused to sell time to him and other black political candidates, and it took sixteen years to settle it. I believe it was under the Carter administration and that the president actually put the pressure on and dictated the terms of the settlement with the Federal Communications Commission. Aaron was chairman of the station board until his death and used to laugh about the change from that rude refusal of selling him equal time to his being board chair.

One of Aaron's main traits was his commitment to follow through. I believe this trait scared the white power structure here, particularly in the sixties, but I think it frightened everybody—black and white—because most people don't live to that standard. On the other hand, I've never met a person who was more forgiving than Dr. Henry. I saw that trait in him, graphically, about eleven years ago. We were having breakfast at one of the local restaurants here, and a couple of white guys came up. They embraced Dr. Henry and talked for a while and were very friendly and jovial—only for me to later find out that these were two of the guys who used to beat him in his head during the civil rights movement.

In my times with Aaron, there have been some so-called friends who have betrayed his trust and his philosophy. It goes all the way back to the day we signed the documents to take over the television station. WLBT was a unionized station, but the union was geared mostly for the white employees who had been there the longest—you know—last in, first out. I had to come in and make some rather substantial and controversial changes. Now, Aaron believed in unions, but when I closed it down at the station, he backed me up.

I have never had a better business partner than Aaron Henry and learned that what you brought to his table better be fair, better be right. He left a lot of room for people to make an error as long as errors were made from the heart and were not errors of viciousness or dishonesty.

What Dr. Henry essentially did over the years was help build a diverse staff of competent people at the station and an asset that's worth over a hundred and fifty million dollars. But we also realized that his history and his vision of the company called for other activities. We implemented a number of new programs and spent five or six million dollars in this state, sending kids to college, helping families out, and demanding performance out of kids. I'm not talking about give-away programs, I'm talking about self-help programs. To me that's what Dr. Henry's life was all about. For many years, Dr. Henry and I never took a dime in dividends out of this company. For the first time in our lives, we took down money in December of 1996, and we turned right around and put that money into a foundation that will continue community work in the future.

And beginning five or six years ago, Aaron allowed me without question to leave this company every May, go down to the Farish Street YMCA and conduct an inner city program for thousands of kids for the whole three-month period while they're out of school. Not only that, he helped fund the entire program. So we literally have been able to influence thousands of young people, not by just cutting a check and sending it to the YMCA, but by hands-on work—teaching swimming, teaching gymnastics, teaching English, teaching reading, teaching computer science, putting a staff together. Dr. Henry came himself during the summer and did a walk-through and met hundreds of young black kids. He didn't say, "Go back to the TV station and make more money." No. He'd be saying, "Get more kids into the program."

Right up until he had the stroke, Dr. Henry kept a hectic schedule. When he was ill in 1995, after a heart attack, we were having a meeting with him at the hospital. The doctor was telling us that he needed to slow down, to start taking it easy, and Dr. Henry is telling us he has a major speech he's got to make in Washington. We're talking about who will sit with him in the hospital, and the next thing we know, Aaron is walking by us with an IV stuck in his arm on the way to the airport in Washington to make his speech. And that's exactly what he did. He left the IV tubes at the front door of the hospital. We all realized then that we were going to let Aaron do whatever Aaron wanted to do. We knew that stopping him from doing what was important to him would kill him quicker than the heart problem.

"Momma" and the Macarena

Sam Simmons directs the National Caucus and Center on Black Aged, Inc. in Washington, D.C.

My nephew Ben Taylor was a student at Michigan State in the sixties, and he and his friend Ivanhoe Donaldson took some food and supplies to Mississippi. They were arrested in Clarksdale, and all I knew to do was to call Aaron Henry whom I had met at an NAACP convention in Atlanta in 1955. Aaron had already gotten them out of jail. I saw him again at a hearing in Mississippi sponsored by the Commission on Civil Rights in 1968, but I really didn't get to know him until 1977 when I joined the board of the National Caucus and Center on Black Aged (NCBA). I was at the National Center for Housing Management, and the caucus had been approved to do a housing project. Lo and behold, Aaron was chair of the NCBA board—he was elected in 1975 and served until December of 1996. I came on as NCBA executive director in 1982, and Aaron helped build this organization to an annual budget of about twenty million dollars a year. We have an administrative staff of sixty-five people and have field offices in ten states and D.C.

With Aaron's help, we went from no money earmarked for housing to about thirteen million dollars' worth of housing projects, including four for the elderly in Mississippi. For many of the projects, Aaron and I would go together to borrow the money. I would ask him, "Do you know so-and-so?" He would give his favorite response, "No, but I bet he knows me," and the person always did.

I don't think the good changes in Mississippi nor the political conventions were the only things that made Aaron Henry popular and added to his notoriety. After the sixties, sooner or later everyone involved in national politics or business had to go to Mississippi, and Aaron was one of the few well-known black business and civic leaders in the state. So when a staffer with a senator over on Capitol Hill said he was going to Mississippi, he would be told right away, "Get in touch with Aaron Henry." And when you look at his NAACP work—state president for thirty-three years and national board membership until his death—he was the only one around from the old days. The rest had died off or been defeated or had become discouraged.

Aaron remained a powerhouse and it helped add to his credibility. He was connected with every social movement in the state and was the softest touch of anybody that you ever met. If he thought your cause was just, he would say "yes" and be identified with it, and housing became one of his causes. Before we even met, he was working in Clarksdale with his friend Bennie Gooden. Bennie used him as a front person for housing built under the Farmers Home Administration, and they probably did more than anyone else in the state to begin housing for low-income people. So you can go to places like Friars Point, Jonestown, Marks—all over the map—I bet there are fifteen low-income Mississippi housing projects named Aaron Henry Homes or the like.

I think Aaron became involved with the NCBA, because, like everything else, the aging thrust was leaving out black people. Hobart Jackson, the main founder of NCBA, was a social worker and pioneer in the field of nursing homes for the black elderly. So he and the other black social workers who were at the 1970 White House Conference on Aging started raising holy hell. They threatened to go outside and have a demonstration and say they were having a "Black House Conference." Dr. Arthur Fleming, who was chair of the conference and later the chair of the Commission on Civil Rights said, "No, don't go any place. I want to work with you. Stay with me." So they stayed, but the group that was doing the protesting started the NCBA, and Dr. Fleming helped them to keep it going. They realized they needed more political clout and that's when they got hold of Aaron.

So he started using his contacts—writing, calling, and going over to the Labor Department to see who could get employment programs going for black elderly. During the Nixon administration, the assistant secretary of labor wrote Aaron that he would not answer any more of his letters and would appreciate it if Aaron did not write or call him any more. But Aaron kept right on, and things changed when Carter came in and brought Ray Marshall as secretary of labor. Marshall and Aaron were old friends—he had been to Mississippi, been to the drugstore and knew all about Aaron Henry. Ernie Green was the assistant secretary in charge of employment training and was told to work with Aaron. There were no employment programs for African Americans or Hispanics at the time, and when Ernie decided to start one, he was going to give a program to his friend Vernon Jordan, the executive director of the Urban League. When we heard this, Aaron and I went to New York one day telling Vernon that he was cutting our throat. Vernon said that he hadn't asked for it and if they wanted to give it to him, he would take it. Aaron kept up the pressure, going through his friend Ray Marshall. So when Ernie Green finally approved a program, initially they gave the Urban League the big cities and gave us the rural areas—the Mississippi Delta and places with no significant black population, like the hills of Tennessee and Kentucky and the panhandle of Florida. But over the years we traded with other organizations to get employment slots, so now we are in every county in the Mississippi Delta.

Through the years, when there was a threat of cuts in Medicare or other programs that benefited the elderly, Aaron would come up and testify before congressional committees. Once, and this is in the Congressional Record, I believe, directed towards President Reagan, Aaron said, "Mr. President, you can mess with me and you can mess with my children, but don't mess with my momma." This became a much-quoted piece, and I believe a poster of it was hanging on his office wall at WLBT in Jackson. He loved collecting things, would ask for anything that you were about to throw away, anything that caught his imagination, but particularly if he thought it was historical or related to the role of blacks in American society. He would carry it back to the drugstore at home, and, if he didn't put it up on the wall, he would put it in the file.

He just grasped onto quotes or poems that he liked and would put them in a speech, and when he would give another speech he would go back and find his favorites and put them in the new speech. He was a great one to sit down with a pair of scissors and put things together. Like the last time that Aaron was here for a board meeting in December of 1996. Clinton had invited him to a Christmas party, and he asked one of our secretaries to go with him, and, of course she was delighted—got her picture made with the Clintons. Then he asked us to help send out a mailing about the inaugural events in January. He was coming up and wanted to let others know. He was telling people in Mississippi, "I hope that you will come and join us at the inaugural here in Washington, and if you come you got to know how to do the macarena. For those of you who do not know how to do the macarena there is going to be a practice session in Mississippi before we come up here." But instead of letting the secretary type up a new message, he laboriously cut and pasted all of this stuff. Then they had to Xerox the whole thing. Then we had to cope with that big brown address book of his, which carried everything he knew and owned. It had gotten so shabby and was held together by a rubber band. (Once, when he dropped it, everything under the sun fell out, receipts and letters and cards and ten or fifteen checks that had never been deposited in the bank.) So we sent that inaugural letter out to all these different addresses—to many people that he knew as far back as freedom ride days—people who had moved ten times since then. It was one of the last things we did for him.

He was just a character. I took some board members to Mississippi for a meeting, and they had never met Aaron. When asked what he looked like, I showed them some pictures and said, "You may see him walking down the main street in Jackson, and he will likely have on a pair of blue bib overalls." They laughed and said it wasn't so. We were to meet him in a downtown Jackson restaurant, and, as we sat there, in comes a man in blue bib overalls and everyone goes up to talk to him. It was Aaron, and my friends just cracked up.

You will be hard put to find anyone as loyal as Aaron Henry. He knew that people were less than perfect. They were still his friends. I would not say that he was a great intellectual, because he wasn't. He just knew people, and he loved people and he wanted to help people. Aaron was the epitome of the "human" in human being. He appreciated everything in the past, but stayed interested in learning about new things. He was often angry with Charles Evers and some of his political choices, but I think he remembered earlier times when he didn't have any money and Charles helped pay for Aaron's daughter's education. That and their times together with Medgar in the worst of days sealed a friendship. So, he could separate out those kinds of things—nine good qualities against one bad one. The one person who I heard him say was "just no good" was Trent Lott. He could talk about all those Republicans and conservatives, but the only one I heard him describe as just an excuse for a human being was Trent Lott.

To be honest with you, I don't know why Aaron ever ran for the state legislature and stuck with it. That day-in and day-out stuff that a legislator does just wasn't his cup of tea. Everybody knew that kind of tedious, laborious stuff did not call him. He was a crusader. He was looking for the latest and the newest battle to be fought.

The Legacy

Aaron McClinton, age twenty-three, is Aaron Henry's grandson. He lives in Clarksdale with his mother, Rebecca Henry, and his sixteen-year-old brother, DeMon.

My earliest memory of my grandfather is his putting a train set together for me at Christmas. My father had died when I was fourteen months old, and my mother and I were living with my grandparents, so, in many ways, he was both father and grandfather for me. I first knew of his civil rights work when I saw him on TV and wondered what he was doing there. Then he started telling me what he stood for, and I started noticing the pictures and posters around the house and at the drugstore.

In the fourth grade, I started looking for his name in the books. There was a lot about Martin Luther King, Jr., and Medgar Evers and others, and even though my mama and grandma said Aaron Henry was right there on the front lines with them, there wasn't too much about him. When I would find his name, I would go up to the teacher and say, "You see this? That's my granddaddy right there." Then I remember he was always getting calls from famous people—presidents and senators—and he just talked to them like everybody else. My grandmother told my brother and me about his pledge to God to help his people if he got out of the war alive, but he never sat me or DeMon down and talked about what he was doing.

I loved him a lot, and I guess the ethic of hard work is one thing that I learned from him. He was so busy when I was growing up, and the house was always full of people, and there was so much to be done. When he couldn't do it himself, I can remember him getting me and DeMon up really early, before school, to go chop or water the garden next to the house. No matter if it's three o'clock in the morning, if you've got something to do you can do it at three a.m., and he would call people at midnight or five in the morning and then go back to sleep. I don't even think he realized what time it was when he was calling these people.

Who He Was 247

Things have changed a lot in Mississippi. Black people can vote, we can go anywhere we want to go, but still, when I look at things now, I realize that we still have prejudices and racial problems. Just a few months ago, some friends and I went to lunch in a restaurant in Holly Springs, and we waited and waited and no one would take our order. I asked the waitress to please take our order, and she said, "Yeah, okay," but fifteen minutes later, no one had come. White people around us were getting served, and we finally left to get back to work. This has happened several times, and sometimes I feel that the white ladies have an attitude, because we were like three black men under twenty-five. Seems like young black men are getting a bad rap everywhere.

My grandfather seemed sadder during his last years. Some of it was losing that last election to the legislature. I still think to this day that the election was fixed. A black opponent beat him, and he had a lot of white supporters that didn't like my granddad—never had since the old days. They had been trying to get him out for a long time, and I believe they fixed it. Then he loved my grandmother a lot and was on edge and sad after she died in 1994. So I lost them both in the space of five years.

Now my top goal is to be chairman of the board of WLBT, the television station in Jackson, like my grandfather. My first job was at WLBT. I worked where they did commercials, where they ran the camera for the news—all over, and I liked it. I majored in mass communications at Rust College, but I want to go back to school towards owning my own radio station—maybe even more than one. I like radio a lot and did an internship at a radio station several summers during college. I feel that communicating with people— the news—all of it—is important. Part of what Granddad taught me was the need to make sure that television and radio are telling the true story. Media is supposed to tell the truth all the time, and it is up to reporters and the people who run these stations to leave the truth in, even when the truth hurts.

Then I want to be a family man, and, if I get a chance, I'll get trained as a cosmetologist and in auto body repair. You know people have a lot of degrees and can't get a job. You may need a little something on the side—a trade to fall back on, or even just to relax. You can always go to a hair salon and get a chair and barber, and the same thing with auto body work. A lot of people go play golf, fishing. I'll cut hair and paint cars.

When I was growing up, I used to go down to my grandfather's drugstore all the time. It was the center of a lot of politics and planning and was very exciting, with people from everywhere coming by. It was like having an on-going history lesson. One of the main things I remember was the sign hanging over the door: "Through this portal pass the best of the persons on the cutting edge of changing for the better life's opportunities for all citizens." Then there were posters and photos all over the walls, behind the ice cream counter, going towards the back door, and even on the ceilings. Posters said "Re-elect Aaron Henry" or to support Mike Espy, Lyndon Johnson, Geraldine Ferraro, Walter Mondale, the Congressional Black Caucus, Jimmy Carter—you name it—all the good Democrats. Then there were photos of Kennedy, Martin Luther King, and many more, and the huge pictures of the murdered civil rights workers, Schwerner, Chaney, and Goodman—I never will forget. My grandfather told me that they were killed so I could vote.

Acknowledgments

I am indebted to many people for their contributions toward making this book a reality. In the beginning, a small chain of events and people burgeoned into a very long one. In 1995, Gloria Carter Dickerson was working for MINACT, INC. in Jackson, Mississippi. She told CEO, B. T. Jones, about my book, *Silver Rights,* which tells the story of the Carter family and their courageous fight during the freedom movement in the 1960s in the Mississippi Delta. Aaron Henry was chairman of the MINACT board at the time, and B. T. Jones gave him a copy. Aaron read and liked the book and in December 1996 consented to my coming to Jackson to meet with him and a committee of six who had been encouraging him to tell his story for many years. Along with Aaron, I met with Constance Slaughter Harvey, B. T. Jones, Robert Smith, Frank Melton, Wydette Hawkins, and R. L. Bolden. We reached an agreement on my working with Aaron to get the story told. I am grateful for the support from that committee throughout the process.

In the short time I spent with Aaron before his stroke, he told me about the three-hundred pages in his own voice in the Tougaloo College archives. Clarence Hunter and Rian Bowie went beyond the call of duty to help with my research of the Aaron Henry Papers and in gathering newspaper articles and many other pieces of information for me. Bill Silver and Henry Hurt, who interviewed Aaron and transcribed those pages in the Tougaloo archives, were most generous in their permission and blessing for my editing and forming the autobiographical part of this book.

Aaron's sister, Thelma Johnson, and his Mississippi cousins, Sallie Montgomery, Snobie McKinney, and Carrie L. Young, gave me a picture of Aaron's early years, and his daughter Rebecca Henry and two grandsons Aaron and DeMon McClinton gave insight into his family life.

I interviewed many of Aaron's friends and colleagues and along with the twelve whose stories appear in the book, my thanks for interviews with Harvey Ross, Bennie Gooden, Bill Minor, Elizabeth Smith, Hodding Carter, Ed King, Reuben Anderson, Fred Banks, R. L. Bolden, Constance Slaughter Harvey, Lawrence Guyot, Charles Evers, Wydette Hawkins, and Gloria Evans. I also thank Joan Browning for transcribing the interviews.

The books or interviews by Neil McMillen, Leslie McLemore, Charles Payne, John Dittmer, Kay Mills, and Worth Long gave me much of the backdrop for Aaron's story.

Reuben Smith, Doris Derby, Carolyn Hackett, Charles Tisdale, Bennie Gooden, Milly Moorhead, and Minnie Watson helped track down many of the photographs in the book.

For their general support, I thank Frances and Ben Hooks, Rheta Grimsley Johnson, Don Grierson, Andrew Carr, Julian Bond, Lisa Rogers, Shirley Bourne, Jackie Gary, K. C. Morrison, and Claude Montgomery. As always, I remain grateful to my agent Nat Sobel and appreciate the fine advice and help from my editor Seetha Srinivasan at the University Press of Mississippi and her efficient staff.

I am particularly indebted to John Dittmer whose enthusiasm for this project has been constant and was manifest in his reading the manuscript early on and in writing a superb introduction to the book.

Finally, my thanks to Chea Prince for his unwavering support and to my sisters Ann and Eileen Curry, brother-in-law Enoch Hendry, and my nephews Coran and Walker Hendry for their encouragement in my writing.

This book is dedicated to Mae Bertha Carter of Drew, Mississippi, the hero of *Silver Rights*, who died on April 28, 1999, and who, like Aaron Henry, was a true "long distance runner" in the freedom movement.

Index

CPSIA information can be obtained
at www.ICGtesting.com
Printed in the USA
BVHW03s1407180818
524673BV00002B/12/P